WRITING

THE BODY

IN MOTION

A CRITICAL ANTHOLOGY ON CANADIAN SPORT LITERATURE

Edited by

ANGIE ABDOU & JAMIE DOPP

21 Feb 19

AU PRESS

For Ron —
One of my favourite
bodies in motion.

Jamie Dopp

Copyright © 2018 Angie Abdou and Jamie Dopp
Published by AU Press, Athabasca University
1200, 10011 – 109 Street, Edmonton, AB T5J 3S8
Cover design by Natalie Olsen
Interior design by Sergiy Kozakov
Printed and bound in Canada by Friesens

ISBN 978-1-77199-228-2 (pbk.)   ISBN 978-1-77199-229-9 (PDF)
ISBN 978-1-77199-230-5 (epub)   doi: 10.15215/aupress/9781771992282.01

Library and Archives Canada Cataloguing in Publication

   Writing the body in motion: a critical anthology on Canadian sport literature /
edited by Angie Abdou and Jamie Dopp.
Includes bibliographical references.
Issued in print and electronic formats.

   1. Sports in literature. 2. Canadian literature—History and criticism. I.
Abdou, Angie, 1969–, editor II. Dopp, Jamie, 1957–, editor

PS8101.S73W75 2018   C810.9'3579   C2018-900427-4
                                         C2018-900428-2

We acknowledge the financial support of the Government of Canada through
the Canada Book Fund (CBF) for our publishing activities and the assistance
provided by the Government of Alberta through the Alberta Media Fund.

Canada   Alberta
            Government

Writing the Body in Motion

Contents

Introduction   3
    Angie Abdou

1   W. P. Kinsella's *Shoeless Joe*: The Fairy Tale, the Hero's Quest, and the Magic Realism of Baseball   11
    Fred Mason

2   The Myth of Hockey and Identity in Paul Quarrington's *King Leary*   25
    Cara Hedley

3   Hockey, Humour, and Play in Wayne Johnston's *The Divine Ryans*   43
    Jason Blake

4   The Poetry of Hockey in Richard Harrison's *Hero of the Play*   57
    Paul Martin

5   Glaciers, Embodiment, and the Sublime: An Ecocritical Approach to Thomas Wharton's *Icefields*   71
    Cory Willard

6   Hockey, Zen, and the Art of Bill Gaston's *The Good Body*   93
    Jamie Dopp

7   The Darkening Path: The Hero-Athlete Reconsidered in Angie Abdou's *The Bone Cage*   107
    Gyllian Phillips

8   "Open the door to the roaring darkness": The Enigma of Terry Sawchuk in Randall Maggs's *Night Work: The Sawchuk Poems*   123
    Paul Martin

9   From Tank to Deep Water: Myth and History in Samantha Warwick's *Sage Island*   139
    Jamie Dopp

10 Identity and the Athlete: Alexander MacLeod's "Miracle Mile" 153
      Laura K. Davis

11 Decolonizing the Hockey Novel: Ambivalence and Apotheosis in
      Richard Wagamese's *Indian Horse* 167
      Sam McKegney and Trevor J. Phillips

    Contributors 185

WRITING

THE BODY

IN MOTION

Angie Abdou

Introduction

Over the past decade, sport literature courses have sprung up at colleges and universities across the continent, in both English and kinesiology departments. As the author of a sport novel, *The Bone Cage* (2007), I have been invited to speak to students in Newfoundland, Ontario, Manitoba, Alberta, and British Columbia, as well as in Maine, Massachusetts, West Virginia, Colorado, Texas, and Kansas. Because I am enthusiastic about sport literature, professors in the discipline frequently contact me with questions. Mostly, they want me to recommend secondary sources. They want strong academic essays to assign to their students, as examples of the critical analysis of sport literature. Unfortunately, there are still relatively few such essays available.

In Canada, an exciting body of critical writing specifically about hockey has emerged, beginning with Richard Gruneau and David Whitson's *Hockey Night in Canada: Sport, Identities and Cultural Politics* (1993). Since Gruneau and Whitson's groundbreaking study, several collections of essays have appeared, including Whitson and Gruneau's follow-up work, *Artificial Ice: Hockey, Culture, and Commerce* (2006); *Canada's Game: Hockey and Identity*, edited by Andrew Holman (2009); and *Now Is the Winter: Thinking About Hockey*, edited by Jamie Dopp and Richard Harrison (2009). In addition, two full-length studies—Jason Blake's *Canadian Hockey Literature* (2010) and Michael J. Buma's *Refereeing Identity: The Cultural Work of Canadian Hockey Novels* (2012)—have offered critical surveys of hockey fiction in Canada. But these scholars have, for the most part, adopted an interdisciplinary approach, rather than offering close readings of the hockey novels and poems that tend to be taught in sport literature courses.

3

Perhaps the critical and commercial popularity of certain hockey novels—classics like Roy MacGregor's *The Last Season* (1983), Paul Quarrington's *King Leary* (1987), and Bill Gaston's *The Good Body* (2000)—has helped to overcome some of the historical prejudice in the academy against the study of sports and, by extension, against literature about sports. At the same time, works of literature about sports other than hockey have largely been ignored. The present collection aims to redress this imbalance, by including considerations of some of the best recent literature in Canada about other sports. In preparing the collection, we intended to maintain an even balance between hockey and "not-hockey" literature, but continually found our hockey list outweighing all other sports combined. The same thing happens each time I teach a sport lit course: if I don't stay vigilant, I easily end up teaching a hockey lit course. This phenomenon is easy to explain: there is an abundance of very good Canadian literature about hockey—which is, after all, an iconic sport in this country, intricately entwined with efforts to summon a pan-Canadian sense of identity. To make room for non-hockey sport literature, we have thus left out some classic Canadian hockey literature: Roch Carrier's *The Hockey Sweater* (1979), Jamie Fitzpatrick's *You Could Believe in Nothing* (2011), Steven Galloway's *Finnie Walsh* (2000), Mark Anthony Jarman's *Salvage King, Ya!* (1997), and Cara Hedley's *Twenty Miles* (2007).

The growing interest in hockey for Canadian writers and scholars also led to a growth in hockey conferences, the first of which was hosted by Colin Howell at St. Mary's University, in Halifax, in October 2001. According to the proceedings, the conference "Putting It on Ice: Hockey in Historical and Contemporary Perspective" was "meant to be the first in a series of conferences on hockey and its historical and social significance" (Howell 2002, vol.1). This conference helped to jump-start an increase in scholarly analysis of hockey and set the pattern for future conferences, which have brought together scholars, journalists, members of community hockey organizations, athletes, and writers and poets from across North America and Europe. In 2002, Howell organized a follow-up conference on women's hockey, and two years later, Andrew Holman, a professor of Canadian studies at Bridgewater State University in Massachusetts, organized a conference called "Canada's Game: Hockey and Identity." Since then, hockey conferences have been held every two or three years. The hockey essays in *Writing the Body in Motion* offer explanations for this wealth of hockey literature and the growing scholarly interest in it, while also examining the association between hockey and Canadian identity.

We hope the interest in hockey literature will gradually extend to other types of sport literature. Sport lit courses allow students the opportunity to critique sport culture and to analyze the role of athletics in today's society. Most of us, at some point in our lives, participate in sport, and many of us also interact with sport as consumers by attending or watching sporting events or following sports in the media. Sport literature courses give us a chance to think critically about that consumption. We intend this collection to complement those courses, both for professors as lecture material and for students as models of literary criticism and as research sources. The essays offer a variety of ways to read, teach, and write about sport literature. Organized chronologically by source text, from *Shoeless Joe* (1982) to *Indian Horse* (2012), the essays in this collection focus specifically on contemporary Canadian sport literature.

The lessons of these literary works—and the essays about them—extend beyond the sporting arena. According to the course website of Don Morrow, who taught one of Canada's first sport lit courses at the University of Western Ontario, sport literature is never just about sport; rather, it explores the human condition using sport as the dominant metaphor. Similarly, Priscila Uppal, perhaps the most well-known Canadian scholar and writer to focus her attention on this topic, explains that the best sport literature functions as "metaphor, paradigm, a way to experience some of the harsher realities of the world, a place to escape to, an arena from which endless lessons can be learned, passed on, learned again" (2009, xiv). Many of the essays in this collection, therefore, examine the various ways in which sport functions metaphorically. Our authors also consider various recurring themes of sport literature, including how sport relates to the body, violence, gender, society, sexuality, heroism, the father/son relationship, memory, the environment, redemption, mortality, religion, quest, and place.

Two theorists feature prominently in the following essays: Joseph Campbell and Michael Oriard. Because writers often represent sport stories as a quest for victory, with the athlete as mythic hero, Joseph Campbell's *The Hero of a Thousand Faces* (first published in 1949) works well as a contextual and theoretical framework. Campbell proposes the "monomyth" of the hero's journey, which involves a departure from home, overcoming obstacles, triumph, and a return to community with new knowledge (see

Campbell 2008). Scholars in this collection study how authors choose to digress from this structure and how the victory that the athletes achieve (self-knowledge) often differs from the one they sought (gold medal). Several of the essays draw on Campbell's notions of rebirth to analyze how these athletes return home with new knowledge and must learn to reintegrate into their (sport) society, as well as how the reborn athletes might change that society on their return. Michael Oriard also offers great insight into myths of the athlete-hero, particularly in his book *Dreaming of Heroes: American Sport Fiction* (1982). Oriard builds upon the work of Campbell and applies Campbell's theories specifically to sport, making Oriard's work especially relevant to teachers and students of sport literature. A professional football player turned academic, Oriard has made important contributions to the field and is widely recognized as one of the foremost cultural historians of American football. His ideas, though, can be extended beyond football. In the following essays, scholars apply his theories to hockey, swimming, wrestling, and baseball. Though published in 1982, *Dreaming of Heroes* is still relevant and remains critical reading for any student of sport literature.

In the discussion of Alexander MacLeod's "Miracle Mile," Laura Davis asserts that MacLeod's story is not your typical sport literature. "Miracle Mile," Davis argues, is "far from a narrative about victory." The same can be said of all the works examined in this collection. For example, Cara Hedley's analysis of *King Leary* reveals that the protagonist was only ever a king in his own mind and that Quarrington's novel works to deconstruct the very notion of sport-hero. Through that deconstruction, Hedley—via Quarrington—also questions the role of hockey in the construction of our nation's identity. Sport lit courses tend to focus on stories that work against the traditional sport-hero narrative. We all know the typical narrative arc from classic sport movies like *Rocky*, *Hoosiers*, *The Mighty Ducks*, and countless others. The movie starts with an underdog who decides to go for it. He (yes, it is almost always a he) trains and trains and trains. He experiences some victory, and the audience becomes deeply invested in his success. But then he experiences an obstacle—maybe he is injured; maybe his dad dies; maybe his girlfriend dumps him. He appears to give up, to quit. Cue the dark, moody music. Zoom in on the hero, sitting on the kitchen floor, the hood of his sweatshirt pulled low over his forehead, his face in shadow. But don't despair! Along comes the coach to give him a rallying pep talk—or a well-placed kick in the butt, followed by an almost affectionate pat on the shoulder, depending on the characterization of the coach—and our hero "digs deep." He decides to "give it all he's got!"—to "go for it!" Of course, sport rewards his efforts. He wins, and we end with our hero on the podium, arms raised high.

Don't get me wrong. I am a sucker for these movies. I cry every single time. Even in *Men with Brooms* (2002), a comedy about a group of beer-guzzling curlers, when they went for it, I cried. Right at that point when the coach finishes his rallying pep talk, with the hero nodding intently, his gaze fierce, my husband always turns to me: "Oh, Ang! He's going to go for it!" My husband mocks me—he laughs at my guaranteed overly emotional reaction to the hero's predictable move towards victory—but let it be known that we *both* have tears rolling down our cheeks. He and I met on a varsity swim team. We went for it, and we have the arthritic shoulders as proof. Neither of our careers ended on the podium. We both get a little weepy at these perfect sport stories. I suppose we like the comforting predictability, as well as the tidy way in which effort and "playing with heart" are always rewarded. The movies offer a kind of simplistic reassurance: by winning in the end, the hero (and the audience) can make sense of everything that has come before—the suffering, the injustice, the confusion, the sacrifice. A victory makes it all right.

Despite the emotional satisfaction that I take in these predictable stories, I have always known that they have very little connection to the truth of athletic lives. I wrote my swimming-wrestling novel, *The Bone Cage* (2007), partly as a response to the discrepancy I saw between sport movies and sport lives. I wanted to write a sport novel that did not end on the podium. I wanted to ask if the Olympic quest might be a misguided quest. Gyllian Phillips takes up that issue in her essay on *The Bone Cage*, explicating the book's literary allusions and drawing parallels with the quest-gone-wrong in Robert Browning's "Childe Roland to the Dark Tower Came." In fact, the quest motif appears in many of the essays in this book. Fred Mason, for example, employs the work of Joseph Campbell in his discussion of quest in *Shoeless Joe*, and Jamie Dopp points out that the marathon swimmer in Samantha Warwick's *Sage Island* might, in the end, have undertaken a very different quest than the one she intended. We find a comparison between hockey and Zen Buddhism in Bill Gaston's *The Good Body*, where engagement in sport helps the protagonist on his journey towards a kind of enlightenment. In each case, sport is a microcosm of our wider society, and the problematization of a certain kind of sport-quest can become a prob-lematization of all quests, an evaluation of all strategies to ascribe meaning and shape to life.

Not only do the texts we have chosen for this volume disrupt the trad-itional underdog-to-podium sport narrative, but they also tend to undermine the very notion of athletic success. Though the characters often come to sport looking for redemption, the redemption they find has little to do with gold medals. In Samantha Warwick's marathon swimming novel *Sage Island,* when Savanna Mason arrives at the Wrigley Ocean Marathon, she thinks: "I wonder if everyone who came here for this race feels like a loser. I wonder if this whole event is fueled by failures wanting to redeem themselves" (War-wick 2008, 52). Initially, Savanna feel like a "loser" who needs to prove herself with this race. In the conclusion, though, this personal affirmation does not take the form readers might expect. Instead, *Sage Island,* like much of the literature discussed in this collection, redefines the very concepts of "winner" and "loser" and the notions of "success" and "failure."

Again, this evaluation of the notion of success can be applied beyond sport. In the introduction to her sport literature anthology, Priscila Uppal compares the work of a writer to that of an athlete, claiming that both artists and athletes "pursue excellence through discipline and rigour, both sacrifice other pleasures in this pursuit, and both are actively engaged in . . . 'pain management' (the ability to turn pain into a creative, dynamic force)" (2009, xi–xii). Uppal adds that "truly great practitioners in both arenas are possessed with the curious ability to actively change the rules the game are played by" because they are "originals rather than followers" (xii). Similarly, both *Shoeless Joe* and *Sage Island* compare novel writing and athletic competition. In *Shoeless Joe,* Kinsella compares the writing vocation (manifested in J. D. Salinger) to life as a professional baseball player. In *Sage Island,* Savanna's brother dreams of publishing a novel, and his creative pursuit is compared to Savanna's athletic pursuits. Savanna's coach (Higgins) feels badly for the parents of these two individuals (the novelist and the athlete) with their non-mainstream dreams. He says, "I was just thinking of your parents, such practical creatures, and both kids turn out dreamers, desperadoes" (Warwick 2008, 81). Here, Warwick portrays sport (like novel-writing) as a kind of rebellion, a rejection of mainstream values and scripts. Savanna's father disapproves of her involvement in swim-ming, claiming, "Swimming is not a vocation, Savanna, it's a diversion"

(96). Savanna, nonetheless, pursues her swimming goals and, because the narrative is in the first person, readers tend to identify with her and wish her success in her endeavours rather than hope that she will give up on her athletic dreams and fulfill her adult responsibilities in her parents' bakery. In this way, the novel presents swimming, and athletics in general, as a way of rejecting society's predetermined script—grow up, finish school, get a job, start a family. Instead, the novel favourably represents the alternative of following individual dreams that may not always seem logical or practical, dreams that individuals might not always be able to justify easily to their parents. Readers are asked to consider whether these athletes, these "dreamers and desperadoes," truly escape from adult responsibilities and obligations: Do they simply delay their inevitable entry into mainstream society? Or do they create new ways of being and thereby redefine what constitutes "success"? Again, sport functions as a vehicle through which to question and critique wider societal values and ways of being in the world.

Perhaps Warwick's devotion to swimming as a lifestyle comes from her own participation in the sport. She still swims competitively and coaches the sport. The same is true of many authors under consideration in this collection. Richard Wagamese played hockey. Randall Maggs played goalie and watched his brother compete in the NHL. Alexander MacLeod ran at an elite level. When I set out to write *The Bone Cage*, I considered using a sport other than swimming, solely because I did not want readers to make autobiographical assumptions based on my own history in the sport. However, I soon realized that no amount of book research could replace those decades in the pool. No matter how much I read about other sports or interviewed other athletes, I would never obtain the visceral knowledge that I have of swimming, a sport I know in my very body. The other athlete-writers represented in this collection bring the same bodily expertise to their exploration of sport, and I invite student-athletes to do the same in their writing.

Because the sport literature analyzed in this collection engages not only in representation of sport for its own sake but also in a rigorous, philosophical examination of everyday life and values, the works lend themselves to various political and theoretical approaches. Trevor Phillips and Sam McKegney, for example, provide an important postcolonial analysis of Richard Wagamese's *Indian Horse*, with its portrayal of the brutal residential school system and the implication of hockey in the violence and abuse. If hockey symbolizes Canada better than the flag, then where is the place for Indigenous peoples and what is the relationship between hockey and the First Nations? McKegney and Phillips explore this question in their analysis of Wagamese's *Indian Horse*.

Turning the political gaze to the environment, Cory Willard offers a consideration of Thomas Wharton's *Icefields* and explores how we can use this mountaineering novel to think about conservation and climate change. His analysis of the novel urges political activism to protect our planet. Rather than being an escape from politics and from pressing contemporary issues, sport lit can offer an arena for vigorous political engagement and activism. To use the words of Jason Blake in his exploration of play in Wayne Johnston's *The Divine Ryans*, hockey and hockey literature "are more than escapist flight from real life" and can, instead, be a place where players (and readers) make sense of their world.

The texts chosen for this collection work to deconstruct the mind/body dichotomy. Each of our essayists makes clear the many ways in which athletic literature can be of great intellectual interest. Of course, there are many more works of fiction we could have included, like Canada's postmodern hockey novel *Salvage Kings, Ya!* (1997) by Mark Anthony Jarman, or the wheelchair basketball novel *Post* (2007), by Arley McNeney, or the mountaineering novel *Every Lost Country* (2010), by Steven Heighton, or the swimming novel *Flip Turn* (2012), by Paula Eisenstein. In fact, sport also plays a major role in many key canonical Canadian literature texts. Think, for example, of the swimmers in Eden Robinson's *Monkey Beach* (2000), Ethel Wilson's *Swamp Angel* (1954), and Margaret Atwood's *Surfacing* (1972). This collection focuses on the texts currently taught most often in sport literature courses, and we hope our book will move the conversation forward.

WORKS CITED

Howell, Colin D. 2002. "Hockey's Many Meanings and Contested Identities." Introduction to *Putting It on Ice: Hockey and Cultural Identities*, vol. 1 of *Putting It on Ice*, edited by Colin D. Howell, v–vii. Halifax: Gorsebrook Research Institute, Saint Mary's University.

Uppal, Priscila, ed. 2009. *The Exile Book of Canadian Sport Stories*. Toronto: Exile Editions.

Warwick, Samantha. 2008. *Sage Island*. Victoria: Brindle and Glass.

1

Fred Mason

W. P. Kinsella's *Shoeless Joe*
The Fairy Tale, the Hero's Quest, and the Magic Realism of Baseball

Baseball is probably the sport most written about by fiction writers; indeed, as David McGimpsey notes, "baseball has in fact gained a highbrow, literary reputation that no other American sport, and very few objects of American culture, enjoy" (2000, 2). McGimpsey (2000, 2) notes that the genre of baseball literature has many consistent tropes: baseball is a natural, God-given sport; it allows people to be judged on quantifiable merit; it is connected to the simplicity of childhood; it brings fathers and sons together. More cynical tropes can also be found: baseball can be corrupted by its fixed monopoly at the professional level, and its "purity" is always under threat, with a nostalgic nod to "how it used to be." W. P. Kinsella's novels and short stories have contributed heavily to the genre of baseball fiction, beginning with *Shoeless Joe* in 1982 (Steele 2011, 17), and his work almost always expresses some of these tropes.

Kinsella's fiction, especially the novel *Shoeless Joe*, has received much attention from literary scholars. Historian Dan Nathan suggests that "in terms of the amount of critical attention it has received, *Shoeless Joe*'s only rival as far as baseball fiction goes is Bernard Malamud's [1952 novel] *The Natural*" (2003, 154). Among other topics, scholars have focused on Kinsella's writing style (Boe 1983; Easton 1999; Fischer 2000), on *Shoeless Joe*'s connection to other literature about baseball's pastoral roots (Carino 1994; Garman 1994; Altherr 1990), on Kinsella's complex portrayal of father-son relationships (Hollander 1999; Mesher 1992; Morrow 2002; Pellow 1991), and on how the novel's nostalgia for baseball's past is overly conservative and excludes women and people of colour (Garman 1994; McGimpsey 2000, Vanderwerken 1998). However, what sets Kinsella's work apart from that of other baseball writers, is his heavy use of the fantastical, such as ghostly ballplayers, and his tendency to slip easily between different spaces and different times on rural ball fields. Drawing on analyses of other academic writers, this essay focuses on how *Shoeless Joe* employs mythical elements of the fairy tale and quest story, as well as metafictional techniques (blending elements of the real world into the fictional narrative), to portray baseball as a spiritual phenomenon.

W. P. KINSELLA AND BASEBALL FICTION

In a number of interviews, W. P. Kinsella indicated that he would be happy to be described as a "baseball writer," even though he insisted that "the best sports literature isn't really about sports. I, for instance, write love stories that have baseball as a background" (quoted in Horvath and Palmer 1987, 186). In addition to *Shoeless Joe*, Kinsella wrote five short story collections related to baseball (1980, 1984, 1988, 1993, 2000) and five baseball novels (1986, 1991, 1996, 1998, 2011). What became the novel *Shoeless Joe* started out as the short story "Shoeless Joe Jackson Comes to Iowa," the title story of his first short story collection. Kinsella wrote the story while at the Iowa Writer's Workshop in 1978, intending to express his love for the land around him. The story became the first chapter of the novel. While he had had previous success as a short story writer, the novel established Kinsella's career and allowed him to take up writing as a full-time profession.

Although Kinsella wrote frequently about baseball, it appears he had little involvement with the sport itself. Like the novel's main character, Ray Kinsella, the writer grew up with his father telling him stories about baseball (Murray 1987, 39). However, the real Kinsella never played as a child and only became a fan as an adult (Horvath and Palmer 1987, 184). As his relationship with the sport developed, Kinsella came to see baseball as a place for myth and dreams. As he told Don Murray (1987, 38), baseball, unlike other sports, is not limited by time or space. A tied baseball game could theoretically go on forever: one of Kinsella's novels, *The Iowa Baseball Confederacy*, features a ball game that goes on for forty days and forty nights. Kinsella also noted that "on the true baseball field, the foul lines diverge forever, the field eventually encompassing a goodly portion of the world, and there is theoretically no distance that a great hitter couldn't hit the ball or a great fielder run to retrieve it. . . . This openness makes for larger than life characters, for mythology" (quoted in Horvath and Palmer 1987, 188). Starting with *Shoeless Joe*, Kinsella, probably more than any other fiction writer to date, turned to baseball for mythic possibilities.

MAGIC REALISM AND THE FANTASTICAL

A marker of much of Kinsella's writing, particularly in *Shoeless Joe*, is his use of magic realism, a literary technique that incorporates surreal or fantastic elements into an otherwise realistic, even mundane world (Hamblin 1992, 3). *Shoeless Joe*, mostly set on a small, simple family farm in Iowa, includes time travel, voices "from beyond," and deceased ballplayers who emerge from a cornfield to display their skills again. The storyline of the novel is largely driven by commands given by disembodied voices. Iowa farmer Ray Kinsella hears a voice that says "If you build it, he will come" (Kinsella 1982, 3). Ray somehow innately knows that the "he" referred to his father's hero, Shoeless Joe Jackson, one of eight Chicago Black Sox players banned from baseball for fixing the 1919 World Series. "It" is a ball field. Despite financial difficulties and ridicule from his neighbours, Ray plows under part of his cornfield to build a ballpark. After three years, he has only managed to create a small section of left field, but it is enough to get Shoeless Joe Jackson to appear. Over time, more players from the Black Sox appear as Ray completes more of the field. The voice also tells Ray, "Ease his pain," which he interprets, with complete certainty, to mean that he should travel across the country, retrieve reclusive author J. D. Salinger, and take him to a major league ball game (Kinsella, 1982, 27-28). Salinger and Ray both see a vision on the scoreboard, and both hear a voice that sends them on a trip back across the country to investigate the life of Archie Graham, who played one inning in the majors. While Salinger initially has doubts, Ray never does, and the voice, as if from on high, always ends up sending those who hear it to do the things they need to do. While the voice is seemingly omniscient and otherworldly, the actions it calls people to do occur in very simple, everyday places, like a cornfield in Iowa, the outfield stands of Fenway Park, and a small town in northern Minnesota.

Chisholm, Minnesota is the site of a major plot turn that links to the fantastical through a form of time travel. While Ray and Salinger are in town, it seems that their investigations into Graham revive the town's memory of him. While out for a midnight stroll, Ray encounters the elderly Doctor Graham, who is long deceased. Ray realizes that he has experienced some sort of time slippage:

> As we walk, I note subtle differences in the buildings and sidewalks. Some of the newer houses on Second Street appear to have been replaced by older ones. There are business signs along Lake Street that weren't there yesterday. Can it be that I am the one who has crossed some magical line between fantasy and reality? That it is Doc who is on solid turf, and I have entered into the past as effortlessly as chasing a butterfly across a meadow? (118)

They go to Graham's office for coffee and conversation, and Graham admits that his one wish in life was to bat in the major leagues. Ray returns to his hotel room, thereby travelling forward in time to his own present. On their way out of town, Ray and Salinger pick up a hitchhiker, a young Archie Graham with bat and glove, headed out west to find a ball club. Ray tells him of his field in Iowa, and Archie agrees to go with them. When the ghost players appear after Ray and his companions get back to the farm, Graham is told that he has a contract with them, and he joins the players on the field. The ghostly Black Sox, like Graham, have a strong timeless quality: they appear in their athletic prime, despite the decades that have passed.

Rebirth and revival of characters are standard features in many fantasy tales, as well as in the origin myths of many of the world's religions. In the novel *Shoeless Joe*, rebirth and transformation are central to everything. We see the rebirth of players, initially Shoeless Joe Jackson and the other Black Sox, and later others, including Ray's father, who was a minor league catcher. However, their presence is largely limited, in space and time, to Ray's field and to game time. One exception is Archie Graham whom Ray and Salinger meet in the world beyond the farm. Once Graham starts playing at Ray's field, though, he transfers from one "realm" to another and exists only as a young player who comes and goes—that is, until he makes the choice to once again become Doc Graham in order to save the life of Ray's daughter, Karin, when she is choking. Graham transmogrifies, ultimately choosing self-sacrifice in being unable to return to the field as a player, much like a mythical hero. Another central character who experiences miraculous transformation is Eddie Scissons, the die-hard Cubs fan who claims to be "the oldest living Cub." One night at Ray's ballpark, the usually wispy opponents are surprisingly visible as the Chicago Cubs from the 1910s. Scissons sees a young version of himself called in as a relief pitcher, with disastrous results. His younger self blows a lead and is pulled from the game. After some initial distress over this episode, Eddie comes to see it as a reaffirmation of his obsession with baseball as a fan; he delivers a speech to the players about baseball as a form of religion and truth for the world. Later in the novel, Scissons dies and we learn he changed his will to request burial in Ray's field. His symbolic rebirth, though a disaster, enables a rebirth of his belief in baseball.

Mythical stories with fantastical dimensions and great heroes serve to impart life lessons and to create bonds and a sense of community (Schwartz 1987, 137–38). Sporting practices in our modern world often take on mythic dimensions, since sport is one of the few cultural practices that can regularly offer us heroes. In his baseball writing, W. P. Kinsella consistently tapped into the mythical potential he saw in the game of baseball. *Shoeless Joe* has many similarities to folk and fairy tales, and it contains a number of elements of the fantasy genre. In a classic essay originally written for presentation in 1939, J. R. R. Tolkien suggests that certain elements bring us into the "realm of the fairy-story," a realm that includes the "real" by focusing on humans and what they do in the fairy realm but allows for the fantastical, like fairies, elves, dwarfs, and dragons—or in *Shoeless Joe*, reborn players and time slippage (Tolkien 1964, 15-16). Crucially, in such stories, magic must be taken seriously: it must not be satirical or comic; it must be presented as true, as part of the story frame itself; and it typically helps with human desires (Tolkien 1964, 17-19).

The plot of *Shoeless Joe* is propelled by magic: several times in the novel, Ray refers to the idea of feeling "the magic" growing before crucial events happen (Kinsella, 1982, 10; 115; 187; 202). But for others to participate in the magic, to see the ghostly players and the ballpark itself, they must believe in the magical possibilities of baseball. While Ray's immediate family members, Salinger, and Scissons experience the ballpark in its full dimension—with announcers, crowds, sights and sounds—others, such as Annie's brother Mark and Ray's brother Richard, initially see only the onlookers, the "real" people, sitting in a ramshackle bleacher on a ballpark surrounded by corn. Richard Schwartz argues that because some characters can see the ballplayers and others cannot, readers of *Shoeless Joe* have to be willing to accept that the phantoms are on the same level of reality in the narrative as the other characters, or the story falls apart. He suggests that "by leaving open the question of the phantoms' reality, Kinsella extends the opportunity for experiencing faith to the readers themselves," requiring that readers take "a leap of faith" (1987, 145).

Writing on the importance of belief in relation to the genre of fantasy and fairy tales, Tolkien noted:

> What really happens is that the story-maker proves a successful "sub-creator." He makes a Secondary World which your mind can enter. Inside it, what he relates is "true": it accords with the laws of that world. You therefore believe it, while you are, as it were, inside. The moment disbelief rises, the spell is broken; the magic, or rather art, has failed. (Tolkien 1964, 36)

Tolkien put the onus for creating belief on the author, the "sub-creator" of the story. Other scholars, such as Neil Randall (1987) and Donald Morse (1998) argue that fictional works with fantastical elements like *Shoeless Joe* make demands upon readers, demands for a willing suspension of disbelief, for cooperation in sustaining belief (Morse 1998, 352). Since readers are required to accept such things as a magical ballpark in the cornfields of Iowa on the same level as the more realistic events in the novel, they must, in some sense, become co-creators of the narrative (Randall 1987,175). Belief is multi-layered in *Shoeless Joe*. The novel criticizes belief in organized religion as being self-serving, and insists that characters must believe in baseball and its possibilities to become full participants at Ray's field. Similarly, the novel demands that readers suspend disbelief in order to enter the story fully. I might suggest that some critics, such as Bruce Brooks (1983, 22–24), or other readers who do not like the novel, may be unable or unwilling to maintain the required suspension of disbelief when faced with such fantastical elements in what is ostensibly a baseball novel.

METAFICTIONAL TECHNIQUES IN *SHOELESS JOE*

To complicate the question of what is believable in his writing, W. P. Kinsella often enters into metafiction, where fact and fiction are blended together so that the reader has difficulty knowing where one ends and the other begins (Morse 2004, 309). *Shoeless Joe* includes a number of real-world people as characters (Salinger, Graham, and Jackson himself) but fictionalizes them in the narrative and places them in all sorts of fantastic situations. Kinsella also incorporates "facts" that turn out not to be true at all. The blending and blurring of fact and fiction so that they are difficult to distinguish is a key feature of the novel.

The most obvious real-world person in the book is the title character, Shoeless Joe Jackson. The Black Sox scandal of 1919, the fixing of the World Series, Joe Jackson's implication in the events, and the subsequent banning of the eight players for life are all historical facts. However, once Joe Jackson steps out of history and onto Ray's ball field, he becomes a fictional character. Kinsella's version of Jackson's past is almost entirely based on the stories told by Ray's father, which sympathetically frame Jackson and the other Black Sox as so-called "victims of the system." Ray's ball field is a place where the players are all absolved of their transgressions and are known simply for their love of the game (Nathan 2003, 155–56). As Joe says, "I loved the game [. . .] I'd have played for food money" (Kinsella 1982, 8). It is notable that Ray avoids actually asking Jackson about his guilt; indeed, he only thinks of it once, on the first night Jackson shows up (Steele 2011, 115). In his cultural history of the Black Sox scandal, Daniel Nathan notes that *Shoeless Joe* was at the forefront of a number of literary works and films in the 1980s that re-envisioned the scandal and shifted the public perception of the players in a much more positive direction (2003, 153–56).

The reclusive writer J. D. Salinger, the author of the classic coming-of age novel *The Catcher in the Rye* (1951), is, of course, also a real-world figure. Like he does in *Shoeless Joe*, the real Salinger stayed out of the public eye, refused interviews, and threatened to sue those who wrote about him (Cutchins 2002, 74). Donald Morse suggests that since Salinger was so reclusive, he was more "real" in the imaginations of fans than he was in reality (2004, 312). Similarly, most of the rumours that Ray uncovers in his research on Salinger were made up by W. P. Kinsella, as was the interview Salinger gave about baseball that convinces Ray to go to him (Boe 1983, 181; Murray 1987, 49). Thus, Salinger's "love of baseball" is the novel writer's fictional creation. W. P. Kinsella could get away with Salinger's inclusion in the novel because his representation of the man is obviously fictional (e.g., "Jerry" goes off into the unknown with the ghostly ballplayers at the end) and reasonably sympathetic, with no malice intended on Kinsella's part (Cutchins 2002, 74n5). Such clearly fictional aspects did little to mollify the intensely private author, however. Salinger did not like his inclusion as a character in *Shoeless Joe* and threatened legal action for the film adaptation, which led to his replacement with the entirely fictional Terrence Mann, played by James Earl Jones (Pellow 1991, 23).

Many readers of *Shoeless Joe* may be surprised to learn that Archie Graham was a real person who actually played only half an inning of major league baseball and went on to become a small-town doctor in Chisholm, Minnesota. The Chisholm newspaper editorial that Ray reads in the novel actually exists and is included in Graham's player file at the Baseball Hall of Fame Library (Steele 2011, 121). W. P. Kinsella read about Graham in a baseball encyclopedia and decided to write him into one of his stories. Kinsella himself undertook a research trip to Chisholm, much like Ray and Salinger do in the novel. In an amusing anecdote that illustrates the confusion of fact and fiction, Kinsella told Don Murray that the librarian in Chisholm maintained that J. D. Salinger actually accompanied Kinsella on his research trip (1987, 48). Furthermore, the inclusion of Graham as a character in the novel and film inspired other researchers to write a biography of his life (Friedlander and Reising 2009), further blending the real and the imaginary.

Another fictional character with a real-world stand-in is Eddie Scissons. Although an entirely fictional character, Scissons is based on a man whom Kinsella met on a street corner in Iowa City (the same way Ray meets Eddie), a man who falsely claimed to have played for the Chicago Cubs (Murray 1987, 48). Kinsella later wrote the short story "The Eddie Scissons Syndrome" (1988, 137–52), in which a psychologist references the character in the novel *Shoeless Joe*—fiction referencing other fiction, as fiction, all by the same author.

The merging of W. P. Kinsella and his narrator, Ray Kinsella, further blends reality and fiction. While it is overly simplistic to conflate author and persona, Kinsella encourages such a reading (Boe 1983, 182), even beyond the shared last name. The similarities are too many to be coincidence. Both W. P. and Ray grew up on their fathers' baseball stories; both have a deep love for Iowa; both had previous unhappy careers as insurance salesmen; and W. P.'s first wife was named Anne while Ray's wife is Annie (Morse 1998, 354; Murray 1987, 7; Steele 2011, 192). Such interweaving of reality and fiction often leaves readers guessing what is true and what is made up. Robert Hamblin offers a clever analogy for the "mix of fact and fabrication" in *Shoeless Joe* and Kinsella's other work (1992, 3). Kinsella's readers, he writes, are like batters facing a pitcher with a mix of pitches, never entirely sure what is coming. The clearly factual material is like a hard, straight fastball. We see a lot of curves, as well, when Kinsella delivers "that spin of distortion that fiction puts on straight fact" (4). Sometimes, what Kinsella offers is so obviously surreal fantasy that it is like a knuckleball—a pitch that we know is coming, yet it still deceives and gives trouble (5). Kinsella's frequent use of "fact-that-turns-out-to-be-fiction, and fiction-that-turns-out-to-be-fact" is like a split-fingered fastball (6–7). It looks like a straight fastball, but then it deceptively moves and the bottom drops out of it, becoming a curve. With Kinsella, we can never be too sure what is truth and what is fiction—at least, not without a lot of fact-checking. Kinsella's metafictional interweaving of fact and fiction complicates the idea of reality, suggesting that reality is multi-layered and may not be that far removed in form or function from what we see in myth (Schwartz 1987, 144).

SHOELESS JOE AS HEROIC QUEST

The fantastical elements of *Shoeless Joe* make strong demands on readers (Randall 1987, 175), but they may be assisted in suspending their disbelief by the fact that the structure of *Shoeless Joe* reflects a familiar form: the "heroic quest" narrative. The idea of the heroic quest comes from a classic piece of literary criticism, Joseph Campbell's *The Hero with a Thousand Faces*, first published in 1949. In this wide-ranging work, Campbell argues that across cultures and over time, many origin stories, fairy tales, and myths have a similar structure, which amounts to a "monomyth." This monomyth suggests that heroes in a story are expected to move through a number of sub-stages (Campbell breaks it down to eighteen in total), which fit into three more general stages: "separation or departure," where they leave everyday life to start a quest; "trials and victories of initiation," where heroes must find within themselves the resources needed to accomplish their goals and overcome challenges; and "return and integration with society," where the now changed heroes bring back the "boon" they have achieved and must find a way to reintegrate, which is often the hardest stage (Campbell 2008, 28–29).

Ray Kinsella's overall journey in *Shoeless Joe* maps well onto the stages and sub-stages of this classic heroic quest.[1] Ray starts with an "openness to adventure" in his willingness to believe that baseball can work magic in people's lives (Campbell 2008, 42). He receives a "call to adventure" in the voice telling him to build a ballpark (42-44). He must "cross the first threshold" and make a leap of faith when he sets out to convince Salinger to come with him (64). He faces many trials and "ordeals by fire": people constantly doubt him and he doubts himself, and he risks losing his farm and his family's future to keep the dream ballpark going (81-84). There is an "apotheosis" (becoming god-like) in Ray's ability to help others achieve redemption, or live out their wishes, and a "receiving of the boon" when Ray gets to meet his own father (127-129, 148-150). Ray's apotheosis extends to the world beyond the farm, as we expect other seekers, others on a journey, to come to his field at the end and receive a boon, as well. There is ultimately a "last threshold" and "reincorporation" when Ray realizes it is Salinger, not he, who will get to travel into the ghost players' world with them (188-189, 196-198). Ray is jealous but realizes he is needed by his family and by the ballpark, as the ongoing caretaker. Through all of this, Ray's journey, although geographically limited for the most part to a cornfield in Iowa, is similar to that of many an epic hero.

In *Shoeless Joe*, sport has the ability to be apotheotic, to lift people into some sort of sacred world. We clearly see Kinsella's use of baseball for its mythic potential in how he uses aspects of the fantastic and sends Ray on a hero's journey. Like other forms of myth, Kinsella sees baseball as a place where life lessons can be learned, rebirth and renewal can happen, communities can form, and people can have a spiritual experience. However, with Kinsella, spiritual does not mean religious, at least not in the sense of organized religion. Much of the academic literature on *Shoeless Joe* focuses on Kinsella's critique of organized religion and his holding up of baseball as a means of spiritual development (see Altherr, 1990; Beach 1998; Joffe

---

1 So much so, that to go into it in really specific detail would take up far too much space. Readers interested in this would do well to consult Brian Aitken's 1990 essay "Baseball as Sacred Doorway in the Writing of W.P. Kinsella," which discusses Ray and the monomyth in fourteen stages. What is discussed here draws on this essay, unless otherwise noted.

1992; Lord 1992). For example, any characters who are identified with organized religion are framed negatively. Annie's mother is described as a woman who judges everyone on religious grounds, who looks with disapproval at just about everyone, and who revels in her self-righteousness: "When there were lulls in the conversation she read her Bible, sneering a little in her perfection" (Kinsella 1982, 23). Annie's brother Mark—who "also has brothers named Matthew, Luke, and John" (24)—subscribes to a form of evangelical Christianity, yet is also a rapacious capitalist and the main villain of the novel. The Christians in *Shoeless Joe* are joyless and allow religion to disrupt their social relationships (Beach 1998, 87).

The believers in baseball, however, achieve spiritual enlightenment. That baseball can be a form of secular religion, and one that substitutes for organized religion that is no longer viable (Cochran 1987, 32), is made clear throughout the novel. Shoeless Joe Jackson says, "This must be Heaven," and Ray replies, "No, it's Iowa" (Kinsella 1982, 16). Before he dies, Eddie Scissons delivers what Timothy Lord refers to as "the sermon on the bleachers" (1992, 47). Looking "for all the world like an Old Testament Prophet on the side of a mountain," Eddie tells everyone that "the word is baseball," and asks, "Can you imagine walking around with the very word of baseball enshrined inside you? Because the word of salvation is baseball. It gets inside you. Inside me. And the words that I speak are spirit, and *are* baseball" (Kinsella 1982, 191-192).[2] In these ways, baseball explicitly supplants organized religion—in particular, Christianity—as a place for belief, redemption, and community in *Shoeless Joe*, taking on the functions of religion and mythos.

CONCLUSION

Shoeless Joe is a canonical work of baseball literature and a fascinating exploration of America's national pastime by a Canadian writer. It departs from other baseball fiction in its magic realism, its demands of readers to buy into fantastical elements, and its sending of characters, and readers, on spiritual quests. The elements that set it apart are the very things that some readers and critics dislike. *Shoeless Joe* certainly has its faults—a naïve optimism,

---

2 Making further connections to Christianity, this text, reworded by Kinsella, is spoken by Jesus in the New Testament, in John 6:63: "The words that I speak to you are spirit, and *they* are life." My thanks to Joyce Hildebrandt for this additional insight.

an excess of metaphor, a nostalgia for a time that makes it less inclusive. However, the combination of real-world people with surreal events, often in simple, realistic settings, contributes to its believability and moves it towards the mythic possibilities of baseball that Kinsella liked so much.

In W. P. Kinsella's 1996 novel, *If Wishes Were Horses*, the character of Ray Kinsella resurfaces and narrates part of the novel. We learn that Ray's field still has its magic and that he has become legendary for helping people achieve various dreams. Ray's little cornfield ballpark in Iowa has become mythic itself. This is appropriate, since magic, dreaming, and myth are at the heart of W. P. Kinsella's *Shoeless Joe*. In allowing all of the characters in ·the novel to have their dreams fulfilled, Kinsella offers baseball (and Iowa) as a social world for dreams and dreamers. *Shoeless Joe*'s focus on myth and dreaming are what draw people into the novel—and often, into sport more generally. Sport is a world where myth sometimes lives and walks and where people can form a sense of identity and community through their fandom. This mythic function of modern sport is something Kinsella returns to again and again in his entire oeuvre of baseball writing.

WORKS CITED

Aitken, Brian. 1990. "Baseball as Sacred Doorway in the Writing of W. P. Kinsella." *Aethlon: The Journal of Sport Literature* 8, no. 1: 61–75.

Altherr, Thomas L. 1991. "W. P. Kinsella's Baseball Fiction, *Field of Dreams*, and the New Mythopoeism of Baseball." *Cooperstown Symposium on Baseball and American Culture, 1990*, edited by Alvin L. Hall, 97–108. Westport, CT: Meckler.

Beach, Charles Franklin. 1998. "Joyful vs. Joyless Religion in W. P. Kinsella's *Shoeless Joe*." *Aethlon: The Journal of Sport Literature* 16, no. 1: 85–94.

Boe, Alfred F. 1983. "Shoeless Joe Jackson Meets J. D. Salinger: Baseball and the Literary Imagination." *Arete: The Journal of Sport Literature* 1, no. 1: 179–85.

Brooks, Bruce. 1983. "Review Essay: *Shoeless Joe*." *Iowa Journal of Literary Studies* 4: 122–24.

Campbell, Joseph. 2008. *The Hero with a Thousand Faces*. 3rd ed. Novato, CA: New World Library. First published 1949.

Carino, Peter. 1994. "Fields of Imagination: Ballparks as Complex Metaphors in Kinsella's *Shoeless Joe* and *The Iowa Baseball Confederacy*." *Nine: A Journal of Baseball History and Social Policy Perspectives* 2, no. 2: 287–99.

Cochran, Robert W. 1987. "A Second Cool Papa: Hemingway to Kinsella and Hays." *Arete: The Journal of Sport Literature* 4, no. 2: 27–40.

Cutchins, Dennis. 2002. "*Catcher* in the Corn: J. D. Salinger and *Shoeless Joe*." In *The Catcher in the Rye: New Essays*, edited by J. P. Steed, 53–77. New York: Peter Lang.

Easton, Rebecca. 1999. "*Shoeless Joe* as Allegory: A Framework for the Writing of Fiction." *Aethlon: The Journal of Sport Literature* 17, no. 1: 121–27.

Fischer, David Marc. 2000. "Dreams, Magic and Peerless Plotting: *Shoeless Joe*." *Writing* 22, no. 4: 12–14.

Friedlander, Brett, and Robert Reising. 2009. *Chasing Moonlight: The True Story of* Field of Dreams' *Doc Graham*. Winston-Salem, NC: John F. Blair.

Garman, Bryan K. 1994. "Myth Building and Cultural Politics in W. P. Kinsella's *Shoeless Joe*." *Canadian Review of American Studies* 24, no. 1: 41–62.

Hamblin, Robert. 1992. "'Magic Realism,' or, The Split-Fingered Fastball of W. P. Kinsella." *Aethlon: The Journal of Sport Literature* 9, no. 2: 1–10.

Hollander, Russell. 1999. "Fathers and Sons in *Shoeless Joe*." *Nine: A Journal of Baseball History* 8, no. 1: 74–84.

Horvath, Brooke K., and William J. Palmer. 1987. "Three On: An Interview with David Carkeet, Mark Harris and W. P. Kinsella." *Modern Fiction Studies* 33, no. 1: 183–94.

Joffe, Linda S. 1992. "Praise Baseball. Amen. Religious Metaphors in *Shoeless Joe* and *Field of Dreams*." *Aethlon: The Journal of Sport Literature* 9, no. 2: 153–63.

Kinsella, W. P. 1980. *Shoeless Joe Jackson Comes to Iowa*. Ottawa: Oberon.

———. 1982. *Shoeless Joe*. Westminster, MD: Ballantine Books.

———. 1984. *The Thrill of the Grass*. Markham, ON: Penguin.

———. 1986. *The Iowa Baseball Confederacy*. Boston: Houghton Mifflin.

———. 1988. *The Further Adventures of Slugger McBatt*. Boston: Houghton Mifflin.

———. 1991. *Box Socials*. Toronto: HarperCollins Canada.

———. 1993. *The Dixon Cornbelt League and Other Baseball Stories*. New York: HarperCollins.

———. 1996. *If Wishes Were Horses*. Toronto: HarperPerennial.

———. 1998. *Magic Time*. Toronto: Doubleday.

———. 2000. *Japanese Baseball and Other Stories*. Saskatoon: Thistledown.

———. 2011. *Butterfly Winter*. Toronto: HarperCollins Canada.

Lord, Timothy C. 1992. "Hegel, Marx and Shoeless Joe: Religious Ideology in W. P. Kinsella's Baseball Fantasy." *Aethlon: The Journal of Sport Literature* 10, no. 1: 43–51.

Malamud, Bernard. 1952. *The Natural*. New York: Farrar, Straus and Geroux.

McGimpsey, David. 2000. *Imagining Baseball: America's Pastime and Popular Culture*. Bloomington: Indiana University Press.

Mesher, David. 1992. "Swing and a Myth: Shoeless Joe Jackson in Fiction." *San Jose Studies* 18, no. 3: 44–55.

Morrow, Don. 2002. "Dreams and Dreaming and the Father in W. P. Kinsella's *Shoeless Joe*." *Aethlon: The Journal of Sport Literature* 19, no. 2: 43–52.

Morse, Donald E. 1998. "Of the Tortoise, Baseball and the Family Farm. Fantasy and Nostalgia in *Shoeless Joe*: A Response to David L. Vanderwerken, 'Reading Race in W. P. Kinsella's *Shoeless Joe* and Phil Alden Robinson's *Field of Dreams*.'" *Hungarian Journal of English and American Studies* 4, nos. 1–2: 351–65.

———. 2004. "W. R. [sic] Kinsella's Postmodern, Metafictional Fantasy *Shoeless Joe*." *Journal of the Fantastic in the Arts* 15, no. 4: 309–19.

Murray, Don. 1987. *The Fiction of W. P. Kinsella: Tall Tales in Various Voices*. Fredericton, NB: York Press.

Nathan, Daniel A. 2003. *Saying It's So: A Cultural History of the Black Sox Scandal*. Urbana: University of Illinois Press.

Oriard, Michael. 1982. *Dreaming of Heroes: American Sports Fiction, 1868–1980*. Chicago: Nelson-Hall.

Pellow, C. Kenneth. 1991. "*Shoeless Joe* in Film and Fiction." *Aethlon: The Journal of Sport Literature* 9, no. 1: 17–23.

Randall, Neil. 1987. "*Shoeless Joe*: Fantasy and the Humour of Fellow-Feeling." *Modern Fiction Studies* 33, no. 1: 173–82.

Robinson, Phil Alden, dir. 1989. *Field of Dreams*. Universal.

Salinger, J. D. 1951. *The Catcher in the Rye*. Boston: Little, Brown.

Schwartz, Richard Alan. 1987. "Postmodernist Baseball." *Modern Fiction Studies* 33, no. 1: 135–49.

Steele, William. 2011. *A Member of the Local Nine: Baseball and Identity in the Fiction of W. P. Kinsella*. Jefferson, NC: McFarland.

Tolkien, J. R. R. 1964. "On Fairy-Stories." In *Tree and Leaf*, 11–70. London: George Allen and Unwin. First published 1939.

Vanderwerken, David L. 1998. "Reading Race in W. P. Kinsella's *Shoeless Joe* and Phil Alden Robinson's *Field of Dreams*." *Hungarian Journal of English and American Studies* 4, nos. 1–2: 345–50.

2

Cara Hedley

The Myth of Hockey and Identity in Paul Quarrington's *King Leary*

In a CBC interview following *King Leary*'s Canada Reads win in 2008, Paul Quarrington responded to the idea that he and other Canadian writers may "overidentify" with hockey in their writing: "Overidentification with hockey in . . . Canadian literature—it seems kind of a funny thing to be accused of, because why aren't more people writing about hockey?" (CBC 2008). Quarrington went on to note the rich potential for exploring "obsession" through the lens of hockey, a potential that he mines in his 1987 novel, *King Leary*.

Quarrington's novel tells the story of Percival "King" Leary, a septuagenarian on a quest for redemption from the offences he committed in order to become the greatest hockey player of his time, the "King of the Ice." Even as he sets off on his quest, Leary is terrified that the title of King and the history that he believes moors it in place will somehow slip from his grasp. And so, through story, he rails against the obliterating forces of time and the ephemeral nature of fan loyalty and hockey history. The recounting of his personal "history" takes the form of a patchwork narrative that is part memory, part "blarney," part elision, peppered with dementia-induced gaps, and strewn with the real-life detritus of hockey history. In his bid to defend his King of the Ice title, then, Leary transforms the material of his life into the stuff of legend, trying to write himself into myth.

Ultimately, the novel suggests important parallels between Leary's personal story and the story of Canada: the anxiety fuelling Leary's quest—his fear that the title will get away from him, that his identity will disappear without it, that he'll be forgotten—is the same psychology as that at the root of Canadian claims to "our national game." Leary's story of how he became King of the Ice thus mirrors both the process through which Canada as a nation has come to be named "King of Hockey" and national history-building writ large.

Relatively speaking in the global context, Canada is young, still in the process of accumulating history and the historical legitimacy that comes with age. As Jonathan Kertzer states in *Worrying the Nation*, "nations are invented not born" (1998, 8). This process of invention is provisional at best, based on uncertainty, experimentation, a perpetual shifting of ground. In other words, our national identity—and the literary "tradition" that reflects it—is ultimately insecure. Enter hockey: the game has been used as a safe and steadfast stake in the nation's self-development, employed as a kind of Prozac for the bipolar tendencies unearthed during the process. With the sport declared a "possession" of Canada, hockey victories may be regarded as promoting national legitimacy. The scoreboard never lies; as long as Canadian hockey teams and hockey players are winning, the nation reigns, in some small way, supreme.

In their introduction to *Now Is the Winter*, Jamie Dopp and Richard Harrison outline several key values forming the ideological constellation in which the narratives of game and nation intersect:

> Canada's great narrative of its own "northern" character, with
> its emphasis on the personal virtues of hardiness, self-reliance,
> and self-sacrifice, and on the social values of small-town life and
> loyalty to the collective good, all leavened with a touch of ironic
> humour, has been told so often in the language of hockey that the
> two stories—of game and nation—can seem like one. (2009, 9)

As Dopp and Harrison suggest, when it comes down to it, any hockey story—fact or fiction—is not about History or Tradition, those capitalized tyrants of narrative; the importance of hockey to Canadian identity is not about our collective domination of the game. Rather, it's about the stories we tell about ourselves, about who we are as a nation, and, most importantly, about why we need these stories. *King Leary* is among the best representations of this psychological process that the nation has to offer. Just as hockey gives Leary identity, a national identity, too, is informed by, or given meaning through, the stories we tell about hockey's importance, as a kind of ice-bound, violent, and graceful representation of who we are. *King Leary* is a highly personal myth about how a hockey legend invents his own myth and tries to redeem himself from the fallout of this process, but it also reflects the larger structures that bond hockey to nation-building myths: how a nation, in Kertzer's words, invents itself. And in the process, the narrative reveals the dangers inherent in the process of affixing identity to static or exclusionary narratives.

It's useful here to corner the meaning of *myth* as it relates to hockey's construction in a national consciousness. In the context of hockey, the buttressing of the game with a mythological foundation implies a spiritual connection between the game and nation; "myth" suggests the presence of some greater significance that resists full definition lurking beyond fact and historical context. In his introduction to the 2004 edition of *Hero of the Play*, Richard Harrison suggests that hockey could be said to offer a "creation myth" underpinning Canadian society:

> Perhaps most important, in terms of the intensity of the
> origin-of-hockey debate, is that creation myth *insists* that the
> distinguishing features of a people's character are things born *with
> them, created when the people were created.* . . . In mythic terms,
> hockey is one of the few things that *could be* said to be ours from
> before the beginning of *Canadian* time. (16–17)

This explanation offers a temporal anchor of sorts for hockey's unwieldy mythological weight. And yet explanations for hockey's role in national identity, when examined closely, are full of crevasses and holes—as are any metanarratives that attempt to encompass a country as vast and diverse as Canada. In *Hockey Night in Canada*, a pivotal investigation into the relationship between hockey and Canadian culture, Richard Gruneau and David Whitson observe that "hockey acts both as myth and allegory in Canadian culture, . . . a story that Canadians tell themselves about what it means to be Canadian" (1993, 13). In their exploration of the machinery of this "collective representation," they point out that the term "myth" is "most often used to suggest something that is essentially false. It implies a contrast between the world of fable or superstition and a 'reality' that the fables often disguise" (132). They invoke instead the Barthesian version of myth as it relates to the role of hockey in constructions of national identity:

Myths are not so much a denial of some actually existing truth as
they are a form of cultural discourse—a way of speaking—about
the world people live in. The problem is that myths tend to speak
a conservative language: their language is static and intransitive;
they represent the social world as something "natural," a fixed set
of relations without a history. (132)

In *King Leary*, Quarrington simultaneously plays into the "fixed set of
relations" structuring hockey's mythology on a national level and shines a
light on their faulty construction, exposing—most frequently through the
use of irony and humour—the static and intransitive language they speak.

The myth of hockey's naturalism forms the foundation of Leary's relationship to the game and his own hockey-playing identity. Quarrington
has Leary buy blindly into this myth, as good, red-blooded hockey-playing
"lads" are apparently expected to do, but Quarrington also subverts the
idea that this myth is static or natural. Citing Barthes's *Mythologies* (1972),
Gruneau and Whitson state that "the myth of hockey as a 'natural' adaptation to ice, snow, and open space is a particularly graphic example of
what Barthes is alerting us to—about how history can be confused with
nature," and they note that the myth is spread through Canadian culture
"by means of signifiers that continually link hockey to the physical environment" (1993, 132). Quarrington directly engages this complex, tangled
relationship between nature and hockey, declaring in a CBC interview that
the "obsession" he explores in *King Leary* has, at its heart, the chill of a
Canadian winter. To him, what *King Leary* is really about is "the winter
and . . . our connection with that. And hockey is . . . one of the things we do
to make our peace with winter" (CBC 2008). Here, Quarrington taps into
the romanticized collective imagining of hockey as an instrument through
which to channel winter energies, a way to play with winter rather than hide
from it, and large parts of Leary's narrative deal directly in these "signifiers"
that, as Gruneau and Whitson say, "continually link hockey to the physical
environment" (1993, 132).

Indeed, some of the most striking, beautiful imagery in this novel depicts
the winter landscape and the imagery of water and ice, cast in the glow of
Leary's revisionist nostalgia. In these passages, winter suffuses the landscape
with a kind of magic that transfers to the game itself as an expression of
the season. Leary describes skating with his old friend Clay Clinton on

the canal of their childhood: "One day after school the two of us laced on our skates and flew down to the canal. She was frozen hard and beautiful. The sunset lay across the river bright and heavy" (Quarrington 1987, 12). Racing Clay on the canal, he shifts into "the hardstep": "Here's what you do. You puff up your spirit till it won't fit into your body anymore. You get your feet to dance across the icebelly of the world. You get empty except for life and the winter wind" (12). Quarrington demonstrates in this scene the ideological mechanisms underpinning the myth of naturalism in hockey, with Leary portraying the intersection of winter wind, skating, and "spirit" in a naturalized tableau.

Leary further establishes his blind belief in hockey as a mythical element of the natural world—a "fixed set of relations without a history" (Gruneau and Whitson 1993, 132)—on both a universal and a personal level in his discussions about hockey's origin. In an anecdote about a seminar on hockey development in North America that he and Clay Clinton attended, Leary describes how another attendee, a young hockey coach from Minnesota, started discussing the origins of hockey, exposing Leary's false, unexamined beliefs: "And the lad from Minn. went on and on about soccer and lacrosse, English foot soldiers playing *baggataway* with the Indians, some Scandinavian entertainment called *bandy*. I bit my tongue, but the truth of the matter is, I never knew that hockey originated. I figured it was just always there, like the moon" (Quarrington 1987, 8).

By connecting the idea of hockey's origins to the ever-present, unquestioned entity of the moon, Leary expands the boundaries of the signifiers through which hockey becomes moored in the myth of naturalism. Leary connects the rink to the moon on several other occasions, cementing this symbolism. He describes the magical "moon-washed rink" on which he first spies the monks playing shinny:

> The rink that the Brothers of St. Alban the Martyr built was [. . .] a circle. There was a full moon, and it filled the window across from my cot, and for some strange reason I could make out all the mountains and craters. The moon was a strange color, too, a silver like a nickel had been flipped into the sky.
>
> Then I heard the sounds, the soft windy sweeping of hockey sticks across the ice. [. . .] The moon was so bright that I do believe I squinted up my eyes. I have never seen it like that since. (145)

The twinning of round rink and round moon reinforces how hockey, in Leary's reconstructed memories, becomes a magical world unto itself, separate from reality. Inside the perfect circle of the rink, the monks' play defies laws of gravity and physiology: Leary describes Brother Isaiah, the blind monk, "skating around like a madman, stealing pucks, passing and receiving," with the moonlight "sitting on his dead eyes like it does on the still surface of a lake," and Brother Simon the Ugly "dancing, jumping into the air [. . .] his monstrous frame silhouetted against the trout silver moon" (146). With the line "I have never seen it like that since" (145), Leary both highlights the childlike wonder of that night and emphasizes the importance of the reformatory as the origin of his creation myth. It is not only a closed-off world, surrounded by a moat, where boys are held to "keep them out of hot water" (34), but also a magical place that defies replication, its memories and mythology accessible only to Leary himself, sealed off from the corrupting potential of the present world.

The oddly circular rink surfaces several times in his memories, offering itself as a potential symbol for Leary's personal creation myth. Dopp suggests that "Leary's quest to redress the wrongs of his life is an attempt to recapture the wholeness of life as represented by the round rink, the perfect outdoor ice, of the monks" (2009, 85). The perfect circle is part of what imbues those days and Leary's magic-laced introduction to hockey with the element of myth: Leary is searching for the innocence and wonder of that time at the reformatory, prior to his obsession with becoming King of the Ice, when hockey was at once just a game played with his friends and a spectacle of magic and myth in which giant men could fly and blind men regain their sight.

As the game of hockey is a natural element in Leary's life, an unexamined part of the natural world, omnipresent as the moon, so too does hockey exist in Leary's own body as a kind of mysterious, natural knowledge without origin: he tells his audience, "I can't remember lacing on blades for the first time. Likewise with hockey. I've got no idea when I first heard of, saw, or played the game of hockey" (Quarrington 1987, 7). In this way, Leary not only establishes the mythological status of hockey as it exists in his world, but he also creates the foundation for the process of his own self-mythologization as he seeks to solidify his King of the Ice legacy; without the proof of memories or stories to represent his entry into the world of hockey, he suggests that his identity as hockey player was fixed from the beginning. This physical naturalization of the game as "bred in the bone" allows Leary to represent, in the "hardstepping" scene discussed earlier, the physical manifestation of the game as a mystical transformation of the body that draws its power as much from magic as it does from physiology:

> The coaches had slide projectors set up to show diagrams of leg muscles and such palaver, and it made me laugh because it was just hardstepping, which I been doing since I was born. Here's what you do. You puff up your spirit till it won't fit in your body anymore. You get your feet to dance across the icebelly of the world. You get empty except for life and the winter wind. (12)

Here, Leary rejects the dismantlement of play into its constituent parts and corresponding muscle groups, relying instead on the mythology of hockey as a natural marriage of winter and the body, mystical yet elemental, tapping into the spirit and creating a union between physical "life" and the "winter wind."

The Learyian logic, then, begins to unfold: if hockey has been a part of Leary's body from the beginning, as natural as breathing, then he must have been born an heir to the King's throne—and it follows that if hockey is a natural extension of the definitive Canadian winter, then it must represent some element or expression of national identity. From here grows Leary's quest to establish himself as King of the Ice. And Leary declares this status to anyone who will listen, in an often desperate bid to cement his legacy. First as a player, then as coach and general manager of the Maple Leaves—whose name operates not only as a grammatically corrected surrogate of the Toronto Maple Leafs but also as a metonymic representation of the nation itself—Leary announces himself, with bluster and bravado, as hockey royalty: "I am the King of the Ice!" Leary declares at the outset of the novel. "I am the high-muck-a-muck hockey player! I have an Indian nickname, *Loofweeda*, which means 'windsong,' referring to the fact that I could skate faster than anyone else" (2).

Leary repeats such claims about his own greatness throughout the novel. This repetition is a key strategy to construct and maintain the naturalness of his self-made, mythologized status as King of the Ice. If myths are a form of "cultural discourse," a mode of representing the world, the myth of King of the Ice can be viewed as a discourse both created and perpetuated by Leary himself, a "complex semiotic system" used to invent his relation to the world, then make it appear "natural" (Buma 2012, 72). In recounting his hockey-playing days, Leary outlines the process whereby he establishes his heroic hockey-playing persona and then adopts this fictional persona as his naturalized identity through performance and repetition. He recalls the early days of his professional hockey career:

> It was in those days that I perfected my swagger, the dragon-head cane flipping. The tykes would call out to me, "Hi there, Little Leary!" this predating when I became the King of the Ice.
> "Ho, there, young pups!" I'd call back, tipping my cap. "Eat yer veggies and you'll grow up like me." (Quarrington 1987, 73)

Here, we are given a glimpse behind the curtain, complete with the props ("the dragon-head cane") and dialogue ("Eat yer veggies and you'll grow up like me") that Leary invents, then repeats to "perfection" as he constructs the myth out of the man. Leary repeats variations of "Eat yer veggies" to children throughout his reign as King of the Ice, not because he believes it but because he thinks it is what a hockey hero would say to adoring young fans.

While Quarrington allows Leary this airtime to construct and defend his King of the Ice mythology, the author also includes ironic slippages and holes in Leary's story that allow the reader to step back from the inflated, mythologized version of himself given to us by an unreliable narrator and view the unstable structures of both the personal myth of King of the Ice and the larger myth of hockey. Jamie Dopp cautions that *King Leary*

> does offer a similar complexity in its treatment of the national
> myths intertwined with hockey lore. This complexity emerges
> in part because Leary is an unreliable narrator, prone to "the
> blarney" as well as to the mental contortions of one engaged in
> an exercise of self-justification; thus, any time Leary waxes poetic
> about his own background or the meaning of the game the reader
> is well-advised to look for irony. (2009, 89)

Leary, as narrator, attempts to convince the reader that his title, King of the Ice, is a pre-existing designation that he both earned and successfully defended through innate talent and hard work. However, Quarrington, as author, gives the reader greater agency than that, allowing us to recognize that we are in the hands of an unreliable and often deluded narrator. Despite Leary's best attempts to exert absolute control of his own story, the narrative slips out of his grasp. It is in these moments of slippage that Quarrington not only displays his comedic chops but also allows readers glimpses of the ironies, omissions, and bits of blarney, large and small, embedded in Leary's telling.

Perhaps the most contradictory counter-story that manages to get past Leary is the origin story of the name "King of the Ice," as told by Blue Hermann. When Hermann says to Iain, their nursing home aide and sidekick, "It's rather interesting about Leary's nickname, 'The King,'" Leary jumps in not as a speaker in conversation with Blue and Iain but as the narrator (Quarrington 1987, 115). "Don't listen to him," Leary tells his readerly audience. "They've given him some very nasty drugs at the home." The back and forth continues, with Leary in narrative asides rebutting or supplementing Hermann's dialogue with his own flourishes of glory. Eventually, Hermann describes the scene in which Leary's nickname was born: "And they take the puck down the ice. Leary applies the St. Louis Whirlygig to his cover and poof, he's in the clear." Leary interjects again to add his own self-aggrandizing commentary: "One of the great wonders of the world, the St. Louis Whirlygig! It's a spit in the eye of gravity and sundry physical laws!" Hermann then, despite Leary's best efforts to steer the story in a different direction, completes his version: "And Leary starts pounding his stick on the ice, you see, so that his teammates will pass the puck. [. . .] But they ignore [. . .] him. Leary throws down his stick in disgust and marches off the ice. [. . .] And Richie Reagan says, 'Well, who the hell does he think he is—the King of the Ice?'" (116). In this story, despite Leary's attempts to divert the reader, we are given a counter-narrative to Leary's mythologized version of the King of the Ice story that uncovers the title's ironic core—an irony that is apparently "lost" on Percival, as is the Shakespeare allusion.

Humour is perhaps the true King of this novel, and, as Don Morrow suggests, Quarrington uses it as a vehicle to "de-mystif[y] the heroic in hockey" (2002, 114). Perhaps the best representation of this style of "demystification" is in the *Loofweeda* origin story. To garner legitimacy for his title, Leary often refers to a second nickname, *Loofweeda*, which, he tells us, is an "Indian nickname" given to him by Manny's Aboriginal grandfather, Poppa Rivers. Skirting the subject of *Loofweeda*'s true meaning when he first calls Leary by that name, Poppa Rivers says, "Oh, a literal translation would be something like 'wind music' or 'windsong'" (Quarrington 1987, 138). Leary flaunts this nickname given to him by the Aboriginal grandfather who appears to Leary as a wise elder or shaman-like figure in his dreams, using it as an affirmation of his elevated status. Through this name, he claims, Poppa Rivers has declared him a kind of mystical athlete with a rare ability to "skate like the wind," as he explains to his audience. However, in another moment of ironic slippage later in the novel, the reader learns that Poppa Rivers never did assign Leary an Aboriginal name and that *Loofweeda* actually means "breaking wind"; Poppa Rivers used the word around Leary, and Leary mistakenly adopted it as his nickname, ascribing to it his own significance in the service of his King of the Ice mythology. As Dopp notes:

> The joke on Leary suggests how credulous he has been in his quest for the kind of "immortality" that such mythic-style names seem to offer. It also hints at all he has repressed or elided in his quest to maintain his "immortal" status. Like his Shakespearean namesake, Leary's hubris has made him cling destructively to his crown, blind to those who truly love him. (2009, 90)

With both accidental and willful blindness, Leary recreates the world around him in the image of King, and it is through Quarrington's frequently comic depiction of these blind spots that the reader is able to identify Leary's tragic flaws.

Perhaps the strongest method of demystifying the heroic through humour is in Quarrington's tragicomic representations of aging and the aged body. While Leary is ruthless in his portrayal of Blue Hermann's failing body, these descriptions also act as a kind of mirror on the aged King himself. Leary and Hermann are, to a certain extent, twinned in the novel, not only forced into the childlike domestic situation of room-sharing but also operating as memory surrogates for each other at times: they are contemporaries, having risen to their respective reigns—Hermann as a journalist, Leary as King of the Ice—in the same hockey world, during the same time period. As such, Leary's farcical representations of Hermann's failing body and the distance between Hermann's elevated status of the past and his current frail, broken-down state in the nursing home operate as a reflection of Leary's own decline, vulnerability, and mortality, showing how far the King himself has fallen. When describing one of the many indignities of old age that Blue Hermann faces, Leary offers a word of caution: "Blue has to wear this underwear gear that resembles diapers, due to his problem with incontinence. But unless you know exactly what God's got in store for you, don't laugh" (Quarrington 1987, 194). In this admonition to the audience, he implicates himself in the same dignity-robbing process of aging that Hermann is experiencing; Leary, too, is a victim of this particular jest of God. He warns us not to laugh, and yet laugh we do as Quarrington serves up uncomfortable but chuckleworthy descriptions of the tragicomic minutiae of Blue Hermann's physical decrepitude.

In keeping with the representations of aging in the novel, the nursing home assumes the role of a halfway house between life and death, with Leary travelling alongside Hermann toward the inevitable in their shared rooms—both at the nursing home and at the hotel during their ill-fated trip to Toronto. At one point, Leary describes Hermann's appearance while sleeping as a person "suffering the torments of hell" (84), and when a maid accidentally opens their hotel room door in Toronto, then flees in terror upon seeing him and Hermann, Leary says, "I can't blame her. Over there is Blue Hermann. He lies on top of the bed sheets (but somehow knotted in them), naked to the world. As he snores, his mouth falls open, his maw both darkly gray and red as blood" (190). In this juxtaposition of the dark gray and blood-red of Hermann's "maw," Leary portrays him as both succumbing to and defying mortality, his body assuming a post-mortem pallor, while the "red as blood" parts announce his stubbornly persistent life. Through Leary's tragicomic representations of old age—the winter of both his life and Hermann's—the audience participates in the demystification of the hero, staring with Leary into the dark gray and blood-red maw of his own imminent death, with Hermann operating as a kind of emissary of this message, a comic curtain behind which Leary finally cannot hide his own mortality. Death, eventually, will get in.

Quarrington ultimately subverts Leary's romanticization of winter, then, dissolving the nostalgic gloss that characterizes the narrator's depiction of the shinny-filled winters of his youth. Not only is the winter of Leary's life not what he imagined he had in store, but winter itself has become an enemy, those beautiful winter landscapes in which he used to shine now treacherous, a battlefield possessing latent danger at every turn. Winter in Canada is not for the elderly or the infirm, as evidenced by this malevolent transformation of a parking lot: "It is a treacherous undertaking, the crossing of the parking lot. The sun and wind are staging a major coup, trying to replace the stubborn winter with fragile spring, and the ground is now half-water, half-ice, slick as bacon fat" (217). In another scene, Leary views the winter landscape through the lens of old age, describing the forests as "dead, drowned in snow" (84). Rather than representing the promise of play, the white slate onto which young boys and men can project their dreams, winter has taken on the symbolism of death.

Through these present-day depictions, Leary inadvertently proves that, through old age, he has become shut out of his own youth-centric mythology, thus demonstrating the larger risk that hockey holds for providing a model of nation-building and national identity that is exclusionary, defined as much by who and what is left out as by what is included. In her analysis of women's shinny hockey in Toronto parks, Anne Hartman notes the sociopolitical significance in notions of sport as an expression of nationalism and shared history:

> Other scholars studying the development of nationalisms have also paid attention to the growth of organized sports. For example, following Eric Hobsbawm's work on sports as "invented traditions," we may argue that constructions of history and memory are not about inert pasts, but are very much about relations of power in the present. (2009, 133)

In this way, we can examine Leary's reconstruction—or reinvention—of his hockey glory days and his reign as King of the Ice for the "relations of power" ingrained in the narrative, reflecting not only his individual experiences but also the larger power structures inculcated in the positioning of hockey as invented tradition, or "our national game."

One early signifier that sets the framework for this exclusionary narrative is the narrator's address to the audience as male. Toward the beginning of the novel, after describing his first encounter with Clay Clinton, Leary states, "Now sir, after an introduction like that, it probably seems strange that Clay and I became friends at all" (Quarrington 1987, 10). This address is reiterated near the end of the novel when Leary admires Duane Killbrew's girlfriend, addressing the reader as "brother": "This lady's got bubs, brother, but I don't have the time to tell you about it" (223). These addresses—so small and brief they could easily be missed—can be read as containing a seed of hockey's exclusionary mythology: the hockey world that Leary describes is a boys' only club. These narrow parameters of inclusion also extend to the version of masculinity defining the population of this world. Michael Buma parses the significance of the description of Killebrew's girlfriend:

> Leary's address to the reader as "brother" is particularly informative, extending the fraternity basis of hockey belonging on the basis of shared appreciation of a woman's body. This throwaway moment, of course, also works to referee the terms of hockey masculinity and team belonging, not only excluding men who wouldn't appreciate the female body (i.e. homosexuals) but also those who would be troubled or offended by this sort of objectification. (2012, 250)

Indeed, the fraternity portrayed in this novel is extremely limited in scope. Women are either the wives or girlfriends of hockey players or are placed under the spotlight in moments of objectification by men, beginning early for Leary when, as a boy, he spies on Clay Clinton's sister "Horseface" having a bath (Quarrington 1987, 12). This is a world in which women are frequently judged by their "bubs" and are perceived as weak. Leary's wife, Chloe, has a heart flutter, which causes her to give "the impression that her poor heart was like a canary in a coal mine, a breath away from death" (134), and she spends much of her limited page-space in the novel in a state of fragile mental and physical health, weak and vulnerable. In contrast, Chloe's sister, Jane, the bold romantic interest of both Manfred and Clay, announces to Leary when she first meets him, "I'm sweating like a stuck pig" (74). She is the strongest female figure in the book, and yet she is still relegated to the stands, becoming a kind of pawn in a romantic tug-of-war between the two men. Had this narrative taken place a few decades later, Jane might have been cast as a hockey player herself (although she is tiny in stature, as are most of the women in this novel), but despite the layered history of women's hockey in Canada, this is not the reality in representations of hockey's "tradition" in this country, which has traditionally excluded women, as well as men who might not subscribe to the limited style of "fraternity" represented in this novel, as Buma points out.

Under these strict limitations, Leary's own sons also fall well short of making the cut. The "gormless" younger son, Clifford, while a huge hockey fan, is spoken of in disparaging tones by Leary; childlike and overweight, Clifford, try as he might, does not fit into his father's exclusionary hockey mythology, nor does he fit into the discourse of masculinity dictated by this world. Likewise, Leary paints Clarence, his deceased eldest son, as a disappointment, a family outcast. Although Leary never states it outright, he suggests through references to Clarence's "queer stuff" and "pornographic" poetry that he is gay (210). As a child, when he is allowed into Leary's hockey world during a Maple Leaves' family event at the arena, Clarence shows up in figure skates and "skates like a girl" (48). However, in this scene, Quarrington also takes a subtly adaptable, subversive approach to representations of the "terms of hockey masculinity" (Buma 250), describing, alongside Leary's initial embarrassment at Clarence's figure skating moves, his grudging admiration—as well as that of his teammates—of his son's graceful and complicated manoeuvres. In part, this reaction can be traced back to the fact that Leary's own signature hockey move, "the Whirligig," is inspired by another player's "figure skating move" (37). Referring to this scene and other figure skating references in the novel, Sarah Jameson suggests that "recent analysis of masculinity and styles of movement in figure skating sheds light on how the novel's representations of skating and dance work to question the narrow conception of masculinity dominant in hockey" (2014, 184). But this is not enough for Clarence to be granted entrance into Leary's exclusive King of the Ice mythology, except in his seldom-spoken-of, yet central role as the villainous child who left out the toy truck (or so Leary believes for most of his adult life) that caused Leary's career-ending knee injury.

These sociopolitical tensions play out in the realm of race as well. As Jameson points out, the fact that Manfred is Aboriginal "suggests the broader historical and political significance of Leary's paranoid bid for hockey supremacy"; she asserts that "Leary can be read as representative of a Canadian, White, male, settler identity whose dominance is founded upon the suppression and expulsion of the Aboriginal" (2014, 186). Citing the trope of the "postcolonial gothic" in Manfred's appearance to Leary as a ghost throughout the narrative, Jameson suggests that "Leary's mistreatment of Manfred . . . draws a direct link between the version of masculinity still celebrated in the game [Canadian hockey] and the violence of colonial history" (186). In this reading, then, Leary's quest for redemption inculcates a larger, national paradigm of reconciliation, suggesting a broader national mythology at work beneath the surface of the narrative.

In order to counter the "static and intransitive" language typifying myths, Gruneau and Whitson, following Barthes (1972), counsel that "it is necessary to develop a way of representing the world that has a more active character—a discourse that depicts human beings as makers of a world that can be continually changed" (1993, 132). Toward the end of the novel, when Leary is facing the ghosts of his past head on, he discovers the ability to change the discourse he has clung to at many a great personal cost, recognizing both that his time as King of the Ice is gone and that the measures he took to preserve the title—specifically, his betrayals of Manny—were not worth it. He tells Duane Killebrew, the hockey star du jour, "I was the King for many years. But now I am an old, old man, and undeserving, what's more. You may be the best there ever was—although I would have loved to have gone toe-to-toe with you in my prime—and you are the King. That's all there is to it" (Quarrington 1987, 218). This admission that he is "unworthy" marks how far our hero has come in his emotional development over the course of this late-life coming-of-age tale. The conversation between Leary and Killebrew continues, with Leary returning one last time to his King of the Ice performance and lines:

> "But now, hey, you're still a pup. Keep eating yer veggies, and try to have a good time now and again."
> "King—Percy—there's something I have to tell you."
> "What's that, son?"
> "I hate fucking veggies!"
> The sunlight is playing on the road, dancing in the melted snow. "So do I, Duane. So do I." (219)

In this admission, Leary reveals the underlying hypocrisies embedded in his King of the Ice persona. Here, we finally begin to see the cleaving of Leary the man from his mythologized King of the Ice identity. It is a moment of illumination, both literal and metaphoric, the outer world reflecting the freedom that Leary experiences once he is released from the burden of defending his title, with all of its inherent contradictions and falseness; when he passes it on, the sunlight comes out to "play [. . .] on the road," penetrating the mythical weight of winter that has influenced so much of his story, melting the snow, then "dancing" in it. This moment reveals the burden of carrying and perpetuating static mythologies. Not only have Leary's fervent attempts to reinforce his King of the Ice title resulted in the betrayal of his best friend; they have also produced an inflexibility of character, an inability to change and grow. Leary becomes locked in an extended adolescence of sorts, trapped in a loop, attempting to recapture the grandeur of his long-gone glory days. Quarrington not only illustrates the destructive effects of an obsessive adherence to a fixed identity like King of the Ice; he also illuminates the dangers of attaching larger concepts of identity to a particular ideology or story. If we attach national identity to the mythology of hockey—our national game, our national religion—we are investing in a story that is, like Leary's King of the Ice mythology, limited in scope, prone to fantasy, and resistant to change. In the end, Leary experiences relief from the burdens of this static mythology, but he also finds final comfort in hockey when he returns to the core hockey memories and images that retain their spiritual significance for him: in his final moments, he comes full circle, returning to the perfectly round rink at the reformatory, where the monks are still at play. "I join them in the circle," Percival "King" Leary tells us.

WORKS CITED

Barthes, Roland. 1972. *Mythologies*. Translated by Annette Lavers. New York: Hill and Wang.

Buma, Michael. 2012. *Refereeing Identity: The Cultural Work of Canadian Hockey Novels*. Montréal and Kingston: McGill-Queen's University Press.

CBC (Canadian Broadcasting Corporation). 2008. "*King Leary*'s Author and Advocate Savour 2008 Canada Reads Victory." *CBC Digital Archives*, CBC Radio, 4 March. http://www.cbc.ca/archives/entry/king-learys-author-and-advocate-savour-victory.

Dopp, Jamie. 2009. "Win Orr Lose: Searching for the Good Canadian Kid in Canadian Hockey Fiction." In *Canada's Game: Hockey and Identity*, edited by Andrew Holman, 81–97. Montréal and Kingston: McGill-Queen's University Press.

Dopp, Jamie, and Richard Harrison. 2009. "Introduction." In *Now Is the Winter: Thinking About Hockey*, edited by Jamie Dopp and Richard Harrison, 7–18. Hamilton, ON: Wolsak and Wynn.

Gruneau, Richard, and David Whitson. 1993. *Hockey Night in Canada: Sport, Identities and Cultural Politics*. Toronto: Garamond Press.

Harrison, Richard. 2004. "Ten Years with the Hero: On Hockey and Poetry." In *Hero of the Play: Poems Revised and New*, 10th Anniversary Edition, 13–27. Hamilton, ON: Wolsak and Wynn.

Hartman, Anne. 2009. "'Here for a Little Pickup?': Notes on Women's Shinny Hockey in Toronto Public Parks." In *Now Is the Winter: Thinking About*

Hockey, edited by Jamie Dopp and Richard Harrison, 123–44. Hamilton, ON: Wolsak and Wynn.

Jameson, Sarah. 2014. "Reading the 'St. Louis Whirlygig': Hockey, Masculinity, and Aging in Paul Quarrington's *King Leary*." *Journal of Canadian Studies* 48, no. 3: 181–99.

Kertzer, Jonathan. 1998. *Worrying the Nation: Imagining a National Literature in English Canada*. Toronto: University of Toronto Press.

Morrow, Don. 2002. "Quarrington's Hockey Shtick: A Literary Analysis." In *Putting It on Ice: Hockey and Cultural Identities*, vol. 1 of *Putting It on Ice*, edited by Colin D. Howell, 111–18. Halifax: Gorsebrook Research Institute, St. Mary's University.

Quarrington, Paul. 1987. *King Leary*. New York: Random House.

3 *Jason Blake*

Hockey, Humour, and Play in Wayne Johnston's *The Divine Ryans*

Many games are played most intensely by disturbed people; generally speaking, the more disturbed they are, the harder they play.

Eric Berne, *Games People Play* (1964)

The Divine Ryans is what some might describe as a "must-read." Hockey fans will delight in references to Maurice Richard, Bobby Hull, and Gump Worsley, that maskless, wisecracking keeper who was always "so indignant when his defencemen allowed so much as one shot" (Johnston 1998, 126). Those who favour the highbrow can feast on allusions to Virgil's *Aeneid*, Dante's *Divine Comedy*, and Shakespeare's *Hamlet*, and those who see hockey in religious terms can appreciate that the "apuckalypse" is nigh and that a sinful soul can become "'puck black,' so black that no amount of time in the fires of purgatory could cleanse it" (51). In short, Wayne Johnston's 1990 novel goes beyond the conventional sports plot about winning the big game and beyond the tired hockey-literature theme of staging Canadianness.

In Johnston's riotous yet sad novel, nine-year-old Draper Doyle Ryan is exiting childhood and learning about sexuality, death, and life in general. Hockey and humour provide him with comfort in a mirthless house belonging to one Philomena Clark (née Ryan), a woman who, for no apparent reason, barks "Don't you smile at me" when she and Draper's mother are looking in the same mirror (91). If Aunt Phil had her way, hers would be a household free of play and smiles. Draper and others who suffer under her are driven to "find release in laughter that subverts the discouragement of their circumstances" (Cook 2004, 129). There is, thus, a sorrow behind their laughter precisely because only fleetingly is Draper soothed by humour's "quality of sudden lightness or lightening ... which we may call *levity*" (Carroll 2014, 41). Draper does, however, have a key ally—his irreverent uncle Reginald, who masterfully uses puns, quips, and laughter as part of an emotional survival strategy.

In this chapter, I examine how hockey, humour, play, and learning converge in *The Divine Ryans*. More specifically, I explore how playfulness stokes Draper's development even as it, like gallows humour, liberates him "temporarily from otherwise inescapable torment" (Lewis 1989, 80). I conclude by pondering the corruption of play and confronting the paradox of forced play—in particular, when Draper is coerced into boxing. Though Draper "wished there was nothing else to think about but hockey" (127), hockey and play are more than an escapist flight from real life: they help Draper make sense of his world. Phil and her ilk, meanwhile, use play and hockey to shame others.

A THEMATIC OVERVIEW

Johnston's novel centres on a four-on-three grudge match between two sides of the Ryan family—on one team, Draper, his sister Mary, their mother Linda (née Delaney), and Uncle Reginald; on the other, the forbidding trio of Uncle Seymour, Aunt Louise, and Aunt Phil. At stake is the future of the Ryan family line. Aunt Phil's squad misuses hockey and other forms of play, including the playfulness that fuels humour. For them, the aim is always one-upmanship, and they constantly seek extrinsic benefits that transcend the play world—that autotelic world that, ideally, has its purpose only within the game. Aunt Phil, who is particularly fond of seeing how soundly the "Catholic" Montreal Canadiens can trounce the "Protestant" Toronto Maple Leafs, is like an athlete who plays only for the salary, never for the sake of play itself. In contrast, Uncle Reginald uses hockey, play, and humour for healthy side effects—in particular, to help Draper grow and learn—but he never loses sight of the enjoyment to be found in the play spirit.

The novel is narrated by Draper Doyle Ryan, a confused boy whose father has recently died. Draper is the youngest male in a priest- and nun-rich family known in St. John's, Newfoundland, as "the Divine Ryans." Aunt Louise Ryan is a nun, Uncle Seymour Ryan is a priest, and Aunt Phil, a laywoman, is more Catholic than the Pope. Phil has little time for the modernizing reforms of Vatican II (1962–65), and years after her husband's death, she remains a woman in black, having "embrace[d] widowhood as her vocation, her calling" (8). Moralistic, dreary, and mean, she drags Draper to wakes, because "boys [. . .] could never be reminded of their mortality too often" (115). Poor Draper. More crucial than Aunt Phil's odd pedagogy, however, is her inability to laugh and enjoy herself, even when at play or involved in games.

The Divine Ryans tracks the year between the Stanley Cup games of 1966 and 1967, which is also the year following the death of Draper's father. Donald Ryan, a closeted homosexual and newspaper editor, committed suicide shortly after his son caught him with another man, "engaged in what might have been some strange form of mimicry, their trousers down around their ankles" (184). The bewildered son cannot understand what he has seen, so he suppresses the memory of that encounter, just as he forgets the traumatic discovery of his father's body a few days later. Aunt Phil, unaware that Draper had already seen the body, proclaims, "'I found him first,' [. . .] as if, by doing so, she had reclaimed him for the Ryans" (205).[1] Moreover, hoping to avoid any scandal through rumours of suicide or, worse (for her), homosexuality, Aunt Phil spreads the false news that a heart attack killed Donald. The aunt's camouflaging story fits what Méira Cook calls the family's "neurotic secrecy leading, inevitably, to repression" (2004, 122) and what Cynthia Sugars refers to as the Ryans' urge to avoid the "embarrassment of . . . homosexuality" (2004, 156).

The Ryans are a family in decline. Former masters of a mini-empire that included "a marbleworks and a pair of flower shops" (Johnston 1998, 1), the mighty Ryans are now down to two businesses: a profitable funeral home and a spectacularly unprofitable newspaper. The newspaper, known in days gone by as *The Daily Catholic Chronicle*, depicts life as Aunt Phil sees it. In

---

1 "Reclaim" is splendidly chosen, as it not only refers to the recovery of ownership but also means "to recall from wrong or improper conduct" (to borrow from *Merriam-Webster*'s definition, https://www.merriam-webster.com/diction-ary/reclaim).

the words of the ribald Uncle Reginald, the *Chronicle* is now "the world's worst newspaper," "a mourning paper, [. . .] a paper in mourning for its own past greatness" (65). Having "ruined the careers of many a Protestant politician" (27), the vampiric newspaper now sucks the money and lifeblood of the Ryan family. To wit, the novel's first line reads, "Our house must be sold to help keep *The Daily Chronicle* afloat" (1), the undertone being that the family itself is sinking, with the passive modal ("must be sold") suggesting agentless inevitability, not a financial decision made by Aunt Phil.

So a mere five months after Donald Ryan's suicide, Draper, his sister Mary, and their mother have to move in with domineering Aunt Phil—but also with Uncle Reginald, who lives in an attic apartment. Decked out in "his waistcoat and his top-hat" (25), Reginald drives the hearse for the family funeral home. For Phil, Seymour, and Louise, dapper and mirthful Reginald is "the embodiment of all that was wrong with Reg Ryan's [Sr.]" funeral home (23). In other words, he's a rare bright spot in Draper's troubled world, which is marked by homelessness, death, funerals and wakes, and sexual trauma, including nightmares.

Draper, in addition to repeatedly seeing his father's ghost (which is always holding a hockey puck), has disturbing dreams about the "Momary," a satyr-like creature that frightens him into wetting his bed. "Half Mom, half Mary," the Momary "was thirty-five years old above the waist and twelve years below it" (42). Johnston neatly inserts these sexual overtures into the plot line and develops them by having Uncle Reginald provide Draper with sessions of "oralysis." He distinguishes oralysis from analysis for Draper, telling him that "[t]he job of an analyst was to take his patient seriously. The job of an oralyst was to make him laugh" (28). Such playful lines, crucial to the novel, highlight the freeing power of laughter while showing just how grim the rest of Draper's life is. However, for all his puns and games, the oralyst Uncle Reginald helps Draper navigate his new life at Aunt Phil's, recover the "missing week" of his father's death, and begin to understand his surroundings as he inches towards puberty (8). Most importantly for Draper's informal education, Reginald never talks down to his nine-year-old nephew.

Like many young hockey fans, Draper looks to the greats for inspiration. Before moving into Aunt Phil's house, he decorated his bedroom with "pictures of all the goalies who had ever played for the Habs, a line of succession beginning with George Vezina [*sic*] and ending with Gump

Worsley, the Gumper" (16). This "line of succession" announces a major theme of the novel: the need to produce a Ryan male to continue the family line. The goalie lineage neatly parallels the Ryan family's lineage, a parallel made obvious when Draper later contemplates the portraits peering down from Aunt Phil's walls. Draper's new household is overseen by the patriarchal eyes of "Grandpa Stern, Grandpa Cross, Grandpa Grim, and Grandpa Disapproving," as Reginald nicknames them (26). These nicknames are particularly biting, since grandfather, great-grandfather, and so on become interchangeable, generic "Grandpas," united in their grimness. Grimmer still is the suggestion that sternness and crossness, like shortness, somehow runs in the Ryan blood. Grimmest of all is the prospect that one day Draper's portrait might hang among them, for he is the "future of the family" (38), in charge of producing a male heir. This novel, then, is very much about "patrilineal genealogy" (Sugars 2004, 156).

Family and hockey are omnipresent and intertwined themes in *The Divine Ryans*. Indeed, Draper imagines the five Ryan siblings—Aunts Phil and Louise, Uncles Seymour and Reginald, and his father Donald—as a hockey team. After his father's death, Draper muses, "All they lacked was a centreman. All they lacked [. . .] was my father, without whom they would be playing shorthanded from now on" (Johnston 1998, 158). Draper thus uses a hockey analogy to come to grips with his father's absence: in other words, this fantasizing is not mere sports escapism.[2] However, the hockey comparison highlights a tragic gap, because Draper's father is not serving a two- or five-minute penalty; he is gone forever. That infinite gap between "shorthanded" and "from now on" illustrates just how difficult it is for Draper to imagine nothingness, as he wrestles with a "world . . . suddenly coloured by his [father's] absence" (Scruton 1996, 458).

Just as Draper uses hockey to understand loss, so too did his father, Donald, use the game as a teaching tool. Because Donald was always toiling for the *Chronicle*, working "impossibly long hours for next to no salary" (69), he rarely saw his son.[3] Instead of bonding in any traditional

---

2 As Michael Messner succinctly puts it, "For most people, 'the sportsworld' is an escape from the pressures and problems of everyday life" (1992, 9). At times Draper "wished there was nothing else to think about but hockey" (Johnston 1998, 127).

3 Of course, Donald also absented himself in order to be "free from the marriage bed" (Johnston 1998, 207) after finally having produced a male heir.

hockey manner, Donald cultivated a textual relationship with the game and his son. When Draper was too young to stay up past the first period of *Hockey Night in Canada*, his father would use an inkless pen to etch game scores into the cover of Draper's *Cartoon Virgil*: "At breakfast, after mass on Sunday mornings, I would put a sheet of paper over the book and shade it with a pencil until I found the score. 'Here it comes,' my father would say, 'here it comes, emerging from the underworld'" (75). Even after Draper is old enough to watch all three periods, he continues the playful practice himself. He engraves the scores into his juvenile version of *The Aeneid*, and the book becomes a "kind of memory slate [. . .] for, in the process of trying to find the score of last night's game, I would call up the scores of games played years ago" (75). Game results are linked to education because Draper must actively seek out the game information his father conceals for him.[4] In this way, the Oxford-educated father introduces his son to the classics and teaches him, however unorthodoxly, to look closely at texts, even if the text is a simple hockey score. As discussed in more detail below, this playful and educational approach to hockey is the exact opposite of Aunt Phil's and Father Seymour's approach to playfulness and sport.

Draper's decoding of "games played years ago" foreshadows the importance of reading documents from the past in order to figure out the present—specifically, documents related to the circumstances of his father's death. In another instance of seeking a past truth from textual evidence, Draper scrutinizes a photograph from his father's Oxford days, when Donald played with the Rhodes Blades. In that quirky team photo, the players sit around a fireplace, sporting blazers and wielding cigars, pipes, or brandy snifters—but they are also wearing skates: "They were all affecting the kind of insolence normal to such photographs, but also smirking slightly, not so much, it seemed to me, to acknowledge the obvious joke as to suggest that there was some further, private joke

---

4 *The Aeneid* is a central reference in this novel. Michael Buma points out the "Virgilian descent into the underworld of Reg Ryan's funeral home" that occurs "during the novel's dream-sequence climax" (Buma 2012, 240). This dream causes Draper to remember his missing week. Equally important is that Aeneas, like Donald, was a reluctant preserver of a line: "though sick with heavy cares, / he counterfeits hope in his face; his pain / is held within, hidden" (Virgil 1971, Book I, 290–92).

involved, some joke behind the joke, some riddle that they were daring you to solve" (157). A few pages later, Draper begins to fathom what the "presumably less innocent reader" (Cook 2004, 143) has already sensed. "The Rhodes Blades. The Gay Blades," Draper muses. "I wonder if that was the real joke in that photograph" (Johnston 1998, 185). Donald and at least some of his teammates were playing a game of hide and seek, an as-if game of hiding in plain sight and daring the viewer to discover their secret, without actually furnishing evidence.

Eventually, Draper discovers that his father left him a more personal message. It was not by chance that Donald was clutching *The Cartoon Virgil* when Draper found his body (205). One year after his "missing week," Draper remembers the incident, retrieves the book, and rubs a pencil over the cover: "The scores of games played years ago began appearing, emerging ghostly from the paper" (206). The words "emerging ghostly" echo the father's playful erudite joke about scores "emerging from the underworld," thereby hinting at a passing of duties from father to son (while also alluding to Aeneas's journey to the Underworld to visit his father, Anchises, in Book VI of *The Aeneid*). Etched among the hockey scores is the suicide note that serves as crucial written proof of what Aunt Phil would deem the double sin of suicide and homosexuality. Donald's heart-rending note reads, in part, "I have come to believe that there is no such thing as forgiveness. You will all be better off without me" (207)—words all the more tragic because Donald committed suicide convinced that he would face "eternal damnation" (193). Thanks to the unusual reading skills Donald taught his son, Aunt Phil's fib about a heart attack is exposed. In exchange for keeping quiet about the suicide, Draper, Mary, and their mother are given enough money to allow them to leave the Ryan home and the confining family environs of St. John's—driven to the airport "in style" (214) by Uncle Reginald in his hearse. As Cynthia Sugars puts it, Draper can actively "purchase his freedom by blackmailing his aunt Phil at the end of the novel" (Sugars 2004, 170).

HOCKEY AND THE PLAY SPIRIT

Hockey, as a game, is a potential source of fun and play. That said, sport and play are not synonyms, nor does a game necessarily engender enjoyment (as anyone who has played Monopoly knows). A game is determined by a set of formal or informal rules, while play is a vague and slippery concept that beggars description: as play theorist Brian Sutton-Smith observes, "We all know what playing feels like. But when it comes to making theoretical statements about what play is, we fall into silliness" (1997, 1). Performance theorist Richard Schechner sees play as a mood or disposition that gives us "refreshment, energy, unusual ways of turning things around, insights, breaks, openings and, especially, *looseness*" (2004, 42). Though an insightful and energizing mood may fall upon us at any time, the play mood is not entirely random. We are more likely to enjoy ourselves at a hockey game, for example, than while living in Aunt Phil's house. In the case of Draper (as we shall see), enjoyment is much more likely during a hockey game than while boxing under the watchful eye of dour Uncle Seymour.

Uncle Seymour is not blessed with a playful disposition. A self-proclaimed hockey fan, he in fact knows nothing about the game, as becomes evident when he watches *Hockey Night in Canada* with Draper and the other Ryans. Worse, with support from Aunt Phil and Aunt Louise, Seymour ruins the communal fun that can come from watching a game in company. Phil, Louise, and Seymour are inept fans. Instead of concentrating on the game, they kibitz about the Toronto Maple Leafs being a Protestant team and amuse themselves over the plural form "Leafs," mocking Protestants for choosing a team name that includes a spelling mistake (Johnston 1998, 79). Their joking reflects an obsessive intolerance, born of a sense of superiority.[5] It is not harmless pre-game banter.

Father Seymour's main hockey peccadillo, however, is that he exploits the game solely to achieve aims beyond the playing field. Rather than enjoying games and sports for their own sake, Father Seymour is radically instrumentalist in using them as a mirthless means to an end; for him, games are "essentially an instrument for some further purpose" (Suits 1978, 147) that lies beyond the game itself. When Father Seymour sits down beside Draper during a game for a heart-to-heart, the scene reads like a description of a creepy date: "'Hello Draper Doyle,' he said, sitting cross-legged beside me. He picked up my Pepsi and took a sip from it, and as if by this, some sort of bond had been established between us, laid his arm lightly on my

---

5 Their type of joking fits the rather caustic "superiority theory" of humour— the idea that humour is essentially "malice and abuse towards people marked as deficient" (Carroll 2014, 8).

shoulder" (Johnston 1998, 80). Seymour's smarmy greeting is cryptically belated, coming as it does in the third period. Was it nervousness that made him wait so long to say hello? Was he planning and plotting? In any case, sitting cross-legged on the floor brings the priest no closer in age to his nephew, stealing Pepsi is no way to establish a bond of any sort, and the draping of an unrequested arm over a shoulder is a flagrant invasion of personal space. No emotional rapprochement or bonding moment ensues.

But Father Seymour's real gaffe is to talk religion during the game. Though some Canadians may speak of hockey as a religion, mid-game sermonizing or theologizing is a bothersome incursion into the game-world. When Seymour asks, "Do you know what the CH on Montreal's uniform stands for, Draper Doyle?" (the answer he wants is "church"), he ruins the playful mood. He follows his question with what Cook aptly describes as an "irritatingly pious disquisition" (2004, 133):

> "But you know," he said, "the word means nothing unless 'u r' in it."
> I must have looked mystified, for he laughed. "Do you get it, Draper Doyle?" he said, looking around the room. "U r in church. The word 'church' means nothing unless u r in it." (Johnston 1998, 81)

What mystifies Draper is the banality and inanity of Seymour's wordplay, not any failure to understand that "CH were the letters with which the words 'church' began and ended" (81). Uncle Seymour's verbal games pale against Uncle Reginald's wit, and Seymour's lack of wit and levity evinces the dispositional gulf between the two uncles. Draper, meanwhile, immediately "considered that UR stood for Uncle Reginald" (81), indicating imaginative fecundity as he searches for an escape route leading to his more playful, perceptive, and helpful uncle.

Unlike Seymour, Reginald is an unabashed hockey fan, one who happily devotes entire oralysis sessions to talking about the Montreal Canadiens with Draper. While watching *Hockey Night in Canada*, he wears a Habs sweater with Maurice Richard's number 9, while Draper, from a younger generation, wears Jean Béliveau's number 4. (Donald Draper, significantly and appropriately for someone trapped in eternity, appears in "a numberless Habs uniform" [158].) When Mary accuses her brother of being a hockey "fanatic" for hating other teams, Reginald nips an argument in the bud by serving up a witty definition: "A fanatic," he explains, "is a fan who is so crazy you have to keep him in the attic" (72–73).[6] Such self-deprecation—after all, Reginald lives in the attic—is foreign to Phil or Seymour and demonstrates the kindlier uncle's playful, tolerant approach to life.

When Aunt Phil and Uncle Seymour mock the Maple Leafs, Uncle Reginald jestingly adopts their viewpoint that hockey is a surrogate religious war against Protestants. Reginald's aim, it seems, is to warn Draper against religious bigotry. Aunt Phil, Sister Louise, and Father Seymour, meanwhile, see the Canadiens as an extension of their church: "None of them had any real affection for hockey. As far as they were concerned, God had created hockey for the sole purpose of allowing Catholics to humiliate Protestants on nationwide TV" (76). Uncle Reginald does not openly refute this delusion. Rather, he pokes fun at the simplistic allegorizing of hockey as a "holy war" that pits "the Heathen Leafs against the Holy Habs" (77, 78).[7] According to Reginald, "the real coach of the Montreal Canadiens was the pope, who was sending Toe Blake instructions from the Vatican, where he and his cardinals were watching the game on closed-circuit television" (78). Reginald's tale exemplifies his teaching method: funny on its own, it also exposes the absurdity of viewing hockey as a religious war. Like Draper's deceased father (but with more humour), Reginald playfully teaches and delights as he nudges Draper away from Aunt Phil's moralistic intolerance.

FORCED PLAY: A DISTORTION OF BALANCE AND MEASURE

Aunt Phil and Father Seymour's game-watching habits reveal a deficiency: they constantly use games and humour as a means to an end. They are all but incapable of playing or amusing themselves or ushering cheer into a room. Though games and play require competition (*agon*), we enjoy them most when they are spiced with frivolity, looseness, or levity; focusing too much on competition leads to *agony* (Golden 1998, xi). The key to enjoyment in sports is balance and measure, and this need for balance extends to moderation of passions. Yes, we have to abide by the rules when we play, and, yes, we have to play seriously by giving ourselves up to the game

---

6 Draper, an intolerant child, will presumably outgrow his belief that Red Wings and Black Hawks and Bruins are not "human beings" (73). Intolerant Aunt Phil, Sister Louise, and Father Seymour, however, seem beyond hope.

7 For a compact examination of *The Divine Ryans* and hockey tensions within Canada, see Buma (2012, 114–15).

(Connor 2011, 172), but there are—or should be—limits to what we are willing to do for victory. Destroying the opponent means destroying the game, while forcing someone to play is as absurd as decreeing fun.

Aunt Phil forces Draper to give up his luxurious third-string goalie role and join Father Seymour's "Number," a group of orphaned boys who, under the muscularly Christian motto "Toughness of body, soundness of mind, purity of soul," are "trained by Father Seymour in the arts of dancing, singing, and [. . .] boxing" (Johnston 1998, 14). Uncle Reginald dubs the group "a cross between the Vienna Boys' Choir and the Hitler Youth" (14). The comparison to the Hitler Youth is grotesquely exaggerated, but it does encapsulate the general mood in Phil's house.[8] Draper, though not an orphan, is soon yoked to Father Seymour's Number and is learning to sing and box (although he is spared the ignominy of tap dancing, defined by Reginald as "the art of making an irritating sound with one's feet" [30]). By forcing Draper to participate in boxing, a violent individual sport, Father Seymour ignores the primary condition of play—namely, that it be voluntary. As Johan Huizinga writes in his seminal *Homo Ludens*, "Play to order is no longer play: it could at best be but a forcible imitation of it" (Huizinga 1950, 7). For Draper, neither boxing nor singing is anything like play: he never loses himself in the autotelic world of the boxing ring, nor does he give himself over to the creative vocal enjoyment of choral singing.

In a rare moment of wit, Uncle Seymour weds boxing and choral singing to jest, at Draper's expense. "'Remember,' Father Seymour said, 'when the bell rings, come out singing.'" He assures Draper that his singing would be sure to put his opponent "down for the count with a combination of shrieking off-key notes" (Johnston 1998, 36). Father Seymour's joke, though stale, is funny. It is also formally similar to how Uncle Reginald teases Draper for being "that unheard-of luxury, the third goalie" (17). Unskilled and not needed on the ice, with no room for him even on the bench, the would-be goalie Draper watches his team from the stands, like a common spectator. Reginald calls him "Draper Doyle, plainclothes goalie" or "Draper Doyle, undercover goalie" (17). So what is the difference between the two teasing uncles? One uncle's teasing is a sign of love, a Nerf dart shot in kind,

---

8 The Nazi parallel reappears when Draper's mom asks him, "Would you lak to join zee Reseestance? [. . .] Eet wahl be danjerous but vary exciting, mon ami" (Johnston 1998, 165). Living with Aunt Phil is like living in Nazi-occupied France.

soothing intimacy; the other uncle demeans Draper in front of his peers, who, as Draper recalls, "roared with laughter" (36). Seymour's aim is to publicly humiliate, not to spur development and confidence.

Father Seymour's extreme competitiveness unmasks itself during his Number's boxing matches against boys from a Protestant club. Not content with mere victory, and apparently oblivious to how sports can bring rival communities and warring factions together, Seymour aims to humiliate his Number's young opponents. As Draper soon realizes, "For Father Seymour, a fight was not really 'won' unless a moral victory came with it. The point was not so much to win as to make the other fighter so resentful of your skill, of your ability to hit him in the face, that he would resort to unfair tactics" (140). This overly competitive mentality is a corruption of any sportsmanship or fair play, since morality itself becomes a combative game of one-upmanship. In Seymour's ideal sporting scenario, his Number's Protestant opponents are compelled to cheat not in hopes of winning—which would entail still being in the game-world—but to forestall a beating. According to Seymour's curious logic of analogy, a child boxer's despair within the ring somehow confirms the weak ways of his form of Christianity.[9] Though Seymour's mindset does not justify Seymour's philosophy as a boxing coach, it does admittedly fit into a long and proud tradition of looking down on other religions, on "others," so to speak.

Aunt Phil, meanwhile, shows her attitude toward gamesmanship in a contest with her own family. Her sporting nadir is far from the locker room; it involves a laundry room. At one point, Draper, Mary, and their mother raid the Ryan laundry hamper (the room is usually kept under lock and key) and parade around in Aunt Phil's bra and Uncle Seymour's underpants. Aunt Phil happens upon them and, understandably, objects to the "riot of fun" (44). Who wants to see her own bra worn on someone's head "like one of those caps pilots wore in World War II" (44)? Though livid, Aunt Phil seems admirably composed when she puts an end to the hijinks and exits the room. Her next move fits the logic of impromptu games and competition, but it is unleavened by any sense of fair play, moderation, or tolerance. She pins Draper's "pee-stained underwear to the bulletin board

---

9 There is poetic justice: when Draper is losing his bout badly, Reginald suggests that Seymour stop the fight. Seymour refuses, only to see how his half-orphan nephew "got down on [his] hands and knees and grabbed [the opponent] by the leg" (147).

in the kitchen," along with a cruel note: "I will not wash such filth" (45). That the soiled undies are on the bulletin board sends a clear message about who is in charge of the joyless household. As Draper realizes, "Aunt Phil had gotten her revenge. She had not only humiliated us, she had made us the instruments of our own humiliation" (45). Her revenge, however, displays an utter lack of equal measure.

Aunt Phil scars her nephew emotionally: when he sees his underwear publicly manifested, Draper thinks, "It might have been my little boy's soul that was hanging there" (45). Her desire to win, like Uncle Seymour's odiously competitive ways at the boxing tournament, eerily combines *agon* and a love of public shaming. This sort of play is the very opposite of how kindly Uncle Reginald uses humour and hockey to help his young nephew cope in difficult times and to coax him towards adolescence and understanding. If Aunt Phil had her way, her house would be a play- and laughter-free zone, with rooms controlled by what Uncle Reginald calls a "dehumourizer" (166). Without Reginald's influence, Draper's world would be uniformly intolerant and intolerable, with or without games. Nowhere is Aunt Phil and Uncle Seymour's win-at-all-costs mentality more obvious than when they are involved in games. Instead of the measured tit-for-tat logic of games, theirs is a vengeful I'll-crush-you-for-that.

CONCLUSION

If a still-common slight against sports is that they are a trivial undertaking and a great distraction from more serious topics, *The Divine Ryans* shows that not to be the whole story. Indeed, Johnston's novel belongs to the contemporary canon of fine sports-related fiction precisely because he explores the many possibilities sports offer in our lives, including hockey-related opportunities for a child's intellectual growth. Ignoring the tried-and-true hockey narrative about who will win the Cup (alas, not the Habs in this case), *The Divine Ryans* thematically intertwines reading and play, while also sounding the boundaries of the play spirit, over-seriousness, and even the moral aspects of instrumentalism. Near the end of the novel, Draper expresses disbelief in the "notion that, although the Habs had just lost the Cup, the world was going on as usual" (192). But, thanks especially to Uncle Reginald and his play spirit, the world does go on, with Draper now equipped to play a mature role in it as he and his family board an airplane to their new lives.

WORKS CITED

Berne, Eric. 1964. *Games People Play: The Psychology of Human Relationships.* New York: Grove Press.

Buma, Michael. 2012. *Refereeing Identity: The Cultural Work of Canadian Hockey Novels.* Montréal and Kingston: McGill-Queen's University Press.

Carroll, Noël. 2014. *Humour: A Very Short Introduction.* Oxford: Oxford University Press.

Connor, Steven. 2011. *A Philosophy of Sport.* London: Reaktion Books.

Cook, Méira. 2004. "On Haunting, Humour, and Hockey in Wayne Johnston's 'The Divine Ryans.'" *Essays on Canadian Writing* 82: 118–50.

Golden, Mark. 1998. *Sport and Society in Ancient Greece.* Cambridge: Cambridge University Press.

Huizinga, Johan. 1950. *Homo Ludens: A Study of the Play-Element in Culture.* Boston: Beacon Press.

Johnston, Wayne. 1998. *The Divine Ryans.* New York: Vintage. First published 1990.

Lewis, Paul. 1989. *Comic Effects: Interdisciplinary Approaches to Humor in Literature.* Albany: State University of New York Press.

Messner, Michael. 1992. *Power at Play: Sports and the Problem of Masculinity.* Boston: Beacon Press.

Schechner, Richard. 2004. *The Future of Ritual: Writings on Culture and Performance.* London and New York: Routledge. First published 1993.

Scruton, Roger. 1996. *Modern Philosophy: An Introduction and Survey.* New York: Penguin.

Sugars, Cynthia. 2004. "Notes on a Mystic Hockey Puck: Death, Paternity, and National Identity in Wayne Johnston's *The Divine Ryans*." *Essays on Canadian Writing* 82: 151–72.

Suits, Bernard. 1978. *The Grasshopper: Games, Life and Utopia.* Toronto: University of Toronto Press.

Sutton-Smith, Brian. 1997. *The Ambiguity of Play.* Cambridge: Harvard University Press.

Virgil. 1971. *The Aeneid of Virgil.* Edited and translated by Allen Mandelbaum. New York: Bantam.

4

Paul Martin

The Poetry of Hockey in
Richard Harrison's *Hero of the Play*

Given hockey's prominence in Canadian life and culture, it might seem odd that there is so little Canadian poetry focused on hockey. In recent years, a substantial body of fiction about hockey has appeared in English Canada—some of the best examples are discussed elsewhere in this collection—but until very recently, Canadian hockey poetry has consisted of only a few passing references and isolated poems. This lacuna is no doubt related to the snobbery with which the Canadian cultural elite has treated hockey historically. As Jason Blake notes in his seminal study *Canadian Hockey Literature*,

> Hockey belongs to low or popular culture, and for much of the twentieth century it was kept away from serious fiction. George Woodcock's observation that "literatures are defined as much by their lacks as by their abundances" says much about perceptions of proper cultural topics. Even while the literati chased distinctively Canadian themes to validate a new literature, they ignored hockey. They ignored the body in favour of the strictly cerebral. (2010, 23)

If those forging the landscape of our country's fiction have avoided hockey for so long because of its association with "low or popular culture," one might presume that our poets would be even less likely to write about the game.

One exception is Al Purdy, whose 1965 poem "Hockey Players" remains the finest and perhaps most influential poem written about hockey (2000, 71). "Hockey Players" famously describes the game as "this combination of ballet and murder." A prolific and important poet whose "everyman" perspective on Canada reshaped the landscape of what was considered literature, Purdy addresses both the dangers of the game—"broken arms and legs and / fractured skulls opening so doctors / can see such bloody beautiful things" (lines 2–4)—and the intoxicating "swift and skilled delight of speed" (l. 65) that make hockey so compelling to play and watch. Throughout the poem, Purdy evocatively describes hockey's intensity as it is experienced by players, fans, and even the nation:

> We sit up there in the blues
> bored and sleepy and suddenly three men
> break down the ice in roaring feverish speed and
> we stand up in our seats with such a rapid pouring
> of delight exploding out of self to join them why
> theirs and our orgasm is the rocket stipend
> for skating thru the smoky end boards out
> of sight and climbing up the appalachian highlands
> and racing breast to breast across laurentian barrens (lines 24-32)

"Hockey Players" was the first hockey poem by a major Canadian poet, and it broke the ground for later poets. Not only did it demonstrate that hockey could be the topic of a powerful and challenging poem, but the poem's rich imagery and thematic network offered a glimpse of how much more could be written about the game. It would take nearly thirty years, though, for another poet to seize the opportunity revealed by Purdy's "Hockey Players."

Richard Harrison's 1994 collection *Hero of the Play* is a landmark of sport literature in Canada. While it is not the first Canadian book of poetry about hockey—John B. Lee's *The Hockey Player Sonnets* (1991), precedes it by three years—Harrison's book is certainly the most recognized and widely read collection of its kind. *Hero of the Play* is the first book of poetry ever to be launched at the Hockey Hall of Fame and the first to be read from at the Calgary Saddledome, two venues that had never before hosted literature in such a way. Since then, *Hero of the Play* has been reprinted six times, including in an expanded tenth anniversary edition—a rare achievement for a volume of poetry in Canada.

Along with the success of *Hero of the Play*, Harrison himself has become a prolific commentator on the game. Between 2004 and 2018 Harrison wrote over a dozen conference papers, articles, and book chapters about hockey. His 2005 poem about the NHL lockout, "NH Elegy," was published by newspapers around the world, and in 2006, he was one of the featured experts talking about hockey on CBC's ten-part television series *Hockey: A People's History*. Shortly after the death of Jean Béliveau in 2014, Harrison's poems were featured in a piece by NBC Sports national columnist Joe Posnanski, "Gordie and Mr. Béliveau," published on the NBC Sportsworld website. Posnanski places Harrison's reflections on meeting Gordie Howe and Jean Béliveau alongside commentary from luminaries of hockey journalism, including Michael Farber, Roy MacGregor, and Cam Cole. Posnanski brings literature and sport together by combining his prose with four key passages from "A Lifetime of Moving the Body Just So" and "Béliveau Teaches Me How to Handle the Puck," poems that Harrison wrote for and read to Howe and Béliveau, respectively (Harrison 2004, 85, 86). Serving as epigraphs to four of the six sections of Posnanski's piece, the passages are the linchpins of the essay, allowing Posnanski to capture both the personal stories of the players and the qualities that made each of them so much larger than life. With the help of Harrison's poems, Posnanski depicts Howe and Béliveau as hockey royalty who are immortalized in verse and legend as much as in the record books.

The larger framework for the poems in *Hero of the Play* is sketched out by Harrison in "Ten Years with the Hero: On Hockey and Poetry," an introductory essay to the tenth anniversary edition. Here, Harrison examines the connections between hockey and Canadian identity. Discussing the debates over where hockey was first played, he argues, "What's important isn't where the origin of hockey is found in Canada, but how Canada finds at least a part of its origin in hockey" (2004, 16). He draws connections among hockey, national myth-making, and what compels him as a poet to explore both:

> And for all its simplicity, like all creation myths, hockey is also
> about Canadian light and Canadian darkness. All creation myths
> have a place for the way their people experience not just the light
> and the dark of the seasons and the day, but the light and the dark-
> ness in themselves. Hockey's simplicity and childish roots offer us

the play that we love for its own sake; its skills and speed give us what we admire in those dedicated to excellence. Its violence gives us a view into our own. (17)

As this passage suggests, Harrison approaches his project from the perspective of a lover of the game and a keen observer of the game's larger place in the Canadian experience.

The form of the poems in *Hero of the Play* is noteworthy. Harrison set himself the challenge of treating the blank page like a clean sheet of ice, with no poem being allowed to stretch beyond the boundaries of a single page. In addition, he "wanted to make the poems look like they came from the sports pages, specifically, sport page columns. I wanted them to look like clippings—the kind of writing that sometimes ends up pinned to locker room bulletin boards."[1] To maintain this structure and appearance in each poem, Harrison created a further restriction, a system he called the "prose-poem line break," which allows him to "take control of the ends of the lines as well as their beginnings" and thus prevent the prose poems from becoming straight prose. If what he wanted to be a single line overshot the right margin, he would either adjust the kerning or the margins "or re-write the line" so that the words would fit on one line. He also typeset the book himself "to make sure all those choices would be preserved." In making these decisions, Harrison was anticipating the responses of potential readers:

If the poems *looked like poems* before they were read, the aversion to poetry in our culture as a whole, and certainly its alienation from our athletic culture, would mean that sportspeople—players and fans and commentators—would rarely if ever read them. But if I approached language poetically within the frame of the appearance of that language that they were familiar with, they'd give the poems a chance. And they did.

Within these formal and aesthetic restrictions, Harrison offers up prose poems rich in imagery and metaphor that address a wide array of themes, figures, and events from the game. The compact form delivers his work to audiences in a way that opens them to seeing poetry and hockey in a

---

1 The quotations in this paragraph are from an email to the author, 21 March 2017.

new light. While it is frequently said that poetry is meant to be read aloud, Harrison takes his hockey poems a step further by regularly performing them aloud from memory. His performances on radio, television, and You-Tube, and in his public readings, suggest that for him, the poetry of sport is enhanced by the physicality of performance. The core hockey poems that Harrison tends to perform in public—including "Stanley Cup," "Rhéaume," and "Elegy for the Rocket"—are those that have also had the widest reach and have been included in many anthologies.

Many of the poems in *Hero of the Play* offer portraits of important figures in the game. In "First Round Pick: Paul Coffey" (43), for example, the poet describes what it is about Coffey, one of the greatest defencemen ever to play the game, that leads him to choose the player first in his hockey pool. In listing the reasons for his choice, Harrison also captures the essence of Coffey's stellar career: "Because two years ago he skated around an entire / team"; "because we / capped him at a hundred points in the pool"; "because he is constantly one behind the / greatest stars, feeding them the puck." The poem culminates, though, in a poignant connection that the poet draws between Coffey and the poet's father:

> because
> his nose is my father's, his look intense as I
> remember my father running the day I finally
> passed him, running my heart out.

This linking of the poet's own experiences and identity with his understanding of the game and those who have played it carries through many of the collection's poems about players.

The desire to feel or play like one's hockey heroes resurfaces in various poems. In "Lindros" (54), for instance, the poet observes how

> Lindros is afraid of breaking
> nothing. I saw him bust a man's collarbone in Maple
> Leaf Gardens, and nearly break another man's leg,
> score one goal and assist on another. The fans went
> wild, and it proves how little we have for ourselves:
> given the chance, I'd be him.

In "Bobby in Africa" (84), hockey becomes the opening for a conversation between the poet and "the manager of the Hôtel Ivoire," who sees the Canadian flag on the poet's backpack:

> he says he loves my country, and he plays on the rink
> that lies chilled like a pie in a land where leaves rot as they
> grow and the air is sweet as apples with their dying.

The mention of Bobby Hull—"a man whose shot I saw push a goalie / into his own net"—builds an instant connection "between men / who've found enough to confirm the world and go on." Anticipating his skate the next day "on this rink way ahead of schedule / and nature," the poet imagines he "will be like Bobby Hull—each time / he touched the ice, he was every boy in love."

The poet considers his affinity for yet another hockey hero in "Béliveau Teaches Me How to Handle the Puck" (86):

> We used to have breakfast together in the 60s; me with
> a bowl and milk and my early-reading eyes, him on the
> back of a box of Shredded Wheat.

Recalling the majesty of that particular photograph of Béliveau "skating the edge between old world and new, Béliveau in charge / the way the eye of a hurricane is in charge," the poet considers what he has learned from his hockey hero:

> He teaches me
> not to look at the whirl of legs and arms and wood, or
> be impressed by the thunder of the puck striking the
> boards, filling the ear of the arena. He teaches me
> *The puck going into the net is silent.*

The juxtaposition at the end of this poem of the noise, violence, and frenetic pace of the action on the ice and the silence of perhaps the only thing that ultimately matters—the small black puck making it past the goaltender and hitting the net—is but one example of many such contrasts and tensions that Harrison explores throughout the collection.

The poems about Hull and Béliveau are two of four poems commissioned by the Calgary Booster Club for a "Sportsman of the Year" dinner in 2000 and included in the tenth anniversary edition. The event was a tribute to four of the greatest players of all time—Maurice Richard, Gordie Howe, Bobby Hull, and Jean Béliveau—and each of these players was in attendance; it was the last time the four men would ever be together, and it was the final public appearance of Maurice Richard. At the event, Harrison read his poems to each of the men and presented them with their respective copies. Getting to meet and pay tribute to one's heroes in such a direct and intimate way was an important moment personally and professionally for Harrison. He ponders the event's significance in "Ten Years with the Hero," his introductory essay in the 2004 edition:

> No longer was I, or could I be, someone responding to hockey
> from the stands. I would be speaking in person, in public, and in
> their company, about men who were freely spoken of as legends,
> whose stories had become part of hockey lore. I would be speaking
> from my world of pages and ink, yet I would be speaking with
> the kind of men whose most trusted and intimate words are never
> meant for ink. (Harrison 2004, 14)

Many of the strongest poems in *Hero of the Play* talk about the complex tensions among masculinity, violence, and identity. "The Use of Force" (52) portrays a fight between Lyle Odelein of the Montréal Canadiens and Randy Moller of the New York Rangers in a game that took place on 9 February 1991 in Montréal. The fight begins with the pre-fight ritual, described by the poet in almost erotic terms:

> Gently, almost like
> leaves on a stream, they drift towards Centre, their
> hands naked now, their heads unhelmeted; this is the
> undressing.

This quiet foreplay ends violently:

> But then Lyle's hand
> pops free and his bared fist goes down and down on
> Randy's face, and the crowd's anticipation, the listless,
> frustrating play of the home team, bursts from the

throats of the 17000 at the Forum that night, a roar
I can feel tremble down the centre of my ribcage, my
stomach, my groin.

Odelein's "offering to the crowd," the poet suggests, influences the outcome
of the game:

> Randy has been brought to the ice,
> his sky filled with Lyle's fist, and the Rangers do not
> fare well this night, while the Canadiens find Caesar's
> tide, and break the game open in their favour.

While the violence of this fight at centre ice propels the Canadiens to
victory and causes a visceral reaction among the home team's fans, the
poem on the page facing "The Use of Force" addresses how the lack of such
a response can leave a team and its fans feeling impotent and let down in
the wake of a tough loss. In "I Watch Him Break Sanstrom's Leg" (53), the
poet refers to a violent hit on the LA Kings' Tomas Sandström in the 1991
Smythe Division Finals and wishes that such an action could be met with
even greater violence:

> and I find myself longing for a big, tough man
> with a nickname like *The Hammer* as if an enforcer
> with the right rink smarts and the will to go the
> distance with anyone on the ice could protect
> his friends from the kind of hit that ends a career,
> the violence within the rules.

In this case, however, violence is not met by even greater violence, and the
poet captures the lingering sense of helplessness this leaves behind:

> Fact is, there is no fight;
> fact is, the Kings go down in six. We've just been
> through a war—even that is not enough when men
> are willing, the outcome is in doubt, and the ache
> in me is to strike, I who am not hungry, not broken.

It would be presumptuous to say that by placing these two poems side by
side, Harrison is arguing that fighting is an essential aspect of the game.

These two poems make it clear, though, that the players willing to sacrifice their bodies—to resort, heroically, to any means necessary to help their team win (even if they still lose)—are those, like "*The Hammer*," who will be remembered by their teammates and fans.

"Stanley Cup" and "Coach's Corner" are but two of the collection's many poems that ponder men's love for the game, and the love and loyalty between teammates, fathers and sons, players and fans. "Stanley Cup" (62), perhaps the best-known poem from the collection, begins with the image of how "Mario Lemieux hoists the Cup, kisses its silver / thigh" and then describes how players over the years have spent their time with the Cup. As the poet reminds us, "Every player on every / team who ever won the Cup gets to take it home," and "even the guy who left it by / the side of the road and drove away, still he thinks / of it as holy." Harrison sums up all the ways in which people have treated and revered the Cup with the final words of the poem: "This way / I have loved you." "Coach's Corner" (50) also points to love as what makes the polarizing figure of Don Cherry so compelling, even sometimes to those who find "the priest of rock 'em / sock 'em" to embody all that they dislike about the game. Even if Cherry "is loud and whiny and complaining" and "slams foreigners, / praises women in all the ways wrong for our time," what makes him, in the eyes of the everyday fan, "their man in a way no / hero of the play could be" is love:

> he is here
> because he is unafraid to love, love the game, the
> journeyman players, love the code that makes a man
> a man—and if you don't know it I ain't gonna tell ya.

There is, certainly, a nostalgic tone to much of *Hero of the Play*, and a sense that its poems work to portray a side of players and hockey that will soon be lost to the growing commercialization and homogenization of the game. Harrison's poems written for Howe, Hull, Béliveau, and Richard each contain a sense of wanting to pay tribute to these players before they are gone. The poem Harrison wrote about Richard for that event, "Maurice" (87), and his later "Elegy for the Rocket" (95) capture Richard's power and determination to persevere. In "Maurice," Harrison pays tribute to Richard's incredible determination and ability to win against all odds by comparing the elderly Richard's decision to come to Calgary shortly before his death to the legendary 1945 play in which Richard scored after dragging Red Wings defenceman Earl Seibert halfway down the rink with Seibert hanging onto Richard's sweater. Richard's ability to make plays that were larger than life, plays that transformed both the match and the sport, are what made him such a special player. In comparing how Richard's "eyes / ablaze and bituminous black" (87), as seen in the famous photo described in "Maurice," had faded by the end of the player's life to "a humble fire at the end of its use" (95), "Elegy for the Rocket" evokes the fading away of a player who redefined the game and, particularly in Québec, people's love for its heroes.

Despite the focus on men and the occasionally nostalgic tone, *Hero of the Play* embraces how hockey and society have changed in recent years, particularly with respect to the roles of women. The poems "Hockey Mom," "The Feminine," and "Rhéaume" delve into the connections between women and hockey, complicating the traditional assumptions about who the "hero of the play" can be. As Harrison writes in his introductory essay, "Hockey Mom," part of "The Hero in Overtime" section added for that edition, "finally addresses a gap in the original book pointed out over the years by hockey moms who've shared their sometimes-secret love/hate relationship with the game" (2004, 13). While the hockey mom in the poem supports and feeds the growth of her son on and off the ice, she cares more for her boy than she does the game. She is not among the

> Spartan mothers
> in the stands screaming in any one of murder's names
> as if a woman's voice could arm her boy for the work
> of wood and bone the men and audience all think is
> part of the game forever. (89)

Although she stays away from the stands and keeps her eyes from the ice, she nevertheless catches herself sharing her son's aspirations:

> you watch his hungry body disappear with
> every bite and healing muscle into the player you surprise
> yourself dreaming with him he'll be.

In "The Feminine" (41), Harrison addresses the identification of players and lovers of the game as men and the caregivers and spectators of the game as women—something that may seem wildly out of date to the reader of 2018, when women's and girl's hockey is exploding at both amateur and professional levels, and boys, girls, and even NHL players are wrapping their sticks in rainbow tape to assert that "anyone can play." Hockey, in this poem, is a divider of men and women. The poet wonders if he could include a feminine figure in an imagined "deck of hockey Tarot cards." Even though "Canada's women's / team is the best in the world," the poet confesses, uncomfortably, that his vision of professional hockey is played by men:

> This is not why I love the game, or why its symbols
> work like runes in my language. This is a game
> the women watch, its gentler moments taken in
> their image.

For the poet and his partner, "the game divides us," not only in how they connect to such a gendered vision of the sport but also in how they communicate:

> Again I've
> come to a profession of love in words I cannot use
> for you, with all the women left in the stands
> where I demand you sit and applaud it all.

Harrison's poem "Rhéaume" (73) provides a counterweight for the unwillingness, expressed in "Hockey Mom" and "The Feminine," to accommodate a less gendered vision of hockey. The poem pays tribute to the pioneering goaltender Manon Rhéaume, the first woman ever to play a major junior hockey game and, by signing in 1992 with the Tampa Bay Lightning and playing for one period in an NHL exhibition game, the first woman ever to play in any major professional sports league in North America. "Rhéaume" revolves around Rhéaume's aspiration to be seen solely as a player and not as a hero or role model. The poem begins with "Here is the desire of Manon Rhéaume: to stop the / puck." Being a goaltender helps, almost, to make those watching her forget that she is a woman: the equipment and the mask give her the opportunity to "disappear into *goalie* the way / a man can be a man and not a man inside the / armour." The poem suggests, however, that her aim "[t]o forget in the motion of the save that we / do not forget she is always a woman and sex is / everything" might be impossible to achieve; even if she is able "[t]o stop the / puck where the best are men," it is less likely that men will suddenly "be better / than they are." The poem ends, though, with an attempt to frame Rhéaume in way that her desire "[t]o be a woman / and have it be her play that counts" might be fulfilled. The poet describes a collage on the wall of the listener that features heroic "women with their arms raised." Alongside other great athletes and activists, goddesses, Catwoman, and Boadicea, we see, as the poem closes,

> Rhéaume
> and a glove save, the puck heading for the top
> corner. Stopped.

More than two decades after both Rhéaume's appearance in the Lightning net and the writing of Harrison's poem, that final image might well be closer to how she is understood today than how she was viewed in 1992.

Given the status of *Hero of the Play* as the first widely celebrated collection of poems about hockey, it is fitting that a significant theme of the book involves the relationship between language and sport. How can you capture in words a sport like hockey, where the action is so quick, multidirectional, and, for the uninitiated, challenging to follow? What can the specialized eye of a poet add to our understanding of the game? In "Using the Body" (51), the poem about the fight between Lyle Odelein and Randy Moller, Harrison illustrates how a moment of hockey can be seen in dramatically different ways. While a fan might see only anger and violence exploding through the fists of a fighting player, the poet is struck by the incongruousness of the fighter's calm deliberation, using his body as "the agent of policy":

> When a fight begins, we say it is emotion, but after
> the game, the goon speaks clearly of the momentum
> of play, doing what he had to do, a strict account
> level in his head. Later, when he wears a suit,
> when he coaches, you can see how he saw the
> entire rink all along: he never looked at the puck,
> the stickhandling, a man's cheek when his purpose is
> clear and there's open ice before him.

The challenge faced by the poet-fan in attempting to articulate this rich tension between how fans and players see and experience the game resurfaces in "The Praise of Men" (42). Faced with a player he admires, the poet finds himself unable to express his reverence for and envy of his talent; yet, as an anonymous fan "with a seat in the blues," he has no trouble finding expression, "hiding my praise in the open":

> Give me these players whom I will never
> meet, to hoot and holler out my deepest riskless love that
> finds no softer words, no shame or venture, merely
> a game.

The poem's opening line, "To their faces, it escapes me, words for the praise of men," distills the challenge Harrison sets up for himself in writing a collection of poems about hockey. In attempting to describe hockey through words and verse, then, *Hero of the Play* reminds us of the many angles from which to see and understand the game. Though Harrison's collection deals with an impressive range of topics and perspectives, ultimately the richness of it all emphasizes how much of hockey has yet to be explored through poetry and other media.

WORKS CITED

Blake, Jason. 2010. *Canadian Hockey Literature.* Toronto: University of Toronto Press.

Harrison, Richard. 2004. *Hero of the Play: Poems Revised and New.* 10th Anniversary Edition. Hamilton, ON: Wolsak and Wynn.

———. 2009. "Between a Puck and a Showpiece: Spectator Sport and the Differing Responses to Hockey (and Its Absence) in Canada and the United States—a Canadian Poet Looks at the Fate of the Game." In *Canada's Game: Hockey and Identity*, edited by Andrew Holman, 151–60. Montréal and Kingston: McGill-Queen's University Press.

Posnanski, Joe. 2014. "Gordie and Mr. Béliveau." *NBC SportsWorld*, 23 December. http://sportsworld.nbcsports.com/gordie-and-mr-beliveau/.

Purdy, Al. 2000. "Hockey Players." In *Beyond Remembering: The Selected Poems of Al Purdy*, 71–73. Ed. Sam Solecki. Madeira Park, BC: Harbour Publishing.

5

Cory Willard

Glaciers, Embodiment, and the Sublime

An Ecocritical Approach to Thomas Wharton's *Icefields*

Icefields, by Thomas Wharton, is a fictionalized account of the early exploration and subsequent development of Jasper National Park, in Alberta's Rocky Mountains. Established in 1907, the park lies to the north of the older Banff National Park and is famed for its glaciers, which are fed by the massive Columbia Icefield. Wharton's novel is imbued with a strong sense of history, not only recognizing the presence of Indigenous peoples in the area long before the arrival of Europeans but also reaching into deep time, through the fascination of its central character, Doctor Edward Byrne, with glaciology. Against the backdrop of the Jasper landscape, Wharton explores the commodification of the natural world as he charts Byrne's journey into the embodied experience of place. Through this experience, Byrne gradually develops an understanding of the interrelationship between human beings and the rest of the natural world and of the connection between ecological and spiritual awareness.

In addition to glaciers, Jasper is the site of spectacular mountains that have long attracted mountaineers, and climbing expeditions play a significant role in the action of Wharton's novel. Like many other arduous physical activities, mountaineering can be taken up either as pure sport or in connection with some other objective, such as exploration or scientific inquiry. Either way, however, mountaineering requires a level of embodiment, physical mastery, and environmental awareness that unifies the practitioner with the field of play. Like the boxer who instinctively knows where the corners of the ring are, or the tennis player who knows her stride on grass or clay or carpet and how these surfaces alter the ball's behaviour, or the skier who effortlessly adapts to the snow pack, the mountain's topography, and fluctuations in weather conditions, the mountain climber develops an embodied connection to the physical environment. In "Why Climbing Matters," an ecocritical exploration of mountaineering literature, Jeffrey Mathes McCarthy writes that "climbing sensitizes the body, opens it to the land's current, and thereby animates it to awareness of the natural world" (2008, 171).

McCarthy argues that the embodied experience of mountain climbing can help us move toward "a new way of knowing nature," one that is urgently needed at a time when "a chorus of environmental voices insists that transforming human attitudes toward nature is the only solution to our ongoing 'environmental crisis'" (2008, 159–60). As he points out, in writing about their experience of climbing, "mountaineers offer a vision of human relations to nature," as well as insight into "how these relations might transcend their cultural context" (2008, 158), both of which hold the potential to heighten environmental and ecological awareness. From a phenomenological perspective, climbing can produce a sense of oneness with nature, a visceral understanding of the fundamental interconnectedness of the human body and the surrounding environment. In addition, narratives about climbing often convey messages about ecological responsibility, expressing "sympathy for a natural world of glaciers and streams and rock faces that merit protection from overuse by industrial culture" (162). As we will see, such themes occupy a prominent place in Wharton's novel.

Icefields opens in August 1898, with Byrne, a doctor from Britain, taking part in a scientific expedition, led by a professor named Collie, in the Canadian Rockies near Jasper. As the party travels across the "Arcturus" glacier, Byrne slips on the ice and falls into a crevasse. This accident, in which Byrne breaks his collarbone, shapes the rest of his life. Trapped in the crevasse, Byrne sees what appears to be an angel embedded in the ice and develops a passionate interest in glaciers, subsequently returning to the place of his accident for study. His injury leaves him unable to climb to the upper reaches of the glacier, effectively limiting his observations to its lower reaches and terminus. This spatial limitation forces an increase in the depth of Byrne's observations, allowing him to perceive subtle changes in the ice. Juxtaposed to this narrowing of physical space is an extension of time. Over the course of his many visits to the Jasper area, Byrne develops a deep attachment to the place, while he also comes to understand the impact of human activity on ecological relationships.

In *Icefields*, the Canadian Rockies are revealed, through the characters' varied relationships to the landscape, as fostering a particularly strong sense of place—so much so that the Arcturus glacier itself becomes a central character in the narrative. Sense of place, as explored by geographer Yi-Fu Tuan, refers to all the distinctive aspects of a specific location that offer human beings a reason to develop an attachment to it. As Tuan notes in his landmark work *Space and Place: The Perspective of Experience*, "Place is a special kind of object. It is a concretion of value, though not a valued thing that can be handled or carried about easily; it is an object in which one can dwell" (1977, 12). For Tuan and those influenced by his work, a place isn't merely a point in physical space, as we so often conceive of it; rather, "space is transformed into place as it acquires definition and meaning" (136). Place thus comprises the many layers of sometimes competing meanings that people give to a particular space. Place is, as Tim Cresswell puts it, "a way of seeing, knowing and understanding the world. When we look at the world as a world of places we see different things. We see attachments and connections between people and place" (2004, 11). In *Icefields*, this variation in meaning and attachment is most clearly illustrated in the differing significance of the glacier for Byrne and for Frank Trask, the expedition guide and indefatigable entrepreneur. Whereas Trask sees the area as something to be exploited for financial gain, for Byrne, the glacier is a source of knowledge about the world and about life itself.

Through Byrne's interests and observations, we gain a sense of the cultural, geological, and historical evolution of the Rocky Mountains. In addition, through his growing environmental consciousness, we are obliged to confront the sometimes troubling relationship between people and places. Cresswell suggests that adopting a place-based perspective can at times "seem to be an act of resistance against a rationalization of the world. . . . To think of an area of the world as a rich and complicated interplay of people and the environment—as a place—is to free us from thinking of it as facts and figures" (2004, 11). This sense of place, as a site of interaction, lies at the heart of the narrative in *Icefields*. With each encounter, Arcturus glacier and the nearby town of Jasper are taken further and further from the realm of inert matter as they are invested with meaning—as what appears to be an endless, empty open space, a frozen wilderness, is transformed into a place of diverse and sometimes conflicting meanings.

ECOCRITICISM: CONFRONTING THE FRAGILITY OF PLACE

Topics such as the relationship of human beings to the natural environment, threats to the sustainability of ecological systems, the commodification of nature, and the weakening of a sense of place are of particular interest to those who view literature through the theoretical lens known as ecocriticism, an interdisciplinary approach to the study of literature and the environment. Before we delve into Wharton's novel itself, a brief overview of ecocriticism thus seems in order. As Lawrence Buell, one of the most prominent scholars of literature and the environment, explains, literary analysts who employ an ecocritical approach attempt to speak "in cognizance of human being as ecologically or environmentally embedded" (2005, 8). While this embeddedness might seem obvious, only in the latter half of the twentieth century did literary scholars begin to give serious and sustained attention to the relationship between people and the natural environment. Buell suggests that ecocritical scholarship developed in response to "a growing malaise about modern industrial society's inability to manage its unintended environmental consequences" (5), consequences that have grown ever more apparent over the past several decades.

In adopting an ecological perspective on literature, ecocriticism is marked by an openness to interdisciplinary scholarship. The work of literary scholars who bring an environmental lens to bear on texts is enriched by the research of scholars in fields such as the natural sciences, geography, history, anthropology, sociology, and so on. As Buell notes:

> Literature scholars who took the environmental turn in the 1980s and 1990s found themselves entering a mind-expanding though also vertiginous array of cross-disciplinary conversations—with life scientists, climatologists, public policy specialists, geographers, cultural anthropologists, landscape architects, environmental lawyers, even applied mathematicians and environmental engineers. (2005, 5–6)

Buell argues that this "environmental turn" was in part a reaction against the so-called linguistic turn in literary criticism, according to which a text constitutes a self-contained and ultimately self-referential whole, an approach that separates "reader from text and text from world" (6). By insisting that texts cannot be adequately understood purely by analyzing their internal structure, without any reference to the surrounding world, ecocritics seek to return both readers and texts to the realm of embodied experience in relation to the ecological world.

As Buell points out, although a work of literature can be viewed as a kind of ecosystem in itself, "in the narrow sense of the text as a discursive 'environment,'" both readers and texts are inseparably intertwined with the world around them. For that reason, "an individual text must be thought of as environmentally embedded at every stage from its germination to its reception" (2005, 44). A narrative cannot be divorced from its social, cultural, and historical setting, and, given that all stories occur somewhere, narratives are inevitably also expressions of place. One may choose to ignore the physical setting of a novel, play, or film in order to focus on some other aspect of the narrative, but because all texts are environmentally embedded, virtually any text can be explored from an ecocritical point of view.

In view of this multidimensional embeddedness, the ecocritic is concerned not only with people and their place in the natural environment but also with the social relations that produce texts, meanings, and critical awareness. In order to write about nature in a way that could itself be considered ecocritical, an author must not only be ecologically mindful but also socially and politically conscious—for the ultimate goal of writing is often to influence the world, as opposed to simply describing it. In addition to ongoing threats to ecosystem integrity, as a society we are witnessing a gradual loss of sense of place. As Buell puts it, "at a time when fewer and fewer of the world's population live out their lives in locations that are not shaped to a great extent by translocal—ultimately global—forces," one must ask whether "'place' as traditionally understood means anything anymore" (2005, 62–63). Indeed, he writes, "one cannot theorize scrupulously about place without confronting its fragility" (62). Now more than ever, it seems essential to focus our attention on the myriad of ecological relationships that exist among texts, people, and the environment as a whole.

One of the central themes of *Icefields* is the importance of embodied experience. Wharton's novel is replete with sensory descriptions of human encounters with ice, wind, and the wild mountainous environment. In *The Spell of the Sensuous*, cultural ecologist David Abram argues that "humans are tuned for relationship": "The eyes, the skin, the tongue, ears, and nostrils—all are gates where our body receives the nourishment of otherness" (1996, ix). As he goes on to note, "For the largest part of our species' existence, humans have negotiated relationships with every aspect of the sensuous surroundings, exchanging possibilities with every flapping form, with each textured surface and shivering entity that we happened to focus upon" (ix). For Abram, the reality that we experience through our senses— that subjective experience so often ignored by objective science—is in fact the means by which we both understand and embed ourselves within the greater ecology of the natural world. We may be able to analyze the mechanics of a homerun swing, but that does not capture the experience itself—the physical sensation of swinging a bat, the knowledge we gain through that action, and the meanings we attach to it.

Abram writes that "the perceiving body does not calculate logical probabilities; it gregariously participates in the activity of the world, lending its imaginations to things in order to see them more fully" (1996, 58). In *Icefields*, it is often this direct sensory perception, this immediacy of connection, that provides the novel's characters with insight into the world around them. Byrne's fall into the depths of the glacier does not introduce themes of adventure and bravery in the face of danger; our attention is focused instead on what comes to Byrne through his senses. Trapped in the crevasse, he sees something he cannot explain:

> He squinted. There was something in the ice, a shape, its outline sharpening as the light grew. A fused mass of trapped air bubbles, or a vein of snow, had formed a chance design, a white form embedded within the darker ice and revealed by the light of the sun. A pale human figure, with wings. The white figure lay on its side, the head turned away from him. Its huge wings were spread wide, one of them cracked obliquely near the tip, the broken pinions slightly detached. One arm was also visible, outstretched, in the semblance of some gesture that Byrne felt he had seen before,

but could not interpret. A remembered sculpture or one of Blake's hovering, pitying spirits. The shape gleamed wetly, like fine porcelain or delicately veined marble. (Wharton 1995, 11)

Byrne sees the image of an angel trapped in the ice—something that simply cannot or should not be.

Initially, Byrne attempts to find a rational, scientific explanation for the phenomenon ("air bubbles, or a vein of snow"), musing on his vision as "a wonder to report to Collie. *A hitherto unknown periscopic property of glacial ice*" (Wharton 1995, 11). However, as his thoughts progress to Romantic poet and artist William Blake, and as the narrative unfolds and Byrne's obsession with solving the mystery grows, we see how direct sensory experience does more than merely foster scientific curiosity: it becomes a new way of knowing, an alteration of his world view. Byrne tells the "scandalous lady alpinist" and travel writer Freya Becker, "I've learned a lot from the glacier itself. A way of looking at the rest of the world. Patience. Control of the emotions" (109, 189). In observing the motion of the glacier over two and a half decades, Byrne does not just see a series of objective scientific laws playing out but comes to understand a way of being in the world. He learns an appreciation for nature and natural processes, as is evident in his conflicts with Trask's entrepreneurial operations, and he learns the patience and sense of balance that comes from ecological mindfulness.

Reflecting on the lessons to be gleaned from mountain climbing, McCarthy writes that "the corporeal, bodily fact of climbing points us toward the possibility of a sustainable relation between human beings and the natural world" (2008, 158). Climbing can, he argues, remind us that "humans and nature intermingle, overlap, connect," as opposed to existing "side by side as active subject and passive object" (170). Although, in *Icefields*, Byrne's injury limits his ability to climb, it is he whose outlook is most fundamentally altered by his initial experience of climbing and who ultimately finds the most intimate relationship with the natural world. This relationship, which begins from his embodied experience in the crevasse, is sustained by his ongoing scientific observations—themselves grounded in direct sensory perception. Byrne studies the ice and comes to know it deeply: as an active subject, he engages in what might seem the passive act of observing, while the apparently inert mass of ice becomes a living thing, with its own direction and movements. Whereas Trask regards the landscape as an object that human action can manipulate for purposes of financial gain, Byrne gains something arguably more precious and more permanent: a felt, embodied knowledge of human interconnectivity with the environment.

EXPERIENCING THE SUBLIME: ECOLOGICAL AWARENESS AND
SPIRITUAL CONSCIOUSNESS

Wharton has said that, in *Icefields*, he wanted to write about Jasper in a way that "would avoid clichés of writing about the mountains and would if possible somehow be close to that wordless experience of a place" (Wyile 2002, 168). That "wordless" experience is wonder, the sense of standing in the presence of the sublime. In nineteenth-century Romanticism, the term *sublime* came, as a noun, to describe "either a landscape that stimulates spiritual awareness or the literary work or painting that captures this elevated quality" (Gaull 1988, 232). The sublime was associated, in particular, with nature at its most powerful, mysterious, and awe-inspiring—"the volcanoes, the earthquakes, the storms, the mountains, caves, and oceans, reminders of God's power and wrath" (232). An embodied connection to the natural world often gives rise to a sense of the sublime, and, as the novel suggests, the desire or capacity of an individual to receive the wonder that nature can evoke lies at the foundation of both ecological awareness and a spirituality rooted in nature.

The relationship between the nature and spiritual experience is established at the very outset of *Icefields*, not only by Byrne's vision of the angel in the ice but also by a reference to Samuel Taylor Coleridge's "Kubla Khan," one of the iconic poems of the Romantic period. As Byrne is recovering from this accident, Sara, the woman who tends to him, reads the poem aloud to Byrne, and Wharton quotes its famous opening lines:

> In Xanadu did Kubla Khan
> A stately pleasure-dome decree:
> Where Alph, the sacred river, ran
> Through caverns measureless to man
>   Down to a sunless sea. (Wharton 1995, 32)

Later in the novel, Byrne recalls "a fact he had always known and yet ignored": "Glaciers are rivers. Water" (169). We understand the Arcturus glacier to be the site of some sort of sacred power, and it is, of course, Byrne's own experience in "caverns measureless to man" that initiates his quest for understanding.

That this quest is a spiritual one is also established early in the novel, by its association with the quest for the Holy Grail. As Byrne is convalescing, Sara tells him about Lord Sexsmith, an English aristocrat and adventurer, who, a generation earlier, set out on a hunting expedition in the area around Jasper. In the course of his journey, Sexsmith dreamt of "an old man in rusted armour," who is carrying "his sacred trust, an object shrouded under a white cloth, across the plain and into the blue mountains" (Wharton 1995, 40). Françoise Besson draws a connection between Byrne and Sexsmith's dream:

> The symbolism of the Grail suggests the mystical quality of Sexsmith's expedition and the "rusted armour" the man wears recalls the image of a knight of the Round Table. Later on, Freya Becker, . . . describing Byrne, says: "he's forged himself an impressive suit of armour" (192). Freya's metaphor echoes Sexsmith's dream and the reader may suppose that, like Sexsmith, and like the old man carrying the Grail, Byrne is a modern knight pursuing his own Grail. Byrne, who had a religious vision of things at one moment in his life—at one point he had even thought of being a priest—is metaphorically and symbolically associated with the old man in the dream. (215–16)

As Besson further notes, the mythical Grail was said to have been carved from an enormous emerald, and "the colour green recurs in the novel like a sign," becoming, she argues, "the symbolical colour of a hidden truth" (2011, 215).

Sexsmith and his party travel deeper into the mountains, moving toward a snow-covered peak that, seen from a distance, appears to Sexsmith as "an Asiatic temple floating in the air." Up close, however, the mountain becomes "a massive presence" (28), and the weary Sexsmith is awed. He "closed his eyes, overcome by sudden vertigo. Here was the edge of the earth, and far below it clouds drifted over an empty blue ocean. [. . .] He was thirty-one years old. A Victorian in the presence of the sublime" (1995, 28–29). The party travels on, climbing up a ridge beside "a gently rising slope of dirty snow and ice. Arcturus glacier, Sexsmith named it" (43). Inspired by his dream, Sexsmith is determined to go further, toward a mysterious source of light—a "spirit place," he is told (43). He ventures out onto the ice of the glacier, but what he experiences there remains unknown to us. He returns in a "black mood" (45), and the party turns around, the expedition at an end.

The parallel between Sexsmith's adventure, which culminates in his mysterious experience atop the glacier, and Byrne's vision of the angel in the crevasse is, of course, unmistakable. Toward the end of the novel, Byrne speculates about why Sexsmith turned back and why, in his memoirs, he mentioned only his disappointment.

> But was that all? Byrne wonders. Why would he keep silent about it? Unless, like me, he encountered something that he dared not set down in his memoirs.
> Disappointment. Nothing but snow, ice, cloud, wind. That was all he found. And what he could not accept. A world with a wasteland like this at its summit. (181)

In many ways, Sexsmith's response to the glacier typifies that of European explorers to the wilderness: it is *terra nullius*, empty space, yet to tamed. He is trapped in what Smaro Kamboureli describes as "the imperial *zeitgeist* of discovery and exploration, the desire to conquer and name the unknown" (2011, 204). Sexsmith also assumes that he knows what "the sublime" should look like and hence will be able to recognize when he is in its presence. Yet his capacity to respond to the glacier is preempted by his expectations—his desire to arrive at some forbidden "spirit place" and to find something he will likewise recognize as a Holy Grail. Caught up in his fantasies, Sexsmith is unable to appreciate what is present before him and so retreats from an experience that Byrne instead explores.

Much the same can be said of Trask, who eventually has his own encounter with the angel in the ice. If Sexsmith stands as a symbol of European exploration, then the deeply pragmatic Trask represents subsequent exploitation: throughout the narrative, he is intent on the transformation of natural beauty into a tourist attraction. Toward the close of the novel, amidst the construction of a roadway into the base of the glacier, Trask decides to climb out onto the ice, admitting to Byrne that he has not "set foot on the glacier" (255) since the expedition some twenty-five years earlier. After parting company with Byrne, Trask heads off on his own, "skirting a small crevasse" (258)—which we infer is the crevasse into which Byrne once fell, now diminished in size—but takes a wrong turn and has to work his way back home by a circuitous route. At one point, he rests briefly at the base of an "upthrust pinnacle of dirty ice": "The pinnacle, sculpted by water and ice, rises in a graceful curve over his head. He nestles for a moment within its scant shelter. Just like a folded wing" (259). The ice is melting, and not long afterward, the shelf of ice on which Trask had paused collapses into the meltwater. Thinking back on his experience later that day, Trask muses that there "must be an artist in the construction crew," an "undiscovered Michelangelo" (260):

> Trask shakes his head. The wasted effort. Didn't the fellow realize how short-lived his creation would be? He probably did. That's why the thing had been unfinished, looking as if it was just emerging from the ice.
> Better stick to building roads and bridges. (261)

Trask is presented as almost wholly bereft of both ecological and spiritual consciousness. Nature is, for him, a resource, rather than a source of understanding.

Wharton once commented in an interview, "I think the story of Byrne at some point deliberately became a story that was meant to show a development of an environmental consciousness. . . . I think over the course of the novel he moves towards what we see today as an environmental, ecologically oriented attitude" (Wyile 2002, 174). If we are to understand Byrne as having an environmental awakening, then the tension that the novel establishes between the conventional exploration and development of nature and nature as the site of a holy quest suggests that ecological awakening also entails an awakening of the spirit.

Fundamental to both religious or spiritual experience is the capacity to feel awe—to marvel at that which is beyond our understanding. In the popular imagination, a religious or spiritual response to the world is often opposed to a rational, scientific one. As Allan Hepburn puts it in an essay on Wharton's novel, "Because science often discounts the inventions of a storyteller, the wonderful, by default, includes the antiscientific" (2001, 76). Yet, as he goes on to point out, "Scientific Byrne, more than any other character in *Icefields*, feels wonder without relinquishing his rationality. Science and wonder are not incompatible; they just offer utterly different approaches to nature. The wondrous is a holdout of what science has not explained, measured, and complicated" (76). Science is, in fact, ultimately founded on the experience of wonder and a confrontation with mystery that prompts a search for explanations.

Hepburn argues that "*Icefields* posits an original wonder that can be glimpsed in and through touristic models of looking at landscape. Tourism doesn't nullify wonder; it merely makes it more difficult to see" (2001, 72). Similarly, a relentless search for rational explanations can easily cause us to lose sight of our original experience of wonder, while it may also tempt us to ignore or dismiss whatever resists explanation and insists instead on remaining a mystery. As Abram observes, there are always those who

> simply will not see any magic, either at a performance or in the world at large; armored with countless explanations and analyses, they "see" only how the trick must have been accomplished. . . . Encouraged by a cultural discourse that disdains the unpredictable and puts a premium on detached objectivity, such persons attempt to halt the participation of their senses in the phenomenon. Yet they can do so only by imaginatively projecting other phenomena . . . or by looking away. (1996, 59)

Byrne refuses to look away; his brush with wonder inspires his obsession with glaciology, but, in his quest for an answer to the mystery, he never loses track of his original encounter with the inexplicable.

Trask, in contrast, is more inclined to explain away what he cannot fathom. Thinking back to his own adventure on the ice, he experiences a brief glimmer of wonder, as he recalls the pinnacle of ice crashing into the water: "But ice floats, he thought at the time. Where did it go? The rock and mud clinging to the pinnacle must have weighted it down" (260). His thoughts go no further, however. Consumed by visions of tourist development, he must ignore or repress wonder in order to maintain his resource-focused world view. He looks away, much like Sexsmith, who, trapped in his expectations, cannot recognize the sublime when he is standing on top of it. He gazes outward and sees only emptiness, a space devoid of meaning.

MULTIPLE VALUES: THE TRANSFORMATION OF PLACE

In Kamboureli's analysis, "*Icefields* explores the structure of colonialism by iterating history," a history "supplemented by a narrative of progress that involves the construction of the Grand Trunk and the building of chalets" (2011, 204). Although the novel is set primarily in the early twentieth century, Wharton provides glimpses of earlier moments in Jasper's history, revealing the contrasting meanings that the area has held for various groups of people. Sara, the woman who takes care of Byrne following his injury, identifies with the local Métis community. Her father, Viraj, was born in India and came to the area as Lord Sexsmith's attendant, while her mother was an Indigenous woman, one of the "Snake people" who now live further west. As we learn from Sara's account of Sexsmith's journey, her mother became the adopted sister of two Stoney brothers and was given the name "Athabasca." The three of them met up with Sexsmith's expedition, and it was Sara's mother who said that the top of the icefield is a "spirit place. Not for the living" (Wharton 1995, 43). "She knew the land better than they did," one of her brothers explains, "because her people had once lived here in this valley, and even deeper in the mountains" (35). Through the encounter of Sexsmith's group with Athabasca and her two brothers, Wharton reveals something of the contrast between European and Indigenous conceptions of the natural world.

In the course of Sara's account, we also learn that Jasper was once a Hudson's Bay Company post and that, by the time of Byrne and Trask's arrival, in 1898, it was the site of a Métis settlement. As Sara explains, "The fur trade had gradually died out and there was no longer any material reason to follow the old overland trail," that is, until people "came looking for the one precious substance that remained here: the gold of solitude and silence" (32). As settlers encroached on the West, the relatively remote Jasper area remained largely untouched by European habitation, at least initially, but already we see shifts in meaning. For Indigenous peoples, the landscape, imbued with spirit, was the source of all life. For fur traders, the area was a source of profit. And, by the close of the nineteenth century, it had become, for white settlers, a place of simplicity and seclusion and, occasionally, of inspiration.

For Trask, however (and for others like him), this silence and splendour translates into a tourist opportunity. Jasper is, for him, a "wild valley waiting for the resourceful young man to see its potential" (65), a potential he is quick to exploit, becoming the part-owner of a newly constructed chalet with its "marvelous glasshouse" (65) and its "immaculate lawns" (66). It is Trask who persuades the "railway magnates to build a spur line from the wide Athabasca valley into this more remote and colder region of the mountains" (65). This is the irony of development: the allure of places like Jasper—their pristine quality, their solitude, the awe they evoke—is destroyed in process of their exploitation. Development brings crowds of visitors, people who have no intrinsic connection to the place or any intention of staying long enough to acquire one. In the process, a relationship embedded in the need for subsistence and founded on reciprocity, respect, and ecological sustainability is displaced by one based on landscape as commodity.

The development of the town and chalet represents a shift from a time "when savage men wrestled with grizzly bears, or were said to have done so" (103), to a time when wildlife is an exotic attraction: "Nineteen-nineteen. A photograph of the era: A black bear, chained to a post at the golf course" (224). Rather than a place where one would dwell, eke out a livelihood, and maintain an embodied connection to place, Jasper National Park becomes a temporary escape for people who are served up lavish comforts. Guests at the chalet are "giddy with joy at the comforts of civilization. Hot running water, wine and cheese, the anticipation of a warm feather bed" (80). As Hepburn points out, "Within an ideology of property and tourism, nature gets packaged for quick consumption" (2001, 72). They are able to gaze on the magnificence of the Rocky Mountains, but the effort once needed to do so is now gone, as is their investment in the experience.

The commodification of the wilderness is further evident in Frank Trask's guided walking tours and in his "four ice-crawlers" with their "military look" (270). For a price, visitors can now travel by motor coach to the terminus of the glacier and then step into an ice-crawler, which transports them safely and conveniently onto the frozen expanse: "The guests step off the bus dreamily. Lulled in the cradle of the machine" (269). In the minds of Canadian sports enthusiasts, ice is, of course, associated above all with hockey, and it is perhaps significant that Trask makes the novel's one reference to the sport: imagining ways to exploit the glacier, he thinks, "And in winter, there could be hockey games right on the ice" (253). Like the landscape itself, sport has also been commodified, and, in the process, the connection of sport to the natural environment has weakened. Games that were once played outdoors now take place in an arena, where spectators can watch, not unlike tourists, in relative warmth and comfort. Moreover, much as formerly pristine landscapes have been overrun by development, sports once pursued purely for the sake of competition and the mastery of skill have become mired in broadcast deals, corporate sponsorships, and colossal revenues.

The differing value put on place is perhaps most explicitly articulated in the exchange between Byrne and Trask about the workmen who are cutting down trees along one of the moraines. Byrne, who understands the implications, is outraged:

> —Do you know how long those trees have been there, Frank? Hundreds of years. It's like a little Arctic up there, everything is fragile. The trees grow very slowly that close to the ice.
> —And now they're in the way. Ned, in this world the trees and rocks have to move, not the men.
> —That's not what you told Sara's people. (250)

Whereas Byrne not only understands but values the glacial ecosystem, Trask does not. Nor is he concerned about the fate of Indigenous communities, such as the Métis families who were also "in the way" and were evicted from Jasper by the government in the face of park development. Unlike the original inhabitants of the area, Trask sees no inherent value in a natural ecosystem, even one that he seeks to exploit. Today, tourists can drive the "Icefields Parkway" from Banff to Jasper, and one senses that, a century later, Trask would be pleased.

TIME AND THE GLACIER

The passage of time is a prominent theme in *Icefields*, and central to this theme is the notion of geological time, or deep time. Each of the novel's five main sections is named for a feature associated with glaciation, and, as Pamela Banting points out, these names "parallel the names given to the parts of a fictional plot: névé (initial incident), moraine (rising action), nunatak (climax), ablation zone (falling action), and terminus (dénouement)" (2000, 72). The action of the novel is thus structured around the phases of glaciation, and, as Banting argues, it is the motion of the glacier that gives the narrative its momentum: "It is not through the human characters' actions but rather through the glacier's movement that the mysteries of the angel figure are re-addressed (though not solved) and Byrne is released from his quest, thus drawing the narrative to its conclusion" (72).

In the novel, the glacier is associated with interruptions in the standard flow of time. Trapped in the crevasse, Byrne becomes disoriented. "How long have I been here?" he wonders. "Minutes or hours. There was no way to tell" (Wharton 1995, 13). He struggles against "the insane thought that he had been wedged in this crevasse for centuries":

> Freezing into absolute stillness, his thoughts crystallized around one idea. He moved an arm, fumbled at his coat for his pocket watch. He had to know the time.
>   Time was the one constant. It did not change or freeze into immobility. Time would go on and so would he. (13)

Trapped in the crevasse, Byrne is grasping for something rational and concrete, some assurance of the continuity of life. In this place of sensory and temporal disruption—a place far older than the human ability to process and experience time—his perceptions are irrevocably changed.

Trask has an analogous experience of disorientation, also associated with the glacier and its angel and also marked by the disruption of time. This occurs near the end of the novel, when he and Byrne are out on the icefield. As Byrne packs up to leave, he suggests that Trask stay for a while to enjoy the silence of the place. Watching Byrne make his way home, Trask vows not to "follow after him like a lost tourist" and heads off in a different direction. In the time that has intervened since Trask last climbed the surface of the glacier, as the guide of the expedition on which Byrne had his accident, he has lost his intuitive, embodied connection to the ever-shifting expanse of ice, and his lack of experience with the current terrain leads him astray. He finds himself down in a gully, his sense of spatial location confounded: "The chalet and all other familiar landmarks are hidden from view" (258). With no choice but to retrace his steps, he scrambles back up to the glacier and "is shocked to find himself bent double, gasping for breath, his head spinning. Too much time spent at a desk the last few years" (258–59). Trask's body does not perform as he would expect, and his ability to predict time also proves unreliable: what should have been a relatively short walk ends up taking hours, with Trask arriving back at the chalet only in the evening.

We often gauge space or distance in relation to time. As Tuan suggests, one explanation for the equation of time and distance is that "units of time convey a clear sense of effort. . . . One hundred paces means one hundred units of a biological rhythm that we know intimately" (1977, 129–30). In this way, a disruption of our embodied sense of physical progress through space entails a disruption in our perception not only of space but also of time. Once we lose our direction, we can no longer predict how long our journey will take us, and we become keenly alert to our surroundings, hoping to find a point of reference. Out on the glacier, Trask spots the red glow of the fire drum at the work camp, which becomes "a beacon to him in the distance"; wedged in the crevasse, Byrne is desperate to pull out his pocket watch. In any situation in which our senses are intensely focused on our embodied experience (including playing a sport), our perception of time changes: events can slow down to a crawl or unfold in an instant.

In *Icefields*, experiences of spatiotemporal disorientation are associated most directly with the mysterious angel of ice, which, like the glacier itself, advances at a pace too slow for ordinary human perception. Byrne is aware of the gap between human time and geological time: "I lean back on the sun-warmed rock, close my eyes, and listen. The glacier moves forward at a rate of less than one inch every hour. If I could train myself to listen at the same rate, one sound every hour, I would hear the glacier wash up against this rock island, crash like waves, and become water" (152). The deep time of geological evolution is not the experiential time of human beings: in geological time, a human lifespan is an inconsequential moment. Indeed, in the context of Christian cosmology, the ability to perceive the world within the framework of deep time presumably belongs solely to God, the Creator, and it is not entirely surprising that Byrne, observing the glacier, turns to religious imagery. As the ice slowly flows over a steep incline in the underlying rock, it "groans, cracks, thunders, and rears up a cathedral":

> When the sun breaks through the cloud, the cathedral fills with light. The warmer air hollows it into a more baroque, flamboyant shape. Spires, archways, gargoyles begin to flow. Waterfalls set festive ice bells ringing.
>
> Then, slowly, the delicate balance that kept it aloft is undermined. Even as light glorifies it, the cathedral is diminished, begins almost imperceptibly to collapse. Sepulchral booms and crashes attest to hidden vaults and hollows, the shirting instability of the foundation. (161)

The creation and demise of the glacial cathedral mirrors the creation, life, and destruction of the earth as described in biblical narratives. Here, Wharton seems to be linking the geological concept of deep time to Christian cosmology.

Eternity is beyond human comprehension: our perception of the passage of time inevitably culminates with our death. Although angels are typically thought of as offering protection, Judeo-Christian tradition also includes the Angel of Death. In the novel, Freya, the intrepid mountain climber, dies trying to reach the summit of the mountain from which the glacier descends. Her camera is broken in her fatal fall, but two images on the film survive, one of them a portrait of Byrne. Looking at it, Byrne realizes that he has aged: "Prematurely white hair, thin white beard lining a long, bony face. [. . .] Chiselled lines at the corners of his eyes" (213). "The markings of time," he thinks. "The ice has been at work here too" (213). He imagines the faces of the soldiers leaving to fight in World War I, their "eyes looking away into some place more distant and unspeakable than the depths of a glacier" (214). Eventually, the slow movement of the ice transports his angel to the terminus of the glacier, where it collapses into the water and is gone forever. Ultimately, the disparity between cosmic time, glacial time, and human time—brought into focus by Byrne's close observations and life experiences—highlights the often myopic nature of human life.

CONCLUSION

Toward the end of *Icefields*, as Trask contemplates the future development of a bus terminal at the foot of the glacier, destined to feature an "igloo-style" façade and a "glacier diorama," he thinks triumphantly: "A sunny pleasure dome with caves of ice!" Wondering whether "it might be possible to import penguins to swim in the melt pool at the terminus," he reflects, "Of course their wings would have to be clipped" (Wharton 1995, 253). Condensed in this brief passage is a theme that has run throughout the novel: that of enchantment versus disenchantment. "A sunny pleasure-dome with caves of ice!" is a line from Samuel Taylor Coleridge's "Kubla Khan," the poem that Sara read to Byrne as he was recovering from his fall into the crevasse. The poem is subtitled "Or, A Vision in a Dream," and, in it, Coleridge writes not only "caverns measureless to man" but also of a "deep romantic chasm"—a "savage" place, "holy and enchanted," from which a "mighty fountain momently was forced" (1996 [1816], 230). While Wharton's use of the poem establishes the glacier and its netherworld as a mystical realm, a world of awe and mystery, Byrne's sense of wonder and dedication to scientific study exemplify how the two can co-exist in one's conception of real places—a meaningful duality that is in fact deeply anti-thetical to Trask's crass, commercial visions.

In contrast, Trask's reference to the clipping of wings brings us back to the start of the novel and Byrne's description of the angel in the ice:

> The white figure lay on its side, the head turned away from him. Its huge wings were spread wide, one of them cracked obliquely near the tip, the broken pinions slightly detached.
> One arm was also visible, outstretched, in the semblance of some gesture that Byrne felt he had seen before, but could not interpret. (11)

Once the light fades, the figure is no longer visible. "A magnificent, impossible figure from a long-forgotten childhood dream," Byrne thinks (13). In his own deep chasm, Byrne has come face to face with something "impossible," something that defies interpretation.

The experience of the sublime is, essentially by definition, ineffable—a form of communion that one can experience but not adequately translate into language. At one point in the novel, Hal Rawson, the poet turned mountain guide, explains to Freya why he has recently found himself unable to write poems: "I realized I'd written about nothing that I'd lived through. None of it was my life, my experience." Freya, herself a writer, is sympathetic: "Words always do that to me," she says, "even when I'm reporting what we like to call the facts. I think to myself, was that really what I saw, what I felt? But I keep trying, I have to try to nail things down with the exact words." To this, Hal replies, "I'll try not to mention the infinite, or the ineffable" (114–15).

The point, of course, is that experiences of the sublime are intimate and deeply felt and that there are no "exact words" with which one can "nail down" the infinite and ineffable. As Tuan observes,

> Intimate experiences lie buried in our innermost being so that not only do we lack the words to give them form but often we are not even aware of them. When, for some reason, they flash to the

surface of our consciousness they evince a poignancy that the more deliberative acts—the actively sought experiences—cannot match. Intimate experiences are hard to express. (1977, 136–37)

In the novel, Byrne, Sexsmith, and Trask all experience the presence of the angel, and all three confront something that they cannot express. But only Byrne is capable of enchantment. Byrne accepts that he has had an intimate encounter with the inexplicable and devotes his life to exploring the mystery, in the course of which he arrives at an understanding of patience and of the human place in nature. In contrast, Sexsmith becomes disenchanted. In actively seeking an experience shaped by his expectations, his hopes of finding a "Grail" of some sort, he overlooks the possibility of wonder and winds up disappointed. Trask is also intent on "deliberative acts": he is so busy planning the future that he cannot simply be still and experience the present.

In his essay on mountain climbing, McCarthy notes that stories about the experience often depict "climbers transcending ego-centered subjectivity and gaining a felt knowledge of human integration with the natural world" (2008, 164). This is, perhaps, the overarching theme in *Icefields*: the human need for immersion, for moments when our senses are so completely given over to our experience that we are no longer conscious of ourselves, or of time and space. Byrne is capable of this immersion, this embodied absorption, an experience that, for him, is triggered by his plunge into the "caverns measureless to man" and sustained by the intimate relationship he develops with the glacier. Like King Arthur's knights, Byrne sets out on a quest to obtain a holy relic, his angel embedded in the ice, but, because he remains open to wonder and enchantment and is attentive to the beautiful complexity of the mountain ecosystem, he finds instead what may be the most divine gift of all—a way of being wholly present in the world, one founded on an understanding of our ecological embeddedness.

WORKS CITED

Abram, David. 1996. *The Spell of the Sensuous: Perception and Language in a More-than-Human World*. New York: Vintage.

Banting, Pamela. 2000. "The Angel in the Glacier: Geography as Intertext in Thomas Wharton's Icefields." *Interdisciplinary Studies in Literature and Environment* 7, no. 2: 67–80.

Besson, Françoise. 2011. "Botany as the Path to Awareness, or the Flower as Grail in Thomas Wharton's *Icefields.*" *Ecozon@: European Journal of Literature, Culture and Environment* 2, no. 2: 211–27.

Buell, Lawrence. 2005. *The Future of Environmental Criticism: Environmental Crisis and Literary Imagination.* Oxford: Blackwell.

Coleridge, Samuel Taylor. 1996 [1816]. "Kubla Khan; Or, A Vision in a Dream." In *Selected Poems*, edited by Richard Holmes, 230–31. London: Penguin.

Cresswell, Tim. 2004. *Place: A Short Introduction.* Oxford: Blackwell.

Gaull, Marilyn. 1988. *English Romanticism: The Human Context.* New York: W. W. Norton.

Hepburn, Allan. 2001. "'Enough of a Wonder': Landscape and Tourism in Thomas Wharton's *Icefields.*" *Essays on Canadian Writing* 73: 72–92.

Kamboureli, Smaro. 2011. "The Sublime of Mobility and Thomas Wharton's *Icefields.*" In *Mobilités culturelles: regards croisés Brésil/Canada / Cultural Mobilities: A Cross-Perspective Between Brazil and Canada*, edited by Pascal Gin and Walter Moser, 189–229. Ottawa: University of Ottawa Press.

McCarthy, Jeffrey Mathes. 2008. "Why Climbing Matters." *Interdisciplinary Studies in Literature and Environment* 15, no. 2: 157–74.

Tuan, Yi-Fu. 1977. *Space and Place: The Perspective of Experience.* Minneapolis: University of Minnesota Press.

Wharton, Thomas. 1995. *Icefields.* New York: Washington Square.

Wyile, Herb. 2002. "The Iceman Cometh Across: An Interview with Thomas Wharton." *Studies in Canadian Literature / Études en littérature canadienne* 27, no. 1: 157–82.

6

Jamie Dopp

Hockey, Zen, and the Art of Bill Gaston's *The Good Body*

At the end of Bill Gaston's *The Good Body*, the protagonist, Big Bob Bonaduce, a forty-year-old career minor-league hockey player, lies in a hospital bed. After a harrowing sequence of events culminating in a car crash and the onset of full-blown multiple sclerosis, Bonaduce is paralyzed, incontinent, and speech-impaired, and has no prospects for future improvement. Yet while others around him are stunned by his condition, Bonaduce seems—for the first time in the novel, really—to have achieved inner peace. He slurs out a joke. He tries to comfort his friend Marg, who huddles tearfully beside him. When Bonaduce implies in the novel's last line that the tears running down his face are not tears of sorrow but of laughter, we are inclined to believe him.

The ending of *The Good Body* is informed by a pattern that runs throughout Bill Gaston's fine and distinctive body of work. His stories and novels often dramatize the encounter between characters like Bonaduce—"everyday" Canadian, sports-loving or -playing guys—and the principles of Buddhism. What Buddhism teaches, Gaston told Tony Tremblay in an interview, is that "the human condition is one of somnambulism. We flounder about, pretending that our concerns matter, focused on little things which in the span of a life don't mean dick" (Tremblay 1991, 207). Gaston's texts often work variations on a plot in which a Bonaduce-like character, living a life of somnambulism, encounters a Buddha figure who inspires that character to experience "a moment of wakefulness or awe or surprise" (204). Indeed, when Bonaduce crashes at the end of *The Good Body*, he becomes awake to himself and the world in recognizably Buddhist terms. What matters, he now understands, is living in the present: from his bed, "he tried to convey with his face [. . .] that what mattered here was not Jason but you, Oscar, *you*, because it is you leaning over the bed. [. . .] What matters is this light streaming glory through the orange curtain" (Gaston 2000, 269).

Yet Bonaduce's journey towards enlightenment is more complicated than it might at first appear. Much of this complication has to do with *The Good Body*'s portrayal of hockey. The novel suggests that Bonaduce's somnambulistic life is largely a consequence of his pursuit of the hockey dream, and that hockey (or at least professional hockey) is emblematic of the kind of life that might lead a person into somnambulism. But the story also suggests that there is more to Bonaduce—as well as to hockey—than a focus on "little things which . . . don't mean dick." The one Buddha figure in the novel turns out to be a goalie whose characterization draws a comic parallel between the ambiguity of Buddha figures and the stereotypical weirdness of goalies—adding further complications. The novel implies that, for all their differences, hockey and Buddhism share uncanny parallels to one another. The encounter between Zen and hockey in *The Good Body*, then, leads to a fascinating and multilayered (not to mention often hilarious) meeting of cultures—an encounter that, I think, is part of what is most impressive about the art of Bill Gaston.

The starting premise of *The Good Body* is that the protagonist, Bob Bonaduce, returns to Fredericton at the end of a minor league professional hockey career in an attempt to reconnect with his son, Jason, who is a student at the University of New Brunswick and a member of that university's hockey team. Bonaduce plagiarizes his way into a graduate school creative writing program and hopes to join the University of New Brunswick hockey team with the idea that the camaradarie of playing hockey together will break the ice with Jason: "Set a guy up, no matter how much he hates you he has to come and whack you on the ass" (167).

From the outset, *The Good Body* makes clear that Bonaduce's pursuit of the hockey dream has had dire consequences for his life. The plot line involving his attempt to reconnect with Jason underlines a profound irony: the quest to be a professional hockey player, which is so often associated with traditional ideals of masculinity, can turn a man into a lousy father and husband. In the case of Bonaduce's ex-wife, Leah, the novel suggests that she and Bonaduce have always had a strong sexual connection but that she was turned off by Bonaduce's role as a fighter. Bonaduce, in turn, was ill-equipped to maintain a relationship. In the case of Jason, Bonaduce lacked the skills to be a good father, and even if he had put in more effort, the demands of his career would have made it difficult to stay connected. As Ken Dryden puts it in *The Game*, the problem with professional hockey from the point of view of a family man is that no matter how hard you try to be a good husband and father, the demands of the season mean that, fundamentally, "your family learns to cope . . . without you" (Dryden 1989, 113). Perhaps the most poignant line in *The Good Body* occurs in the dressing room when it dawns on Bonaduce that the indifference Jason is projecting towards him is, in fact, not an act: "the catchphrase he'd for two hours been breathing to himself, 'We're both pretending I'm no one special,' now transmuted to the thought *He's not pretending*" (Gaston 2000, 201).

Bonaduce's story suggests that the problems associated with hockey in his life reflect deeper existential issues. An important clue is the body imagery that appears throughout the text. As a professional athlete, Bonaduce is a "body-person," and his attention to his own physique leads him to judge others through the lens of physicality. For example, Daniel Kirk, the first "manprof" he meets, is a "buttclenched male animal" (17), and Margaret, the student who will become his closest new friend, "probably thought a bit about food" (15). Bonaduce's identification with the body—and his related tendency to use a head-body dichotomy to categorize people, with "head-people" understood as the irreconcilable other—can be read as symptomatic of the limited quality of his hockey-focused life. Chögyam Trungpa considers a key aspect of Buddhist practice to be the synchronizing of mind and body, which he describes as "a basic principle of how to be a human being" (1984, 52). Similar claims could be made about various Western philosophies (especially feminist philosophies). In contrast, Bonaduce's singular identification with the body reveals an extreme version of the human tendency to deny bodily weakness and what that weakness points to.

That Bonaduce has lived in denial about aging and death is underlined by the event that most directly triggers his attempt to reconnect with Jason—his discovery that he has multiple sclerosis. MS is described in the novel as virtually an incarnation of death itself. Bonaduce recalls the morning of his first MS attack as a continuation of "sleep's dreamscape," a transformation of himself into the kind of living dead creature found in nightmares: "You wake up with vision so fuzzy it's like sleep's dreamscape has continued, and then you find the legs don't work too well. Couldn't even bloody walk, he was a big nightmare puppet with packed rag legs. It wasn't some awful new injury, because he'd been feeling so weak and weird lately he hadn't even been playing" (Gaston 2000, 43). As a disease, MS involves a step-by-step withdrawal of feeling and function from the body, sometimes slowly over years, sometimes very quickly. For Bonaduce, it means different parts of his body going dead in a foreshadowing of the overall death of his body: "Hold your fork. Dead hand on the lap under the table" (234).

Bonaduce's response to his MS, until the very end of the novel, is to deny the reality of the disease, just as his body focus has meant a lifelong denial of human weakness, aging, and death. His attempt to play hockey for the UNB team goes directly against the medical advice he has received, which is not to overexert himself. When the overexertion has the predicted effect—an acceleration of his symptoms that turns him into "a limping mummy"—he responds in classic hockey player fashion by attempting "to walk it off" (235). Eventually, he hits moral and physical bottom, breaking the leg of a player on Jason's own team to try to win Jason's favour and triggering an almost debilitating onset of MS symptoms; then, in a last attempt at denial, he gets into his car and tries to "get gone" (247). The crash that follows is like a forceful, final assertion of the body. Bonaduce wakes up in the ditch to find that he is paralyzed and has soiled himself, his body "emptying itself, muscles he couldn't feel" (262). Only when he is forced to experience his utter helplessness before the weakness of his body, with the terror and panic that comes from a clear awareness of his own mortality, is Bonaduce able to glimpse what it means to be truly alive.

The deeper existential issues faced by Bonaduce in *The Good Body* are the primary focus of Buddhist philosophy. Buddhism takes as its starting point the view that human suffering arises not so much out of the inevitability of change and death as out of our attempts to "solve" these facts of existence in some final way, either by denying their reality or by trying to explain them in a way that transforms them into something other than what they are. As Steve Hagen puts it, "We think we have to deal with our problems in a way that exterminates them, that distorts or denies their reality.... We try to arrange the world so that dogs will never bite, accidents will never happen, and the people we care about will never die" (1997, 18). Buddhism teaches the folly of such thinking. Rather than try to "solve" the facts of existence, Buddhism encourages us to cultivate nonattachment. Hsing Yun puts it like this: "Prajna [wisdom] teaches us that nothing should be clung to because there is nothing that can be clung to. Everything is empty" (2001, 78). Nonattachment is not a means of escaping reality but of "dealing with the fundamental nature of reality," which is its lack of an essential nature or meaning and the inevitability of change (90). The pay-off for achieving Buddhist wisdom is to live more fully in the present. This is all that is meant by "enlightenment" in Buddhism. Indeed, as Hagen points out, the term "Buddha" simply means "awakened one" (1997, 3).

Gaston's first three novels all revolve around Bonaduce-like protagonists who are startled towards wakefulness by an encounter with a Buddha figure. In *Bella Combe Journal* (1996), Vaughn, a hockey-playing wanderer, is challenged by Bert Flutie, a far-seeing bum; by Lise/Annie, whose only rule is "wakefulness" (192); and by Connor Peake, a poet who goes from the extremes of meditating to performing weird antics in order to shake up the people around him. The Baal twins in *Tall Lives* (1990), who struggle equally with the opposite extremes of order and chaos that dominate their lives, are challenged by Felix, a Buddha-shaped French-speaking philosopher, who ultimately sees the futility of attempting to "change the world" and, as a result, burns up his life's work, an encyclopedia, along with his house (207). And in *The Cameraman* (2002), the protagonist, Francis Dann, also a hockey player, is challenged by his friend Koz in much the way that Vaughn is challenged by Connor Peake. Koz, like Connor, is a tricky agitator whose antics seem designed to shock people into wakefulness—but as a film director rather than a poet. Koz's ideal is to think of life as a very expensive movie with only one chance to do things perfectly. "The way we waste time," he says, "you'd think we forgot we're going to die" (156).

There is a characteristic ambiguity in all of these figures: they all seem as much tricksters as agents of enlightenment. Koz is typical. He is described throughout *The Cameraman* by way of antinomies. He is an ordinary guy with extraordinary abilities, a popular jock who is also an uncannily top student, the kind of kid who "was absent a lot, yet always got perfect scores on tests" (25). Koz is both "the maze and the map out" (232), a maker of films that suggest both "silliness and genius" (61); he has eyes that suggest "a wise man, or a wise guy" (187). To Francis, some of Koz's deeds might have been intended to "shed light" but others "could easily mean nothing at all" (60–61), which adds a destabilizing layer of irony to the catch phrases Koz uses to draw attention to his work—"watch this" and "trust me."

The ambiguity of Gaston's Buddha figures reflects an ambiguity in Buddhist teacher figures more generally. There is much reverence towards teacher figures in Buddhist literature, and many stories are told of the journeys towards enlightenment experienced by these teachers, journeys that become object lessons for others to follow. There are also many stories about the tests posed by teachers in order to prepare students to learn. Often the tests involve hardships or frustrations that at first seem extreme or inexplicable. In *Zen in the Art of Archery*, for example, Eugen Herrigel describes long periods of apparently fruitless repetition at each stage of his learning to shoot. At the beginning, he spends the better part of a year simply practicing to draw the bow (incorrectly, as it turns out). Eventually, he learns that the repetition is necessary to "detach him from himself," for "all right doing is accomplished only in a state of true selflessness, in which the doer cannot be present any longer as 'himself'" (1953, 67). Another way to put this is that the tests set by the teacher are designed to break down the ego-investments of the student, investments that are expressed, among other ways, in the student's desire to be a "good student" or to "get" something from the teacher. As Chögyam Trungpa explains, "the impulse of searching for something is, in itself, a hang-up," and only when this hang-up is exhausted can enlightenment take place (2002, 42). That the teacher's role is to challenge the student to give up his or her ego-investments implies that the teacher wields a great deal of power. In order to thwart the desire to "get" something, the teacher will inevitably make what seem like arbitrary or inexplicable demands, acting, apparently, as a wise guy and not a wise man—and the student must submit to this. Herrigel points out that the teacher-student relationship in Zen depends upon the student's "uncritical veneration of his teacher" (1953, 62). For Trungpa, the basic condition of true learning is an openness in the student that comes from a kind of "psychological surrender" to the teacher. "It is essential to surrender," he writes, "to open yourself . . . rather than trying to present yourself as a worthwhile student" (2002, 39).

Coupled with this reverence towards the teacher, however, is an awareness of the limitations of the teacher's role. There is a crucial distinction in Buddhism between the wisdom that the teacher might convey and the nature of true wisdom. The teacher is, in an important sense, only an agent, only someone who might help the student achieve his or her own experience of truth. Ultimately, enlightenment has to be experienced directly. The role of the teacher is very much like the role of the "sacred" texts of Buddhism.

While these texts are revered, it is understood that they do not contain truth in some concrete or extractible way. As Hagen puts it, "Buddhist teachings and writings can assist you, but you won't find Truth in them, as if Truth somehow resided in the Buddha's words" (1997, 10). One of the most famous metaphors in Buddhism compares the Buddha's words to a finger pointing at the moon. The finger can point the way, but ultimately, to see the moon, you have to look for yourself. The same is true of the teacher. To think of the teacher as some superior being who possesses wisdom or truth is to mistake the finger for the moon. This is why Trungpa, in the same chapter that describes the need for "psychological surrender," cautions against the idea that this might lead to any kind of "master-servant relationship." Instead, he suggests that the way to think of the teacher is as a "spiritual friend"—someone who assists the student from a position of equality. The process of learning, then, becomes "a meeting of two minds" and "a matter of mutual communication" (2002, 39).

The Good Body takes Gaston's portrayals of ambiguous Buddha figures a step further by making the Buddha figure a goalie Bonaduce rooms with for the last part of his career in the minors. In the character of Fournier, Gaston draws a comic parallel between the ambiguity of Buddha figures and the stereotypical weirdness of goalies, who are usually understood to be either the most thoughtful players on a team or the craziest (another version of "a wise man or a wise guy"). The usual goalie weirdness of Fournier is magnified by "his accent and Montreal suave," which make him stand out even more than the other Canadian hockey players in Tulsa, Oklahoma, where Bonaduce's team is based. Bonaduce senses what is special about him: "His English wasn't great, but the glint in his eye leapt easily over language. He had a way of smiling at your subtle question, looking at you with understanding but saying nothing. If you persisted, he might wave it away and say happily, 'No matter!' [. . .] He read so much" (Gaston 2000, 119). Eventually, once Fournier gets to know Bonaduce well enough, he admits that "his lifestyle was in keeping with the traditions of Zen": he shopped "only for the food of one meal," had only two sets of clothes, and so on (119). Unlike the other players, who tended to pick up women in bars, Fournier met women in libraries or the grocery store, and the ones he dated tended to be "Zen or health-food types themselves" (120).

Fournier appears on only a few pages of *The Good Body*. He plays the role of concerned friend, checking in on Bonaduce by telephone (114), sending his new girlfriend's book about yeast infections as a treatment for Bonaduce's MS (186), and helping to arrange a last, large pay cheque from Bonaduce's former hockey team (266). He is not the immediate catalyst for Bonaduce's enlightenment. The extremely New Age–like quality of the therapies he suggests for Bonaduce's MS (by way of his extremely New Age girlfriend) underlines the extent to which he may be a flake. His presence in the novel, however, suggests the availability of another way of approaching life from the somnambulistic one that has defined Bonaduce's approach so far. Bonaduce, importantly, is open to Fournier's ideas. When he goes along with Fournier's Zen lifestyle, Bonaduce feels "lighter, more ready for the game, party, movie, or call-up to the bigs" (120).

Bonaduce's openness to Fournier's Zen-like ideas is one of a number of clues that there is more to Bonaduce than the stereotype of a "stupid rough hayseed hockey player" (41). Long before his fateful crash, Bonaduce is shown to have other important qualities: he is genuinely literate, a guitar player and aficionado of contemporary music, and a clear-eyed observer of both hockey and the larger world. For example, early in the novel, he looks out the window to see a landscape where nothing is happening and has a Buddhist-like thought: "You could think of it as an empty stage waiting for something to happen. Birds. Deer. They had to come. In two months, snow. There were worse things to watch than an empty stage" (35). Later, he remarks upon the "trivial ugliness" that a career in hockey must seem to someone like Leah, whose own work involves helping refugees and "victims of war and torture" (54–55). And at various places, he makes astute—and funny—observations about the world of academia. His most telling observations in this area involve comparisons between academia and hockey. There is macho posturing in the academy, he points out, that is not unlike that found in hockey, as his hilarious account of Phil "presenting" in a graduate seminar shows (40). The graduate students are good at irony, he observes, because they practice it "like pros" (85). And, most significantly, the intelligence on display in academia is not foreign to the hockey dressing room, where there is also a great deal of "wit" as well as "nightclub and taxi savvy," not to mention the "sound public management of pride and envy, something academics were famously inept at" (42).

An important aspect of Bonaduce's astuteness is that it occurs not only in spite of his being a hockey player but also because of it. Bonaduce's interest in music and literature, as well as his openness to the ideas of Fournier, marks him as a "freak" in the eyes of his teammates—hence, not your usual hockey player (34). At the same time, the astuteness of Bonaduce's observations are not unrelated to the "savvy" he has absorbed from the hockey dressing room. Beyond the worldliness of the dressing room savvy, there is a sense that Bonaduce's astuteness is a result of his ability to observe with an innocent eye practices whose absurdity is hidden to those who are immersed in them. This is particularly true in his satire of academia. What this suggests is that the point of view of "regular sorts, even hockey-jacket types" is not only a source of somnambulism but also, potentially, of critical insight (220).

That Bonaduce's astuteness occurs not only in spite of his being a hockey player but because of it is itself reflective of the ambiguity of hockey in *The Good Body*. Yes, hockey is associated with somnambulism, but hockey, the novel suggests, also contains elements that point the way to enlightenment. Take Bonaduce's body focus. Though his self-identification as a "body-person" suggests an unhealthy division of body from mind, the body-focus of his life as an athlete also contains clues about a way out of this unhealthy division. As an athlete, Bonaduce has daily physical rituals not unlike the practices of meditation. Exercise helps to quiet his busy mind: "Jog the legs, the spine, the body into a pleasant stupor, hard breathing" (10). Gaston's first novel, *Bella Combe Journal*, makes an explicit connection between the "hard breathing" of physical activity—especially skating—and the awareness of breath that occurs in meditation (Gaston 1996, 77–78, 142). Though the connection is not made as explicitly in *The Good Body*, a number of passages show Bonaduce's awareness of breath—with the implication that this awareness has been heightened by his activities as an athlete. Take this one from his first night in his new bed in Fredericton:

> [This] pure and gentle going-in that almost erased you, a tender secret muscle the size of your body that turned you to air if you flexed it right—if you stayed here like this, you could be one of those people, and he knew they existed, one of those people who know only what matters, who can play life like the game it is.
> (Gaston 2000, 47)

The goal of an athlete's physical practice is to achieve that elusive state referred to as "the zone," which Gaston, in his hockey memoir, *Midnight Hockey*, likens to the mental state that might come from meditation: "The funny thing is, the zone appears to be exactly what meditators are seeking when they meditate. Go ahead, read any book on meditation and check out how they describe the sought-after state: a heightened clarity, a stillness, a place beyond words, and effortless. [. . .] It's mind and body together, in perfect union" (99). Bonaduce himself has an extended experience of the zone during a period in Kalamazoo when he scores an amazing number of goals, "first of a bunch of flukes and deflections," and then others when he is actually trying to score (191). The clarity Bonaduce achieves at the end of *The Good Body*, then, is very much consistent with the characteristics of the zone he aimed for—and sometimes experienced—as an athlete.

Perhaps the most fascinating intertwining of Zen and hockey in *The Good Body* has to do with the treatment of luck. Luck is foregrounded in the opening pages of the novel with the description of the antique air freshener that dangles from Bonaduce's rear-view mirror (3). Marg identifies this talisman as Bonaduce's "rabbit's foot" (29) and tries to increase his chances of good fortune by giving him another good luck charm in the form of a dream catcher (34–35). References to stars (49), astrology (61), and fireflies (those living embodiments of stars; 101) help to maintain the profile of luck in the novel. All of these references underline the significance of Bonaduce's observation that the confluence of events that brings him to Fredericton—the folding of his minor league team, his MS diagnosis, and a rare letter from Jason—suggests that he is taking his turn "under luck's big magnifying glass" (13).

Luck, of course, has a powerful mystique in sports. The prevalence of superstitions among athletes has to do with the fact that success or failure often seems determined by factors over which an individual has no control. A lucky bounce here or there can make all the difference. When Bonaduce is in the zone, he experiences it as a form of luck (191). The challenge for an athlete is that this zone of apparent good luck is both elusive and fragile— hence the tendency to think of it in mystical terms and to try to control it by magical means. Bonaduce describes the tendency like this: "The good zone you seek is delicate and there's nothing of it to hold on to, which is why the guys have their little thing. [. . .] Shamrock, Buddha, girlfriend's bandana, lucky rock" (262–63).

Luck, from a Buddhist point of view, is complicated. The idea of luck implies something outside of ourselves, some external force that might work either for or against us. Good luck charms are intended to "charm" this external force into acting on our behalf. But given the Buddhist teaching that "you are your own refuge, your own sanctuary, your own salvation" (Hagen 1997, 19), the idea of appealing to some external, quasi-supernatural force to fix your life is deeply flawed. As Bhikkhu Shravasti Dhammika explains, the Buddha "considered such practices as fortune telling, wearing magic charms for protection, fixing lucky sites for buildings and fixing lucky days to be useless superstitions" (2005, 41). Yet there are psychological aspects to luck that have affinities with the goals of Buddhist practice. Richard Wiseman summarizes the results of his ten-year study of self-identified "lucky" and "unlucky" people as follows: "Lucky people generate their own good fortune via four basic principles. They are skilled at creating and noticing chance opportunities, make lucky decisions by listening to their intuition, create self-fulfilling prophesies via positive expectations, and adopt a resilient attitude that transforms bad luck into good" (2003, para. 13). One of the truisms in sports psychology is that it is important to have a positive attitude. Being positive is no guarantee, but doubting yourself is a sure way to failure. Bonaduce knows this: "Doubt can kill luck all by itself" (191). At the same time, success requires that you can't want to succeed too badly. To be lucky in the deepest sense—to be in the zone—requires nonattachment. As Gaston puts it in *Midnight Hockey*, "you can't force your way into the zone—it has to simply happen" and "it has more to do with relaxing than it does with straining" (2006, 98–99).

A Gaston story that develops these ideas about luck in a particularly illuminating way is "Saving Eve's Father," from the collection *Sex Is Red*. This story tells of a boy named Alex who discovers that his girlfriend Eve's father—a man who has the good or bad fortune to have the same name as a famous hockey player, Mike Gartner—is addicted to a particular video gambling machine. Alex takes all his savings out of the bank in loonies, goes to the store with the machine in it, and proceeds to play for hours upon hours as Eve's father and other local addicts look on. His plan is to play until all his money is gone (minus one dollar he leaves in the bank to keep his account open). When asked by Eve why he is doing it, he replies that he isn't sure except that "as long as I'm playing, they're not," referring to her father and the others looking on (Gaston 1998, 9). The store owner understands that Alex is sacrificing himself. "The boy's dyin' for your sins is what he's doin," he tells the addicts (12).

The larger context of the story makes clear that the video gambling machine preys on the desire of the men to fix their lives by a stroke of luck.

Even Alex recognizes its seductiveness. When he wins a game, "the pealing angel-song of the electronic bells" and the "cartoon-blue" of the screen are "like some version of paradise" (11). Unlike men like Eve's father, however, Alex recognizes that the game is fixed, that not only do you always lose in the end, but along the way, the machine creates unlikely lucky streaks to "suck you in" so that you play on in hope until it has "all your money" (11). The machine, the story implies, is an analogue for life itself. Life contains good fortune and bad, but, in the end, our luck always runs out. The wise response to this condition, from a Buddhist point of view, is nonattachment. Real luck has to do with not clinging to luck. Alex discovers this for himself when his desire to fail at the gambling machine is spent. At this point, twelve loonies short of losing all his money, he has to stop, because "[h]e knew now what luck was, how it came of truly not caring if you had it or not. And, knowing this, he saw that if he kept playing he would start to win, and keep winning, and ruin it all" (13).

The analogue between the video gambling machine and life brings us back to the comparison between Buddhism and hockey. The ultimate point of affinity between the two is hinted at in a comparison Bonaduce makes between readers of novels and fans of hockey:

> When you read a book you are nothing but a fan. And fans of
> books have nothing—nothing—over fans of hockey. That a puck
> is an utterly meaningless thing to chase is exactly the point. They
> might never think of it this way, but hockey fans are drawn to the
> spectacle of men who are the best in the land at using their bodies
> to fulfil *pure desire*. (Gaston 2000, 136)

As a game, hockey is, in one sense, not "serious"—it is not part of the world of striving and doing and transforming of the material world that we associate with "real work." Hockey is, for this reason, "utterly meaningless." Then again, so is life. Hockey is fundamentally like Buddhism because they are both part of the reality of life itself. Human beings are creatures of desire, and our desires (to do things, to accomplish things, to get lucky—even to be a "good" student of Buddhism) can make us mean and make us suffer, but they can also lead us, in spite of our meanness and suffering (and sometimes because of them), towards enlightenment. "Pure desire" implies a desire that has worn itself out, that has become devoid of the impulse to desire any specific thing. Pure desire doesn't search for something. Another way to think of what happens to Bonaduce at the end of *The Good Body*, then, is that his luck runs out in the way Alex's coins run out in "Saving Eve's Father." His desire wears out; he stops searching, hoping, and craving. And at the moment when he no longer cares whether he is lucky or not, luck returns to him in the form of "the light streaming glory through the orange curtain" (269).

Nothing should be clung to because there is nothing to cling to.

WORKS CITED

Dhammika, Shravasti. 2005. *Good Question, Good Answer.* 4th ed. Singapore: Buddha Dhamma Mandala Society.

Dryden, Ken. 1989. *The Game.* Toronto: Harper and Collins. First published 1983.

Gaston, Bill. 1990. *Tall Lives.* Toronto: Macmillan.

———. 1996. *Bella Combe Journal.* Dunvegan, ON: Cormorant.

———. 1998. *Sex Is Red.* Dunvegan, ON: Cormorant.

———. 2000. *The Good Body.* Dunvegan, ON: Cormorant.

———. 2002. *The Cameraman.* Toronto: Anansi. First published 1994.

———. 2006. *Midnight Hockey: All About Beer, the Boys, and the Real Canadian Game.* Toronto: Doubleday.

Hagen, Steve. 1997. *Buddhism Plain and Simple.* New York: Broadway Books.

Herrigel, Eugen. 1953. *Zen in the Art of Archery.* New York: Vintage. First published 1948.

Tremblay, Tony. 1991. "Tall Tales from a Genteel Hoodlum: The Artful Exaggerations of Bill Gaston." *Studies in Canadian Literature* 16, no. 2: 197–215.

Trungpa, Chögyam. 1984. *Shambhala: The Sacred Path of the Warrior.* Edited by Carolyn Rose Gimian. Boulder, CO: Shambhala. First published in 1973.

———. 2002. *Cutting Through Spiritual Materialism.* Boston: Shambhala.

Wiseman, Richard. 2003. "The Luck Factor." *Skeptical Inquirer: The Magazine for Science and Reason* 27, no. 3.

Yun, Hsing. 2001. *Describing the Indescribable.* Boston: Wisdom Books.

7

Gyllian Phillips

The Darkening Path
The Hero-Athlete Reconsidered in Angie Abdou's *The Bone Cage*

Every sports novel begins with a hero.

Michael Oriard, *Dreaming of Heroes*

If you continue doing something you've done for such a long time, you can't really grow in other ways.

Hannah Kearney, skier and Olympic Gold Medalist

Spoiler alert: Angie Abdou's novel about two would-be Olympians does not end with a gold medal. In fact, this novel does not end at all, at least not in any way that we have come to expect from the movies or media coverage of sport. Even in sport literature, we are accustomed to some kind of "win," though it might not involve a podium or a trophy—Smith's refusal to cross the finish line in Alan Sillitoe's 1959 short story "Loneliness of the Long-Distance Runner," for example (another spoiler!).

Abdou's novel traces the parallel—and eventually, intersecting—lives of a swimmer, Sadie Jorgensen, and a wrestler, Digger Stapleton, both of whom train at the University of Calgary. Each wins in the Olympic trials and faces the thrilling but daunting task of taking it to the next level, "The Show."

107

However, Sadie's plans go drastically awry, and she is left to struggle with her identity as a non-athlete and to support Digger in his "quest for gold." The novel ends not with triumph or meaningful defeat but with a question mark: How does Digger perform? We'll never know, since the narrative ends with Sadie seeing Digger off at the airport and then prosaically going home to shave her legs. With its surprise (non)ending, *The Bone Cage* challenges us to expand our idea of the elite athlete as a lone hero by placing as much importance on the "play" of training and competition as on the end result, and as much importance on building community as on personal excellence.

Abdou's novel begins with Robert Browning's 1865 dramatic monologue "Childe Roland to the Dark Tower Came," and with that allusion, it draws on a significant interpretive paradigm, but with a twist. *The Bone Cage* adopts a version of the heroic monomyth—the athlete as hero on a quest for glory and self-knowledge. The heroic monomyth is an archetypal form for the sports novel and its hero, but Browning's poem presents a variation: it leaves the hero's fate undecided. Joseph Campbell, in *The Hero with a Thousand Faces* (1949), emphasizes that the monomyth has a particular structure: the departure from home, with the hero "crossing the threshold" into adventure; the initiation, during which the hero overcomes obstacles and triumphs, thus achieving "apotheosis"; and the return to community with new knowledge, or what Campbell refers to as "the boon." By referring to a poem that omits the return, Abdou sets up the seemingly incomplete ending of her story and, in turn, emphasizes how the athlete-hero is conceptualized popularly as an individualist. As Michael Oriard argues, this ideal of the athlete-hero represents an immature version of the mythic hero, one that ignores the crucial return to community (1982, 40). Browning's poem, moreover, focuses attention on the psychological middle ground of the journey, in which the hero goes deep into self-examination to find new resources for coping with impossible challenges. Abdou's athlete-heroes are represented on the cusp of potential transformation, one that leads them out of the isolated and ultimately self-destructive models of athletic success. Though they have not returned to their communities by the end of the novel, both protagonists represent models of the hero that are more potentially open to community. Leaving the narrative open-ended suggests that this "new" model of athlete might be less inclined to be lured into the entrapment of objectification (in the "bone cage") and more willing to experience sport in the spirit of play and to bring that spirit back "home."

Although mythic in structure, *The Bone Cage* does not read in any way like a fantasy novel; it is grounded in the reality of athletes' lives and in the commodification of those lives by the culture industry. Hannah Kearney, quoted in this chapter's epigraph, is an American Olympic medalist who has spoken out about the psychological challenges faced by athletes who are eventually forced to define themselves outside the all-consuming world of sport. Much like Sadie in *The Bone Cage*, Kearney acknowledges the joy that training and competing has brought her but also points out that she is ten years behind her peers in terms of life, career, and family, and that she has only ever really trained for one thing—skiing (Crouse 2015). For Canadians, the list of national heroes also waxes and wanes with each Olympics, leaving many athletes to pick up the pieces of their lives. One example of an athlete represented as truly heroic in her Olympic win is Silken Laumann, who came back from a catastrophic training injury to win a bronze medal in Olympic rowing in 1992. She was justly praised for her superhuman struggle to medal, but celebrity came with a cost. Having been dogged by scandal during her career, with, for instance, a questionable doping accusation, she published a memoir, *Unsinkable* (2014), that laid bare some of the realities faced by real-life heroes in the single-minded pursuit of excellence. Karen Hartman has noted the contradictions inherent in a media culture that simultaneously builds an athlete up as "the traditional hero who is understood to display high morals, consummate sporting behaviour, courage, loyalty and bravery" and relishes the celebrity scandals of cheating in sport or criminal behaviour off the field: "These conflicting stories and perceptions of sport and athletes create an interesting dichotomy that cannot be easily assessed or sorted" (2014, 172–73). In fact, the real-life athlete has little time to develop into a well-rounded hero since "athletes may have to be selfish and self-absorbed in order to succeed at sport" (172). While readers and media consumers yearn for athlete figures to be all-around outstanding people, these athletes actually live lives circumscribed by their isolated pursuit of the personal best.

The construction of athlete as hero is a constant motif in *The Bone Cage*; it is an ideology unconsciously reinforced by parents, coaches, and media and ultimately absorbed by the athletes themselves. The fantasy of personal triumph cancels out almost any sacrifice made along the way: "As Digger falls off to sleep, he sees himself in Sydney on the middle podium (a Cuban to his right and an American to his left), the Canadian flag rising high above the rest and everyone clapping" (67). By combining the modern-day story of Sadie and Digger with the (possibly) failed and primarily psychological quest of Childe Roland, Abdou's novel implicitly challenges the popular cliché of athlete as hero.

IN THE BELLY OF THE WHALE: TRANSFORMATION FROM "CHILDE" TO HERO

The first allusion to "Childe Roland" comes in the epigraph to the novel:

> I had so long suffered in this quest,
> Heard failure prophesied so oft [. . .]
> And all the doubt was now—should I be fit?

This quotation sets up the analogy between Roland's quest to find the Dark Tower and the athlete's quest for Olympic glory, implying that the athlete, comparable to Roland, "suffers" in training and competition. Here, "to suffer" means not only to feel inflicted pain (as in "no pain, no gain") but also to endure, to go through, without necessarily having a positive outcome. "Suffer" can mean pure experience for both Roland and the athlete. As well, athletes are on a quest, meaning that they will have to overcome obstacles to achieve a goal and that the achievement will mark a rite of passage to maturity: since the word "childe" originally meant untested knight, perhaps Roland achieves knighthood. Athletes, like the knight, persevere in spite of the odds against them. And finally, once athletes are completely committed to their journey, with no turning back, all that is left to motivate them is the thought that they, like Roland, might miss something—might lack that little edge of fitness to be just that much better than the competition or than those who have failed before. As Sadie and Digger embark on their journeys from the trials to the Olympics, they ask themselves if they are fit—not just physically, but mentally—for this final test of athleticism that will (they hope) help them pass from trainee to mature hero.

Simply by alluding to Browning, the novel immediately generates a critical context for the athlete's quest since the poem is notoriously open-ended. In *A Map of Misreading* (1975), Harold Bloom identifies Childe Roland as having failed in his quest for maturity and self-understanding. Other scholars have read the quest as successful, if it is seen as a trope of writing, since Roland's final triumphant act is to "sound" the title of the poem itself (e.g., Strickland 1981, 301). Or they have read Roland's quest as mythic, suggesting that his "failure" to return home indicates that the poem focuses on Roland's middle stage, after the hero enters what Joseph Campbell calls "the belly of the whale" (e.g., Williams 1983, 28-29). This reading is most compelling for my understanding of the poem's function as an intertext in *The Bone Cage*. In Campbell's reading of the archetypal function of mythology, the hero, in order to attain new knowledge, leaves behind the old certainties—hence the departure from home and the journey. To achieve full maturity, self-knowledge, and self-mastery, the hero must pass a threshold into nothingness, into the annihilation of ego, in order to be reborn: "The idea that the passage of the magical threshold is a transit into a sphere of rebirth is symbolized in the worldwide womb image of the belly of the whale. The hero, instead of conquering or conciliating the power of the threshold, is swallowed into the unknown, and would appear to have died" (Campbell 1949, 90). In Browning's poem, we never see the speaker's departure from home; we only see the point at which he crosses the threshold. When Roland takes the road to the Dark Tower, he has a moment of panic when he looks back, "pausing to throw backward a last view / O'er the safe road, 'twas gone, grey plain all round" (Browning 2003, lines 51–52). There is no way to return on the "safe road"; he can only move forward.

On his journey, Roland discovers a geography that is more mindscape than landscape: rather than encountering enemies who must be vanquished, he must confront his own doubts, fears, and failures at every turn. Once he reaches the Dark Tower, he can do nothing but contemplate those who have failed before him:

> Names in my ears
> Of all the lost adventurers my peers,—
> How such a one was strong, and such was bold,
> And such was fortunate, yet each of old
> Lost, lost! (lines 194–98)

In the end, all Roland can do is blow his trumpet, from which issues the last line of the poem—which is also its title. The poem focuses on the middle ground of the knight's attempt to lose his status as "childe" in order to contemplate the process by which a man might achieve maturity—by confronting and overcoming the psychological barriers of ego. The fact that the poem ends where it began signals, perhaps, that becoming a "hero" is more properly process than product.

Both Sadie and Digger, in their different ways, recognize that their focus on elite athletics inadvertently generates a state of prolonged adolescence, where they are in between child and adult. Sadie still lives at home, trying to minimize her intrusion into her parents' lives and feeling that it is "enough that they put up with a grown daughter in their house at all" (Abdou 2007, 5). Digger still depends on occasional handouts from his parents to get by. After Sadie, like the knight overcoming his trials, wins her Olympic trials, she realizes that this victory is also a trap; she imagines "herself a late-twentieth-century incarnation of Childe Roland, the black line at the bottom of the pool her own darkening path" (9). Seeing no way back, she turns inwards, not conquering or absorbing the "threshold" but dissolving her own ego in order to find a new self. This dissolve happens literally and figuratively in a number of ways. Not long after the win at the trials, Sadie's grandmother dies. Since she is closer emotionally to her grandmother—interestingly, also the one who cares least about her swimming career—than anyone else in the narrative, this death has the effect of severing Sadie further from herself as a person in the world, from her ego. The loss drives her into a cocoon of sleep where she sinks into a womb-like state of mourning:

> During the three days before the funeral, she conducts her life
> largely from the confines of her bed. Its warm darkness envelops
> her, holds her. From her cave of blankets she hears what goes on
> beyond her little realm—muffled condolences, flower deliveries,
> meetings with the pastor—but she has no desire to participate in
> any of it. [. . .] [C]losing her eyes and pulling the covers far over
> her head lets her ride out those waves of anxiety, ride them straight
> back to deep sleep. (85)

Although this retreat into sleep is a natural response to overtraining and powerful emotional loss, it also carries obvious womb-like connotations: the dark, warm cave; the muffled sounds of life; and of course, for Sadie-the-swimmer, water imagery, riding the waves. When she emerges, Sadie does not achieve a miraculous rebirth, but her former single-minded focus on swimming has certainly broken down, and she begins to question her identity as solely an athlete.

However, this crisis of transformation is simply a precursor to the major event that sends Sadie into "the belly of the whale"—the car crash on the way to Fernie. In this moment, and during the trials that follow, Sadie is literally shattered and has to rebuild herself anew: "[T]he pain has only whispered to her from a distance. *You're hurt. You're wrecked. You're broken*" (164). In a more conventional novel—definitely in a sports film or even in the popular media representations of "real life," as with Silken Laumann—the catastrophically injured athlete would triumph by rebuilding her former self, go back over Campbell's threshold, and return "home." However, Abdou does not allow us that tantalizing comfort. Instead, Sadie has to put aside her massive ego-investment in being an Olympic athlete and cast about to find a new way of being. Even more than winning the Olympic trials or losing her beloved grandmother, Sadie's accident signals the painful transformation of growing up and coming into maturity as a fully developed hero. Like Childe Roland, once she goes down that road, there is no way back. By the end of the novel, Sadie completes her final act of rebirth when, after dropping Digger off at the airport for his flight to Sydney, she goes home to have a bath and shave her legs. Whereas before the accident, she had planned to shave her body in preparation for her Olympic swim, this moment of personal grooming, mundane for most women, takes on the symbolic resonance that Sadie is ready to enter life again as a transformed adult. In *Anatomy of Criticism*, Northrop Frye points out that many heroes, such as Moses or Perseus, are generated by or conducted through a watery environment. While Campbell focuses on the womb-like rebirth from the belly of the whale, both critics highlight that the hero is born or reborn in water or a water-like space, signalling transformation and transfiguration, as the origin of the word "protean" suggests (Frye 1957, 98). Sadie, as a swimmer, is perhaps naturally prone to a protean transformation. While she does not leave swimming behind, she realizes that she has more to offer the world than simply being a vehicle to a gold medal.

DEFINING THE ATHLETE-HERO: SELFISH OR MYTHIC?

In popular culture and in representations in the media, the athlete-hero is often represented as courageous, honourable, and fighting for a larger cause, such as national glory or the spirit of teamwork. However, the labour and measure of the athlete's triumph are always located in the individual performing body. In *Dreaming of Heroes*, Michael Oriard traces the development of the American sports novel from its inception in the early twentieth century with the juvenile sports story. Using the paradigm of Campbell's monomyth to understand the cultural relevance of the sport-hero figure, Oriard notes that these early athlete protagonists often suffer from a kind of arrested development:

> The prototypical athlete-hero celebrates unlimited human achievement and potential, but at the point at which his virtues should transform him from a pedestrian "star" to a mythic, god-like hero, he fails. His accomplishments are self-directed and not other-directed as are those of the heroes of myth. Thus he represents the potential of the athlete hero to be a genuine hero and his too-frequent failure to be one. (1982, 40)

As Oriard notes, Campbell's critical model of the monomyth understands the transformation of the hero through "the belly of the whale" and the trials that follow as one of complete loss of the "old" child-like ego and of movement into full maturity. Mythic heroes are destined to return to their community with "the boon" that they have achieved—metaphorically, a wisdom that looks to others rather than to themselves. However, the narratives of the early sports novel usually end with the personal triumph of the athlete ("apotheosis") and not with the mythic model—the loss of ego, the transformation into a mature and powerful self, and the return home to benefit the community. Oriard notes that it is tempting to dismiss these stories as naïve, childish fictions that appeared early in the development of the genre, and indeed, he goes on to make the case that contemporary American sports fiction dramatically complicates the figure of the athlete. However, this vision of the athlete-hero has stayed with us through popular culture and embodies "the major hero for American adults as well" (40).

Though Oriard's book was published in the 1980s, this vision of the hero is still the predominant one in sports media, as Karen Hartman points out when she notes that, fan desires aside, "the athlete is not a free agent like the old fashioned hero—he or she is a created product (in huge numbers) by an industrialized process" (2014, 181). The currency of this idea is a problem represented in *The Bone Cage* with Digger's trials-by-TV. With the media coverage of Digger as an Olympic hopeful, the novel overtly underlines the connection between the heroic ideal in the popular imagination and the work of the athlete. Just before Ben's breakdown over his own loss of status, the three friends—Digger, Fly, and Ben—gather to watch the "Digumentary," a CBC profile on Digger called "Quest for Gold." Unlike Digger's other media experiences, this profile is positive and even tries to be realistic when Digger downplays the glamour of being an Olympian. In the end, however, it seems false, and Digger "feels exposed, as if they [his friends] have just caught him masturbating" (Abdou 2007, 98). The analogy of being discovered masturbating highlights the self-centred qualities of this kind of immature (as Oriard would describe it) hero-building. Heroes who are only focused on their own narrow accomplishments are implicitly engaged in narcissistic self-pleasure, which is better suited to adolescent fantasy.

Digger's other media encounters reinforce not so much the self-absorption of the competitive athlete as the way in which sport is overdetermined by popular culture. As a "knight" of sport, Digger's first trial is the Olympic trials, which are held not in a wrestling venue but in a television studio: "CBC said they'd only televise if the wrestlers came to them. Now they're supposed to bus to downtown Toronto tomorrow to wrestle in a cramped studio, just so CBC can pre-tape the matches and plug them in to some dead TV spot on a Sunday afternoon three or four weeks from now" (22). This relocation of the competition has an obvious practical effect on each athlete's performance: there are fewer amenities for the wrestlers, and their focus is bound to be compromised by the change in routine. The language of this passage also emphasizes the metaphoric element of this media-driven competition: the studio is "cramped"; the taped matches will be "plugged" into some "dead spot"; their rooms are "close and dank" (23). The language conveys a feeling of entrapment because the wrestlers are confined by the media construction of their sport. Their performance and identity is determined not just by their own rules of training and competition but also by the requirements of the "industrial process" of culture (Hartman 2014, 181). The absurd bookend to the novel's opening is Digger's final visit to the TV studio before he leaves for Sydney, during which he is eclipsed by other athletes whose sports are more easily translated into spectacle; his battle-scarred body is "edited" for the camera, and the host of the show misnames him. In other words, his identity is managed, or mismanaged, to suit the narrow requirements of the medium.

Digger is, to some extent, caught in a Childe Roland–like fixation on the "quest for gold" as the marker or proof that he is ready to drop the "childe" status and become a fully fledged mature hero. He is caught, however, because the terms of this proof are defined purely through personal achievement. Sadie, in contrast, seems to be undergoing a transformation from personal achievement to genuine mythic hero. The difference between them lies in the relationship between personal identity and achievement, on the one hand, and responsibility for community, on the other. In addition to being herself a hero-in-training, Sadie also functions as something of a guide to Digger, since she seems a little further down the road to self-understanding. Her directions for Digger take the form of both warning and encouragement. As a guide who is also a former English major, Sadie expresses her wisdom in the form of literary allusions to not only "Childe Roland" but many other texts. For example, when they are on the road to Fernie, just before her accident, Sadie, in true English major mode, takes Digger through an interpretive exercise with a reference to Ray Bradbury. She compares the athlete to the astronaut in the story, who triumphantly lands on the moon with no means of return: "Countries take their athletes to these great heights in the name of glory," she says, "but when they're done with them—" (159). The hero in Sadie's metaphoric reading is stranded, reflecting Oriard's reading of early American sport fiction and contemporary pop culture. If the identity of an elite athlete is entirely invested in personal achievement, he or she is incapable of a measure of maturity.

Digger recognizes the warning in this story and also feels the tension, on a practical level, between the requirements of his sport and the pull of relationships. After the accident in which Sadie and he are involved and from which he emerges unscathed (not ready for growth perhaps?), he has an unconscious confrontation with his own need for transformation: "Digger doesn't know why being badly hurt and recovering in a hospital makes Sadie so inexplicably terrifying, but his head feels detached from his neck and his hands far away from his body, everything disjointed and out of control" (169). While Sadie is literally broken apart and has to rebuild or rebirth herself, Digger expresses his terror of a similar fate with this strange fantasy of dismemberment, a fantasy that is not just about his fear of losing bodily integrity—when having a perfect body is so necessary for his identity as an athlete—but also expresses an anxiety about the pull of Sadie's need for him. His responsibility to his friend—and potential lover—is directly at odds with his need to be entirely selfish if he is to win gold. In other words, he is not ready to take on the true mythic hero role in returning to community. This unfortunate reality of the single-mindedness required of athletes is reinforced when Saul, Digger's coach, tells him that he is "spending too much time with the crippled girl" (209). This is, of course, part of the deliberately tough talk that coaches sometimes engage in to motivate athletes with anger, but it also reveals, perhaps, that the bodily integrity seemingly required for perfection in physical achievement is aligned with the solipsism required for psychological strength in competition. To be a great athlete, it seems, one has to cut oneself off from other people and go it alone.

So what are the alternatives? If being a hero-athlete is not a fully mature expression of heroism, does Sadie reveal another path? Does the novel? The beginnings of an answer to these questions can be found in the novel's last references to "Childe Roland." After Digger cuts himself off from contact with Sadie to focus on his training, she sends him a greeting card to wish him well in the Olympics. The card Sadie picks for Digger says, "Life is a journey. [. . .] Enjoy the road, wherever it ends" (227). In a sense, this message is an indirect allusion to Browning's poem in that it redirects Digger's focus to the process of training and overcoming rather than the product. In "Childe Roland to the Dark Tower Came," the knight-to-be struggles with his own internal demons throughout the entire poem, only realizing near the end of the poem that he is already "there":

> For, looking up, aware I somehow grew,
> 'Spite of the dusk, the plain had given place
> All round to mountains—[. . .]
> How thus they had surprised me,—solve it, you! (l. 163–67)

In other words, rather than attaining some marker or achievement of heroism, Roland finds his destination, his achievement, to be the very process of overcoming. In spite of fear, he is fit, but he is fit because he forges on, not because he wins some thing in particular. Sadie's message to Digger sounds a little like the one his friend Ben receives from his (non-athlete) doctor: "'[The doctor] says I need to focus on the process rather than the end,' Ben tells Digger, 'says that I need to recognize the value of my experience in sports was in the process'" (143). This is part of Sadie's message too, but she and Ben's friends are justly suspicious of the ease with which Ben converts to some version of mindfulness practice. There is achievement in the process of high-level training, but high-level training cannot take place without an "intense burning desire" for an outstanding performance (84); otherwise, this experience of the "journey" would be recreational fitness, keeping in shape.

The message from Sadie is more complex than just a greeting card or a mindfulness maxim, and it is more completely expressed by her last direct allusion to Browning. The significance of this gift, for Sadie, is signalled by her embarrassment. A platitudinous greeting card is one thing, but an actual poem, especially one as cryptic as "Childe Roland," is a much more intimate gesture:

> She feels heat sliding up her neck. Poetry? Not your usual
> pre-Olympic gift for a wrestler. Her first instinct had been to
> highlight the lines near the end of the Browning poem: *How such*
> *a one was strong, and such was bold / And such was fortunate, yet*
> *each of old / Lost, lost!* Fortunately she'd fought off that instinct.
> Too dark. [. . .] Instead, she'd highlighted the very final lines where
> Childe Roland knowing what he knows, eyes wide open, forges on,
> raises his trumpet to his lips and blows. (231–32)

Sadie's initial but rejected choice is part of her message too, but it's a message for us, not for Digger. He will have to make the discovery himself that he, the "he" he is now, is "lost" no matter the outcome of the games. His ultimate task is to leave the self-focused identity of the athlete-hero, just as it is everyone's task to leave youth or even life. As the poem suggests, facing self-doubt is the hardest obstacle to overcome. The result of overcoming that obstacle is a renunciation of illusions and an acceptance of self-knowledge. The message from Sadie to Digger, however, suggests a triumphant ending to the poem and to Digger's quest, regardless of the outcome of the games. The triumph is simply to be there and to be ready to risk everything, to risk "losing" the gold medal but also losing his old, familiar self.

PROCESS AND PLAY: ANOTHER WAY OF THINKING ABOUT SPORTS

The Bone Cage retrains our focus, as readers of narrative, on the process of the story rather than its goal, and in so doing, questions the conventional assumptions about the value of sport, training, and competition. The conventional values of winning as the end goal and of the narrowly focused athlete-hero, rather than the expanded mythic hero, are supplemented if not replaced by other values: achievement in the very processes of overcoming; the athlete as a properly mythic hero, as community-centred rather than self-centred; society's appreciation of the mythic qualities of athletes and the whole person, not just the athlete or goal as object; and finally, the embracing, as a sport-loving culture (in which a majority of people are overweight and out of shape), of the spirit of play as much as competition. *The Bone Cage* clearly works against the overdetermination of the athlete in isolated glory. The simple fact that the novel has two protagonists instead of one tells us that an athlete not only *cannot* do anything alone but also *should* not. Sadie, pushed by the accident, more quickly appreciates her full capacity as mythic hero than does Digger, but both will need to let go of their ego investment in the athlete identity and bring what they have learned from the experience of being an elite athlete, from those trials, into the world of other people. Sadie's first "boon," it seems, is to be Digger's support and guide as he follows her through the process of maturation. But the potential for Digger to bring his boon to a community is clear from early in the novel. In fact, Digger's success in wrestling can partly be attributed to the strong friendships he has with his teammates; these friendships are tellingly stronger than those of Sadie with her peers on the swim team. Those friendship bonds support Digger—for instance, when Fly prompts him to call Sadie: "'I'll say it again,' Fly sighs dramatically. 'I don't know how you'll manage without me'" (229). However, they also make him into a supporter, as when he and Fly look after Ben during his breakdown. All of this shows the potential to bring good into whatever community Digger and Sadie develop as they move out of becoming into full adulthood.

While Abdou's novel builds a more positive and fully developed notion of the athlete as mythic hero than more conventional sport discourses do, it also leaves us with the possibility of sport as having value beyond the outcome of a game. Oriard notes that many contemporary sport novels examine the darker elements of sport in society, and *The Bone Cage* certainly adds to that genre. However, as Oriard also points out, these novels ultimately celebrate sport: "Although the reality of sport culture can be brutal or dehumanizing, in their essence the games celebrate life, the vitality of the spirit, and human potential; the best novels understand both sides well" (Oriard 1982, 21). Often, when I teach Abdou's novel, students are drawn into the critique of a society that essentially treats athletes as disposable; however, I end this chapter by pointing to the novel's expanded understanding of what it means to participate in sport. This too is a celebratory novel. One of the elements of it that I personally love is that it eloquently describes the feeling of pure physical power and accomplishment in doing a sport: "Sadie belongs in the water. Only here, her body performs as trained. Heat tickles her neck, mingles with the cold fluid enveloping her. She's near the end, should be exhausted, but today she feels she could swim forever, motoring full speed at the water's surface. Hot, cold, pleasure, pain" (4). This is the moment just before Sadie's triumphant win at the trials, and while that win feels wonderful for her, I would argue that this moment *during* the race is perhaps the greater victory. The pleasure-pain of accomplishment, of pure physical power, is precisely the "process" that should be the focus of the experience of sport. As with Childe Roland, the athlete's pure engagement with the trials, overcoming and transforming the barriers of the self, is as much the goal as the medal is.

The feeling of swimming as joyous effort is more properly defined as play than sport, and it is the spirit of play that Abdou's novel gestures towards as a solution to the problem of extreme goal-orientation in sport. In writing about sport fiction written by and about women, Michael Oriard identifies this shift in focus from competition to play as a specifically feminist narrative strategy. He shows how Dorey, the main character of *Water Dancer* (1982), by Jennifer Levin, moves through a kind of existential crisis as a competitive long-distance swimmer, shifting from being obsessively goal-oriented to coming back to a love of swimming for its own sake: "In surrendering herself to the water, in dancing in her element, Dorey discovers a different kind of strength, an intense feeling of being alive. Not competition or mastery but surrender becomes a new kind of freedom. . . . To be a water dancer is neither to dominate nor to be dominated but to live in one's body in the world" (Oriard 1987, 18). Although he does not quite put it in these terms, we might describe Oriard's characterization of this feminist reappraisal of excellence in sport as "play." For Christian Messenger, the idea of play is in powerful tension with the structures that contain and delimit the identity and activity of the athlete; consequently, the critique of culture in sport fiction is partly a yearning for the return to play. He argues that "we need a structural model in which play and sport may co-exist in a full field of relations where play may be seen as the basis for sport but also as its implied opposite and critic in many ways" (Messenger 1990, 11). *The Bone Cage* explores something like this structural model as it shows the creation of the athlete in isolation but within the structures of the narrowly defined cultural hero. Abdou shows the single-mindedness and internal struggle of the mythic hero-in-training in tension with the need to serve a community. And she shows that athletic excellence grows out of the pleasure in pure physical mastery, which then is often distorted and cramped by the external requirements of competition and results.

CONCLUSION

I hope I have made a convincing case that Browning's poem about that ambiguous quest helps to lend structural meaning to some of the unconventional narrative elements and some of the central problems raised in the novel. While "Childe Roland" is a central intertext in *The Bone Cage*, it is not the only literary reference by any means (and, in fact, a discussion of all the literary allusions could generate a productive understanding of the novel). Sadie's last allusion in the novel is to another questionable hero, F. Scott Fitzgerald's Tom Buchanan from *The Great Gatsby*, "a man at the pinnacle of such an acute limited excellence that everything afterward will savour of anti-climax. Win or lose. And she has promised to bring him [Digger] back from that?" (233). This reference to Gatsby's lonely— and ultimately empty—hero reinforces the importance of community for high-achieving individuals: the hero can be tragic and glorious but should not have to journey alone. It might also be noted that this reference, along with discussions of the athlete-hero in Oriard, Messenger, and Hartman, all refer to American fiction and culture. I would argue that Abdou gives her critique a specifically Canadian character by ending with an emphasis on community and a challenge to the supremacy of ego. But that may be a topic for another paper.

WORKS CITED

Abdou, Angie. 2007. *The Bone Cage*. Edmonton: NeWest Press.
Bloom, Harold. 1975. *A Map of Misreading*. Oxford: Oxford University Press.

Browning, Robert. 2003. "Childe Roland to the Dark Tower Came." In *The Victorian* Age. Vol. 2B of *The Longman Anthology of British Literature*, edited by Heather Henderson and William Sharpe, 1323–28. New York: Longman.

Campbell, Joseph. 1949. *The Hero with a Thousand Faces*. Princeton, NJ: Princeton University Press.

Crouse, Karen. 2015. "After Moguls Come Life's Bumps." *New York Times*, 13 January.

Frye, Northrop. 1957. *Anatomy of Criticism: Four Essays*. Princeton, NJ: Princeton University Press.

Hartman, Karen. 2014. "Fields of Dreams and Gods of the Gridiron: The Trinity of Myth, Sport and the Hero." In *Myth in the Modern World,* edited by David Whitt and John Perlich, 165–84. Jefferson, NC: McFarland.

Laumann, Silken. 2014. *Unsinkable*. New York: HarperCollins.

Messenger, Christian. 1990. *Sport and the Spirit of Play in Contemporary American Fiction*. New York: Columbia University Press. First published 1981.

Oriard, Michael. 1982. *Dreaming of Heroes: American Sports Fiction, 1868–1980*. Chicago: Nelson-Hall.

———. 1987. "From Jane Allen to *Water Dancer*: A Brief History of the Feminist (?) Sports Novel." *Modern Fiction Studies* 33, no. 1: 9–20.

Sillitoe, Allan. 1959. "The Loneliness of the Long-Distance Runner." In *The Loneliness of the Long-Distance Runner*, 7–54. London: W. H. Allen.

Strickland, Edward. 1981. "The Conclusion of Browning's 'Childe Roland to the Dark Tower Came.'" *Victorian Poetry* 19, no. 3: 299–301.

Williams, Anne. 1983. "Browning's 'Childe Roland,' Apprentice for Night." *Victorian Studies* 21, no.: 27–42.

8

Paul Martin

"Open the door to the roaring darkness"

The Enigma of Terry Sawchuk in
Randall Maggs's *Night Work:
The Sawchuk Poems*

The second poetry collection ever to be launched at the Hockey Hall of Fame, fourteen years after Richard Harrison's *Hero of the Play* (1994), was Randall Maggs's *Night Work: The Sawchuk Poems* (2008). *Night Work* delves into the life and career of Terry Sawchuk, perhaps the greatest hockey goaltender of all time. The collection explores the psychology of a single player and offers a very different example from that of Harrison of how sport, and particularly hockey, can be viewed through the lens of poetry. The poems are longer, grittier, and, on some levels, more difficult to access than those in *Hero of the Play*. While Harrison's concise and focused single-page poems stand alone, each one a new game on a fresh sheet of ice inspired by a specific player, idea, or event, Maggs's lengthier poems work off of one another to create a richly intertextual, three-dimensional, and occasionally contradictory portrait of a player whose impact on the game was matched by his enigmatic nature.

Since its publication in 2008, *Night Work* has earned considerable critical and popular success. The collection was awarded the 2008 Winterset Award, an annual recognition of the best book published by a writer from Newfoundland and Labrador; the E. J. Pratt Prize for Poetry (2007/2008) at the Newfoundland and Labrador Book Awards; and the Kobzar Literary Award, presented biennially for the best Canadian literary work in any genre that addresses a Ukrainian Canadian theme. The book was also named one of the top one hundred books of the year by the *Globe and Mail*. As with Harrison's *Hero of the Play*, the obvious excellence of Maggs's literary treatment of such a popular topic brought about a degree of attention rarely afforded to a new collection from a Canadian poet. Maggs was interviewed about Sawchuk and *Night Work* on the CBC national radio shows *Q* and *The Next Chapter*, but his work also saw media coverage in more unusual venues. It was featured in an extensive interview of Maggs by sports journalist Bruce McCurdy on the hockey blog *Copper and Blue*. Then, as Martin Brodeur broke Sawchuk's seemingly untouchable record for career shutouts, *Night Work* was discussed in the *New York Times* by US hockey writer Stu Hackel, who referred to it as "a remarkable set of poems . . . that deserves a place on every serious fan's bookshelf." The praise by Canadian writers was even more effusive. The back cover of *Night Work* includes Dave Bidini describing the collection as being "poised to become a Canadian classic," while Stephen Brunt, one of Canada's pre-eminent sports journalists and the author of several important books about hockey including *Searching for Bobby Orr* (2006), writes that *Night Work* "may be the truest hockey book ever written." The impact of *Night Work* would also reach beyond the literary world, inspiring both a short film based on the poem "Night Moves" (Simms 2009) and a powerful song, "Sawchuk," by the late, great Newfoundland singer-songwriter Ron Hynes. The song's lyrics, co-written by Maggs, draw from the general depiction of Sawchuk's life in *Night Work* as well as from the words and themes of the poems themselves.

Picking up *Night Work: The Sawchuk Poems* for the first time, one is immediately struck by the book's length. At 189 pages and with 74 poems, 12 photographs, extensive acknowledgements, and a bibliography, the volume gives the impression that it is as much a biography as a collection of poems. The poems themselves are bookended by two unforgettable documents that capture the pain and injuries Terry Sawchuk suffered for the game over the course of his remarkable career. The book's epigraph is an excerpt from the autopsy report that describes in excruciating detail the many scars found across Sawchuk's face at the time of his death. These thirty-one lines of text that inventory the "multiple fine scars present over the forehead and face" (Maggs 2008, 9) give the reader a glimpse into the beating Sawchuk took in the net over a career that began when no goalies wore masks and when no goalie ever wanted to leave the ice for fear of losing his highly coveted spot on the roster of one of only six NHL teams. Over his twenty-one seasons in the NHL (1949–70), in an era when few goalies had a career lasting more than a decade, Sawchuk recorded 447 wins and 103 shutouts, NHL records that stood for decades. The price his body had paid by the time of his early death at the age of forty included broken bones (including a poorly healed broken arm that wound up two inches shorter than the other), six hundred stitches, torn tendons, a devastating eye injury, ruptured discs in his spine, a swayed back from his famous crouch stance, and a nervous breakdown.

While many of these injuries are discussed or alluded to in the poems in *Night Work*, Maggs's choice to open the book in this way reminds us that the poems to follow constitute just one attempt to articulate the complexity of Sawchuk as an individual and as a player. The excerpt from Dr. Gross's autopsy report, a clinical and objective assessment written in the hours just after Sawchuk's death, tells us a great deal and, at the same time, almost nothing about Sawchuk's life. While a doctor can catalogue all the marks on a player's face, the stories and suffering behind the scars—the prominent "oblique scar, 1½" in length" or the "suture cross scars" that lie across it—remain buried under this purely objective writing (9). *Night Work* ends with the famous *Life* magazine photograph of Sawchuk for which a makeup artist enhanced many of the goalie's scars, making them all look recent. While the photograph aimed to depict all the facial injuries Sawchuk suffered over his career, its inclusion at the very end of *Night Work* reminds the reader that, like the autopsy report and each of the poems in the collection, any efforts to capture Sawchuk's inner nature and experience are just that: attempts, through art and words, that are doomed to fall short. *Night Work*, then, aims to paint a portrait of Sawchuk that is true to both the spirit of the subject and the vision of the artist, rather than to document every aspect of the goaltender's life and provide an objective biography. Maggs's collection is not an autopsy report, nor does it focus on telling the story of Sawchuk's death; it is, rather, a set of stories that no photograph or medical narrative can tell. *Night Work* is Maggs's foray at breathing life into the enigma of Terry Sawchuk and his experiences on and off the ice.

Dividing the book into eight sections, Maggs generally groups together poems that deal with specific periods in Sawchuk's life and career, although later sections include poems that do not directly address either of these topics. The biographical poems stretch from Sawchuk's childhood in Winnipeg to his dying hours in the hospital, which are captured in the final section, "Last Minute of Play." Photographs of Sawchuk from throughout his life are interspersed in the text, and epigraphs from other poets precede each section, ranging from Homer's *Odyssey* to twentieth-century poets such as Elizabeth Bishop and Denise Levertov. Only one epigraph deals with sports directly: the fourth section, "Goaltender Suite," opens with a quotation from Thomas Boswell's baseball book "Why Time Begins on Opening Day." The wide and distinctly literary scope of these epigraphs reminds the reader that *Night Work* is as much a book about poetry and its possibilities as it is about hockey. The tension between these two seemingly incompatible worlds is one of the most striking characteristics of Maggs's book.

The first section of the book, titled "The Question That He Frames," introduces us to Sawchuk through the words and imagined perspective of Red Storey, one of the subjects whom Maggs interviewed during his research for the book. Storey—himself an athlete who played hockey, lacrosse, and professional CFL football, winning a Grey Cup with the Toronto Argonauts—is a member of the Hockey Hall of Fame for his career as a highly respected NHL referee. Though Storey was a referee for only a decade (1950–59)—he resigned abruptly after NHL President Clarence Campbell was quoted as questioning Storey's performance in a controversial and riotous game six of the Stanley Cup semifinal that saw Montréal advance to the finals—he was on the ice throughout Sawchuk's prime, including his three Stanley Cup wins with Detroit (1952, 1954, 1955). The poems "Neither Rhyme nor Reason" (19–20) and "The First Wife" (21) compose the entirety of the book's first section. "Neither Rhyme nor Reason" recounts the poet's visit with the elderly Storey "that long afternoon in his home / with his souvenirs and his second wife" (19). In this poem, which sets up a key incident described in the later poems "Big Dogs (1)" and "Big Dogs (2)," Storey mentions "that crazy question" that Sawchuk asked him at the start of a game:

> *Where to begin with the guy?* Even after 50 years,
> it nags him like a wrinkle on his ankle. *What he came to me*
> *wanting to know, Jesus, I thought he was joking.* (19)

This incident—which is mentioned again in "The First Wife"—begins to give a sense of the complex and enigmatic character of Terry Sawchuk, a character that fascinates, according to Storey, because it seems connected somehow to Sawchuk's legendary abilities as a goaltender:

> And why would you fret about Sawchuk
> anyway? Jumping Jesus, what the guy could do.
> He'd felt the agony in the Forum tonight [. . .]
> as Terry turned them back wave after wave in the terrible storm
> of the crowd—48 shots against 12, the Rocket in twice,
> but the Wings take the game 3 to 1. (21)

The longer, linked poems "Big Dogs (1)" (58–63) and "Big Dogs (2)" (109–12) go on to recount in full the incident that troubled Storey for so long. "Big Dogs (1)" returns to the setting of the poet's interview with the aged referee. The eighty-three-year-old Storey spends a great deal of time in silence during the conversation as he works to remember the events of fifty years earlier—another way of stressing how hard it is to understand the past. Finally, in "Big Dogs (2)," Storey reveals the conversation first mentioned in "Neither Rhyme nor Reason." He tells the poet how, one night in Detroit, after clearing the crease of the players who had piled on top of the home team goaltender, Storey asked Sawchuk if he was all right. Sawchuk's angry response, "go fuck yourself / you drunken *deaf* son of a bitch" (111), earned him a misconduct penalty. A couple of days later as the game is about to get underway in Montréal, "Terry skates out from his net to ask me a question I'll / never forget" (110). Sawchuk asks why he received a penalty in the earlier game:

> 'What was it for, you big Palooka?' I say, 'You told me to eff off. You
> can't say that to a referee.' What I was really wanted to say was you can't
> treat friends that way. He just stares at me a moment and you know
> how dark and scary his eyes could be, I don't even know what he was
> feeling, sad or sorry or angry. 'I don't remember that,' he says.
> 'I don't remember any of that.' (111–12)

Half a century later, Storey remains haunted by the incident. Sawchuk's question might point to how, in the heat of a game, his focus on the puck was so intense that he failed to register all that was going on around him.

Storey, however, seems to feel that he caught an unsettling glimpse of something darker and more mercurial. As he explains to the poet in "Big Dogs (1)," "'But there was something about him, something / more than just how good he was. [. . .] That's what you want to know about, I suppose'" (58).

Storey's frustration at never being able to fully know or explain Terry Sawchuk—"'Did I ever get him figured out? Ask me something easier'" (63)—is a metaphor for the challenge faced by the poet as he works to understand his subject from a variety of angles. Maggs skillfully dekes the temptation to look past the contradictions and depict Sawchuk as a knowable, unified subject. Instead, he takes a more postmodernist approach, showing us Sawchuk from many different angles, including through a number of poems that try to imagine the goaltender's own personal experience.

The second and perhaps most important section of *Night Work*, "Kings and Little Ones," takes the reader from Sawchuk's childhood in Winnipeg to the early years of the goalie's playing career in Detroit. It is the lengthiest section of the collection, spanning forty-two pages and nineteen poems, and it includes some of Maggs's finest work. The first poems in this section work through some of the well-known facts about Sawchuk's childhood growing up as a Ukrainian Canadian in Winnipeg. We see him in school at twelve years old in "Initia Gentis" (Latin for "the beginning of"), and in "Sheet Metal," we learn more about his immigrant father, a "strong / but gentle man, shaped by the sound of violins / and un-flat land" (27), whose devastating workplace injury sent the sixteen-year-old Terry to work to support his family. Understanding what is at stake for Terry and his family allows the reader to empathize more deeply with the young man, particularly in "Writing on the Walls," as he sets off on the train in 1946 to join the junior Red Wings. In the poem, he loses to a card shark "the ten dollar bill in a pocket, still folded." His mother had given him the money, and he thinks:

> I would have sent home what she gave me, doubled,
> just so she'd know, but I didn't know how
> to get out ahead of the game.
>
> I might have learned that then about myself. (33)

Like "Writing on the Walls," the poems that detail Sawchuk's formative years in Winnipeg all contain elements of a near mythic origin story that presages both the goaltender's future greatness and the darkness that will sometimes surround him. The second and third stanzas of "Initia Gentis" address how Sawchuk and his friends, in their working-class neighbourhood, were unable to play hockey at night since their rinks had no lights. The "trouble with time" that "[b]egins in school" and the "black hand's gloom" of the long winter nights are set in the context of the opening stanza lines of the poem (25). The first stanza, the only section of the poem in the first person, is, through its italicization, visually distinct from the rest of the poem:

> All my life I'll know this restless tilt of eyes,
> the upward glance before you get set, how much
> time you have to save your skin. (25)

The image of Sawchuk in net looking up at the clock and the way players—goaltenders especially—perceive time in a particular way comes up in later poems as well, most notably in "Different Ways of Telling Time" (49-53). In "Sheet Metal," Terry's one workplace injury "slicing open his catching hand" (28) is echoed years later, when "Pulford would skate across / that same hand," severing Sawchuk's tendons and jeopardizing his career. The brutal toll on Sawchuk's body and mind are detailed in later poems, such as "An Ancient Fire" and "The Thousand Things," but this early poem helps connect Sawchuk's many hockey injuries with the workplace injuries and mishaps experienced by his blue-collar father.

Another significant event in Sawchuk's childhood that shaped the future Hall of Fame goaltender was the loss of his older brother Mike when Terry was ten years old. Mike played goal and the younger Terry was deeply influenced by the brother he idolized. It was only after Mike's death, when Terry inherited his old equipment, that the younger brother got the chance to be in net. Terry never played another position after that. In "The Back Door Open Where She's Gone to the Garden," the poet imagines, through Terry's perspective, the family's struggle to cope with Mike's death:

> How do the rest of us deal with him being gone?
> [. . .] And I wear the pads in the family

now. I bring the bruises home, the aches and taunts
that wake me in our moon-bleak room. (30)

"The Famous Crouch" provides greater detail of Mike's influence on Terry,
including on his technique as a goaltender:

All those nights I'd hear him
in his sleep. *Stay low, stay forward, balance*
on a ball. Forget the names they sing you through the screen.
See the shot before it leaves the stick. (31)

At the end of the poem, Terry notes that Mike's influence on him remains
strong through his career:

But now it's me who's bending low and looking for
the bullet shot. All my life, I'd heard the warning
in his voice and in the moment's heat
I hear it yet. (31)

Poems such as "The Famous Crouch" help to build a narrative of how
Sawchuk's early life in Winnipeg formed the roots of both his Hall of Fame
career and what at times would be his battle with his dark, troubled psyche.

While the section "Kings and Little Ones" contains several other notable
poems that follow Sawchuk through to the first part of his career, including
"A Clever Dog" (39–41), "Let's Go Dancing" (55), and "Desperate Moves"
(64–65), no discussion of this section would be complete without examining "Different Ways of Telling Time" (49–53), one of *Night Work*'s finest
poems and one that anchors the theme of time that infuses the collection.
The passing of time on the clock is the one unerring constant in any game
and the preoccupation of every player:

They know time's rough
and tumble. Space and time, that's where they live,
arcs and angles, a quick move into open ice.

The players most conscious of the time on the clock, the poet reminds us,
are the ones who never leave the ice:

Left out on the ice—they might as well be
on the moon—both goalies eye the clock,
one's for zero, the other likes infinity,
but things can change.

Get going clock.
Slow down slow down. (49)

Although "no one in the building likes time's pace," the referee can add more
seconds to the clock: "imagine the power, / to kick time's arse like that"
(49). Divided into six sections, with titles like "(iii) *sudden death*" and "(v)
carpe diem," the later sections of the poem take us away from the ice into
the hours in the dressing room and the personal rituals before the team hits
the ice. The final section, "(vi) *big river*," sees Sawchuk awake in bed beside
his sleeping lover, wishing that time would slow down and that he could
leave behind the thoughts of his past and the threat of the up-and-coming
goalie Glenn Hall taking his place in net.

While the early parts of *Night Work* follow a chronological structure, the
poem "A Clever Dog" marks an important shift. It describes Jack Adams,
Detroit's general manager, preparing for a meeting with Terry Sawchuk and
deciding to slash his salary offer to the goaltender from three thousand dol-
lars to two thousand. Adams's decision to trade Sawchuk to Boston at the
peak of his career in 1955 and replace him with Glenn Hall damaged Sawchuk's confidence and, by all accounts, troubled him for years afterward.
Midway through his second season with Boston, Sawchuk became over-
whelmed by stress and, on the verge of a nervous breakdown, announced
an early retirement. After trying several other careers, he returned to play
for the Red Wings the next season. His confidence was shaken, though, and
his career and life would spiral downward from that point on. As Maggs
explained in an interview with Bruce McCurdy, *Night Work* is deliberately
structured to reflect the impact on Sawchuk of his first trade from the Red
Wings: "I break off that [chronological] pattern intentionally. What appears
from there on is perhaps less orderly in appearance, which reflects what
happened in Terry's own life as a result of Jack Adams's handling of him.
From then on there are sections more or less grouped together having little
regard for any orderly historical unfolding of time" (McCurdy 2010).

The remaining sections of *Night Work*, then, zero in on particular
moments of Sawchuk's career. For instance, the third section, "Two Goalies

Fishing in the Dark," deals exclusively with the Bruins' ten-day, seven-game tour of Newfoundland in April 1956. While most of the poems either feature Sawchuk as the speaker or tell something about his performance there, they are equally poems about Newfoundland and this important moment in the history of the five communities in which the Bruins played exhibition games against local teams. As the Bruins kick off the tour with a rough ferry ride from North Sydney, Nova Scotia, to Port aux Basques, Newfoundland, the speaker in "Night Crossing in Ice," presumably Terry Sawchuk, asks himself "Who could call this heaving darkness home? / Who'd go out of his house in this for a game of hockey?" (Maggs 2008, 69). The remaining poems in this section serve to answer that very question; the reader sees Newfoundland and the exhibition games through the eyes of Sawchuk and, in poems such as "String and Bones," witnesses Sawchuk through the eyes of Newfoundlanders. "String and Bones," which became the basis for the short film *Night Work: A Sawchuk Poem* (Simms 2009), tells the story of the local hockey player who scores on Sawchuk in a penalty shot with an ill-advised "bullet / right at Sawchuk's head" (Maggs 2008, 78). The first half of the poem includes quotations from a variety of unnamed sources, each seeming to offer their own take on this story and on why "Terry took such exception" (78). In the second half of the poem, the poet tracks down Gerald, "the man who scored on Terry Sawchuk" (79):

> "Maybe he did come after me,
> but he was only kidding. Yes, he did say
> something. Just like it was yesterday."
>
> Long silence, looking out over the water,
> then he turns to me. "He said, 'How come a guy with the shot
> you got isn't up with us in the NHL?'" (79)

The conversation between these two men is a humorous reminder of how, as the decades pass in a storytelling culture like that of Newfoundland, a tale can grow in ways that make how it is told more important than the long-lost truth that may or may not be at its core. This is a theme, of course, that has particular relevance to the poet's quest to come to an understanding of Sawchuk through poetry and story rather than through player statistics or historical records.

Aside from the inclusion of "Big Dogs (2)" and "Transition Game," two poems in which the unnamed narrator appears to be Sawchuk, the fourth section of *Night Work*, "Goaltender Suite," comprises poems that pay tribute to a variety of legendary and lesser known goaltenders from the early to mid-twentieth century, ranging from Gump Worsley and Jacques Plante to Percy LeSueur and Frank "Ulcers" McCool. The section also contains two remarkable poems about the position of goaltender—"Rough Calculations" and "One of You." "Rough Calculations" talks about the physics of hockey, beginning with a comparison between the "subtle baseball with its endlessness, / its pendulous invitation" and the inherent "winterness" of the puck: "Flat and squat, a puck's / inert, needs a lever, needs ice" (95). The poet imagines physics equations that, by taking into account a puck's mass, velocity, and *"the time the puck is in contact with the player's head,"* one might be able to calculate *"the amount the head is deformed,"* something "goaltenders / know in their bones" (95–96). The final section of the poem reminds the reader of how the invention of the slapshot, "the '50s leap in firepower [. . .] blending the games / of boys and murder" (96), "for goalies meant a whole retooling / of reflex, a new code for heart" (97). Above all, the poem helps to contextualize how and why so few goaltenders in Sawchuk's day were able to withstand the pressure and danger of putting their poorly protected bodies between the puck and the net; Sawchuk's unparalleled longevity at the time speaks to both his incredible resilience and the deep price he paid with his body and mind to do what he did. As the poem "One of You" reminds us, hockey is a different game for the goaltender than it is for any other player:

> Denied the leap and dash up the ice,
> what goalies know is side to side, an inwardness of monk
> and cell. They scrape. They sweep. Their eyes are elsewhere
> as they contemplate their narrow place. (98)

The poems of "Goaltender Suite" explore how goaltenders have more in common with each other, perhaps, than with the others on their own teams. Collectively, these poems offer another way of understanding why Sawchuk may have been seen by his teammates as distant and disconnected and why the pressure of his role gradually ate away at him.

The fifth section of the book, "Canadian Dreams," collects a variety of other hockey poems, including two about the great Montreal Canadiens defenceman Doug Harvey, who struggled with alcoholism and bipolar disorder later in life. Other poems, such as "Guys Like Pete Goegan" (125–26), recount stories and experiences that Maggs learned about from his brother Darryl Maggs, who played in the NHL and the WHA for teams including the California Golden Seals. The Golden Seals come up in "No Time to Go," the only poem in this section to include Sawchuk. Sawchuk, the speaker in the poem, is second-guessing his decision to play for the LA Kings in 1967–68: "Shitty ice. Shitty crowd again this afternoon, biding / their time from brawl to brawl" (121). A story about how a young player's wisecrack to the Chicago coach gets him traded to the Seals, a team that wears white skates, leads Sawchuk to reflect on the fate of hockey and hockey players in California:

Prairie boys wearing white skates.

There's guys getting hold of this game
been out in the sun too long. (122)

Although now, half a century later, hockey is well established in California, "No Time to Go" reminds today's reader that, especially to veterans like Sawchuk, NHL expansion must have been seen as a dramatic lessening of the game.

The contrast between the game of hockey today and that of the era of the original six and of the post-expansion years becomes more apparent in the final three sections of *Night Work*. The brutality of the game in the 1950s and 60s and its impact on Sawchuk's body and mind described in the later poems in the collection is unfathomable today; with today's goaltenders now protected by pounds of equipment and padding the experience of the goalie has changed dramatically from the mask-free era during which Sawchuk began his career. The sixth section of the book, "Saints at Home, Soldiers Between Wars," depicts the border between the pressures of the game and Sawchuk's personal life starting to become more unstable. Sawchuk's difficulties sleeping because of the lingering effects of his injuries comes up in both "Game Days" (130) and "How Things Look in a Losing Streak" (131–32):

slept on my bad side again, the elbow
slowly disintegrating. More bone for the jar when the season's
done. (130)

In the poem "Things in Our Day" (135–39), Sawchuk's former Detroit
teammate Gary Bergman speaks to the poet about Sawchuk: "that's when
he was most alive. Out on the ice with the / game on the line. Even with all
it cost him in the end" (139).

The price Sawchuk paid to play the game as he did is detailed exten-
sively in the seventh section, "Hurt Hawks." The poem "An Ancient Fire"
(145–46) begins with a 1967 photo of Sawchuk, then a Toronto Maple Leaf,
after he had been injured by a slapshot from Blackhawk Bobby Hull. The
poet observes that in the photo, which occupies the page directly opposite
the poem,

> in the deep slump of his body you see his agony
> and sagging spirit. [. . .]
> The signs of defeat are clearly there. The taped-up
> hand that holds the damaged arm. The body that only
> wants to curl into itself. (145)

In "The Thousand Things," a poem that addresses the same incident from
that 1967 semifinal series, Maggs imagines Sawchuk's perspective as he
sees the shot coming:

> His choices were few: come out and cut down the angle
> or go take that job with his father-in-law. A hundred and twenty
> miles an hour, he takes one full force on the shoulder.
> The crack of bone like a roof beam giving way. (147)

Somehow, Sawchuk manages to play on. "No Country for Old Men" details
how, following game five, Sawchuk's teammates come to realize the extent
of his sacrifice and heroic resilience:

> one by one they sense a deepening silence in the room
> and turn to look where Terry's resting, panting, having
> wrestled off his sodden shirt. Their eyes tell them
> armload of plums, say peacock's plumage.
> Their fingers pause in their intricate task. *Jesus, Ukey,*

someone breaks the silence. The whole room
gapes at the hammered chest and belly. Easy to count
the darker nine or ten from Hull. They can't even look
at the shoulder. (153–54)

That year, the Maple Leafs defeated Chicago in six games and, thanks
in part to some of the greatest goaltending ever seen, went on to defeat
Montréal and win the Stanley Cup. Maggs describes the Stanley Cup run
over several poems in this section, ending it with the poem "Tidal Fears"
(163–64). "Tidal Fears" asks how Terry could keep wanting to play after
nearly two decades in the NHL during an era when no other goalie had
lasted more than eleven seasons. Even "getting drilled by pucks, his nose
half ripped away, / his eyeball sliced, the backs of both hands / opened up
by skates" is not enough to make him quit for good. The poet asks, "What
always brought him back / for one more year?" (163–64). He imagines
Sawchuk's answer at the end of the poem: "'Hell, you saw me out there—I
can play this game forever'" (164).

Terry Sawchuk, of course, could not play the game forever. Thus, the
closing words of "Tidal Fears" provide a fitting transition into the final section of *Night Work*, titled "Last Minute of Play." The poems in this section
address Terry's return to Detroit as a backup goaltender for the 1968–69
season and the final season of his career as a New York Ranger for 1969–70.
The collection's final poem, "New York I.C.U." (176), focuses on the last few
hours of Sawchuk's life. Recuperating in hospital after a series of surgeries
to address injuries suffered in a fall after a scuffle with his roommate and
teammate Ron Stewart, Terry tells his coach, Emile Francis, who has been
at his bedside for days, to go home to his family. Later that day, Sawchuk
dies from a pulmonary embolism. Given the topic, Maggs's thoughtfully
restrained treatment of his subject's final hours showcases his craftsmanship
as a poet. Tragically, Terry wanted to keep his accident a secret, so Francis
was the only one there. Maggs, though, sees the kinship of goalies as part
of Francis's devotion to his friend and player:

Emile, the Cat, the only
coach he'd had who'd known the life of playing goal.
That was why he kept the four-day vigil all alone. (176)

In Sawchuk's insistence to police investigators that he alone was responsible for his injuries, Maggs observes

[h]ow dextrously
a goalie hangs the chains of culpability around his neck.
Open the door to the roaring darkness, let him go first. (176)

As Sawchuk faces his death, Maggs closes the poem by tying everything back to all that Sawchuk faced as a goaltender:

Fear what was on the way?
What could there be about fear he didn't know?
Open the door.
Infinity is just another fucking number. (176)

While Terry Sawchuk realized the dream of many a Canadian child by becoming one of the greatest hockey players of all time, the pain and torment that came along with that achievement also led to his tragically premature death. As Jamie Dopp suggests, Maggs finds in Sawchuk the same fascination we find in great literary characters like Dr. Faustus or Jay Gatsby. "Figures such as these," Dopp writes, "speak to recurring human anxieties about success. Does success always involve moral and personal compromise? Is there behind every successful person some kind of Faustian bargain?" (2009, 112). In the end, Sawchuk is no longer here to reflect on his life or to answer any of Maggs's or the reader's questions.

Although *Night Work* is Maggs's attempt to delve into the enigma that was and is Terry Sawchuk, he signals throughout that we will gain no singular, incontrovertible understanding of the man. This indeterminacy, however, should not be seen as leaving us without any sense of the truth about Terry Sawchuk. As Maggs points out in his afterword, although the historical facts about Sawchuck are elusive, poems like those in *Night Work* aim for a "greater truth" (2008, 180). Maggs's contention about poetry is reminiscent of Demeter's question about the relationship between art and the subject of art in Robert Kroetsch's 1969 novel, *The Studhorse Man.* Writing about the "superlative grace and beauty of Chinese art," Demeter, the novel's narrator, asks: "Ah, where to begin? Why is the truth never where it should be? Is the truth of the man in the man or in the biography? Is the truth of the beast in the flesh and confusion or in the few skillfully arranged lines?" (155). The power and immediacy of Randall Maggs's *Night Work* poems suggest that art may lead us closer to "the truth of the man" than facts and statistics ever will. Maggs's portrait of Terry Sawchuk is so rich and three-dimensional that it is hard for any attentive reader of *Night Work* to close the book without thinking that, as *Globe and Mail* sports writer Stephen Brunt puts it plainly in his endorsement on the book's back cover, "his Sawchuk is real."

WORKS CITED

Dopp, Jamie. 2009. "The Face Before the Mask: Review of *Night Work*, by Randall Maggs." *The Fiddlehead* 238: 112–14.

Hackel, Stu. 2009. "The Morning Skate: King of Shutouts, King of Pain." *Slap Shot: News from the World of Hockey* (blog), *New York Times*, 8 December. https://slapshot.blogs.nytimes.com/2009/12/08/the-morning-skate-king-of-shutouts-king-of-pain/.

Kroetsch, Robert. 1969. *The Studhorse Man*. New York: Simon and Schuster.

Maggs, Randall. 2008. *Night Work: The Sawchuk Poems*. London, ON: Brick Books.

McCurdy, Bruce. 2010. "An Interview with Randall Maggs, the Sawchuk Poet." *SB Nation: Copper and Blue* (blog), 19 March. https://www.coppernblue.com/2010/3/19/1376288/an-interview-with-randall-maggs.

Simms, Justin, dir. 2009. *Night Work: A Sawchuk Poem*. Book Shorts Production, MovingStories.TV. https://www.youtube.com/watch?v=a3cWW-6un9Y.

Jamie Dopp

From Tank to Deep Water
Myth and History in Samantha Warwick's *Sage Island*

One of the most famous Canadian literary works about swimming is A. M. Klein's 1948 poem "Lone Bather." The poem describes a man who seeks refuge from city life by going to a deserted pool for a swim. He dives from an "ecstatic diving board" and "lets go his manshape" as he hits the water. The imagery of the poem emphasizes the fantastical transformations the man undergoes while in the water, where he becomes "mysterious and marine," a "merman" whose thighs "are a shoal of fishes." He enjoys a deep sense of freedom until he is forced by "a street sound throw[n] like a stone [. . .] through the glass" to return to the world and his regular life. As he towels off, the man rubs away "the bird, the plant, the dolphin" until he becomes again "personable plain" (Klein 1974, 321).

Representations of swimming in literature often contain mythic resonances similar to those of "Lone Bather." According to these representations, swimming is an activity that takes a human being out of his or her natural element, thus offering a break from everyday existence and creating a space of temporary freedom. Such texts often use imagery that hints at connections between ourselves and other water creatures as well as between our modern and ancient selves. These connections, in turn, allow us to make contact with something timeless or more meaningful within ourselves—a process often figured by the surface and depth imagery evoked by water itself. Think of Maggie Lloyd in Ethel Wilson's *Swamp Angel* escaping from her oppressive suburban life in 1950s Vancouver to the interior of British Columbia, where she rediscovers her strength in part by swimming in a secluded lake, an activity that "transforms her" and helps her to forget "past and future" (1990, 130). Or consider Lisa Marie at the end of Eden Robinson's *Monkey Beach*, who swims out into the ocean in an attempt to resolve the mystery of her brother Jimmy's disappearance by contacting the underworld of the dead (2000, 372–73). Or—in perhaps the most famous Canadian literary example of all—the unnamed protagonist in Margaret Atwood's *Surfacing*, who dives below the surface of a northern Ontario lake to make contact with the hidden truths of her own life (2010, 147).

The opening of Samantha Warwick's *Sage Island* portrays swimming in a way that is within this tradition. The epigraph to the novel, from Richard Angell's *The Long Swim*, begins: "The feeling within you, the urge to crawl out of your skin and get away, get away, is so strong that it couldn't be uniquely personal." The prologue elaborates on the feeling evoked by Angell: "That feeling when you first enter the water, straight as a needle; that underwater glide, the flying, weightless sensation of being suspended—free." The prologue goes on to describe a swimmer's hand as an "amphibious paddle" and swimming itself as a return to "prehistoric simplicity." Like Klein's lone bather taking his respite from the complexities of the modern city, the swimmer in Warwick's prologue becomes "a drifting speck, divorced from the patter of thought and city scream"—an experience that "wipes the mind's slate clear" and creates a "*tabula rasa*" (2008, 1).

The protagonist of *Sage Island*, Savanna Mason, attempts to redeem her life by an act of swimming with recognizably mythic dimensions. She travels far away from home to swim in a long-distance ocean race called the Wrigley Ocean Marathon. The extreme nature of the challenge seems to allow her to shed her previous sense of failure and embrace a positive new identity, in the manner of a traditional hero completing a quest (see Campbell 1949). And yet, in important ways, the novel complicates—or makes problematical—the mythic meaning of Savi's act. Much of *Sage Island*, in fact, foregrounds how the historical environment of the United States in the 1920s conditions—and limits—her attempt to redeem herself through swimming. The limitation of myth, according to Roland Barthes, is that it is "constituted by the loss of the historical quality of things" (1972, 109). *Sage Island*, however, emphasizes that the mythic dimensions of swimming are only made available by—and are deeply intertwined with—the historical quality of the thing.

The events leading up to Savi's involvement in the Wrigley Ocean Marathon are conveyed in a series of flashbacks that help to establish Savi's character and motivation. As a seventeen-year-old, Savi is a competitive swimmer from New York City who is in the running for the 1924 Summer Olympics in Paris. At the Olympic Trials, however, she finishes in a tie for the final team spot and is ruled to have lost on a "Judges' Decision" (Warwick 2008, 36). After a period of disappointment, she regains her sense of purpose—as well as her enthusiasm for swimming—when a rich patron, Peter Laswell, supports her in a bid to become the first woman to swim the English Channel. Mere weeks before her attempt, however, Trudy Ederle, the same woman who had beaten Savi on the Judges' Decision at the Olympic Trials and who has gone on to become an Olympic medalist, swims the channel herself. Laswell withdraws his support for Savi because a second swim would lack "punch and originality" (162). He also, not coincidentally, commands his son, Tad, to end the romantic relationship he has begun with Savi. Hit by this double loss, Savi sinks into a deep depression. In the midst of her desolation, she learns of the Wrigley Ocean Marathon, a long-distance swimming race that is to take place off the coast of California. The main narrative of the novel consists of Savi's preparation for and participation in this race—an act she hopes will redeem the multiple failures of her life.

Interestingly, the backstory does not describe Savi's first encounter with swimming. There is no childhood scene of discovery, nothing comparable to, for example, Johnny Weissmuller's blissful account of swimming for the first time in Lake Michigan, at Lincoln Park, Chicago, when he was eight or nine years old (1930, 132). In fact, one of the notable aspects of Savi's early career is how little joy or childlike pleasure it contains. What beauty she perceives in swimming has to do with the artificial environment of "the tank." The Olympic Trials, for example, occur in a "deluxe facility in New York" with "marble lips" and "brass bars" that give it a "Renaissance appeal." But this same environment tends towards harshness. At the Trials, Savi recalls a sickening "humidity," a "violent blaze" of reflected light on water, and "shrill whistle-bursts" that "split through the noise" (Warwick 2008, 25).

The flashbacks suggest that Savi's motivation for swimming comes from a desire to escape the oppressive conditions of her life. Her everyday life is defined by work in her family's bake shop and the constrained role available to her as a young woman in the 1920s. Early on, the novel draws a contrast between her own limited choices and the relative male privilege enjoyed by her brother, Michael, who blithely drops out of college (which Savi wouldn't be allowed to attend) and takes off to Paris to find himself (14). Later, as she clings to the remnants of her swimming career, Savi recognizes that swimming is all that stands between her and an "ordinary life." The thought of being reduced to a traditional woman's future, married with children, makes her, she says, "perfectly sick to my stomach" (56). Competition, in contrast, gives her a thrill. One of the most powerful passages in the early part of the novel has to do with the physical experience of being in a race: "I felt a burst in my centre, a burst like the magnesium flare of flash powder. I carved into the water and ploughed into the tumble and chaos of a one-hundred-metre sprint" (30).

The backstory suggests that the thrill Savi feels is a result of the contrast that competition offers from her ordinary life. The thrill is further intensified by the exceptional nature of competitive swimming for young women at the time. As Savi's best friend and fellow-swimmer, Maizee, puts it, there are few girls who swim competitively at all in this period, much less who swim as fast as they do, which makes it feel as if they're participating in "some top-secret operation. Operation Girls' Team—as though it's still taboo, all that stuff about the strain not being good for us" (22).

Maizee's comment reflects the sexism that Savi encounters throughout her career. Sexism challenges her as a woman in everyday life but also specifically as a female athlete. Allen Guttmann describes the post–World War I era as a time of "stops and starts" for women's sports, just as it was for the women's movement more generally (1991, 135). The complexity of the broader social situation is perhaps best embodied in the dominant female figure of the 1920s, the flapper, who represented a resistance to traditional female behaviour, with her scandalous dress and claims to greater social freedom. These claims were enabled by the social changes for women of that era, such as women working outside the home, acquiring the right to vote, and so on. Yet the flapper ultimately reinforced the stereotype of a woman defined almost entirely in sexual terms: flappers were not emancipated career women; they were party girls. As Barbara Harris describes the life of the flapper, "When her dancing and drinking days were over, she settled down as wife and mother" (Harris 1978, 140-1). Warwick reflects this aspect of the historical environment by making Maizee a flapper. Maizee seems more rebellious (and wiser) than Savi at first, but after her own swimming career stalls, she meets Robert Bobrosky Jr., the son of Peter Laswell's business partner, and reverts to the traditional female role. By the time Savi arrives on Catalina Island, Maizee is "already engaged to Bobrosky after only two months of courting" and is learning Spanish for her honeymoon. One of her first phrases, appropriately, is "Me he perdido"— meaning "I am lost" (Warwick 2008, 182).

Tensions between the seeming emancipation of women in the 1920s and resistance to this emancipation can also be seen in the career of the woman who is Savi's archrival in the novel, Trudy Ederle. From the time she swam the English Channel in 1926 until her place was taken by Amelia Earhart in 1928, the historical Trudy Ederle was the most famous sportswoman in America. The authors of *America's Girl: The Incredible Story of How Swimmer Gertrude Ederle Changed the Nation* see Ederle as one of the "brash women" who swam the Channel "to try and strike a blow for their gender and show everyone that the weaker sex wasn't so weak at all" (Dahlberg, Ward, and Greene 2009, 3). At first glance, Ederle was wildly successful: her crossing time of fourteen hours and thirty-one minutes beat the record time of the five previous male Channel swimmers by about two hours (Guttmann 1991, 148; Campbell 1977, 58). Ederle's subsequent fame, however, was sustained in part by the crafting of her image as a "normal" American girl despite her physical prowess. For example, in an article about her in *Evening World*, "she was shown doing housework and talking about how cooking was one of her favorite things" (cited in Dahlberg, Ward, and Greene 2009, 4). Ederle's explicitly marketed wholesomeness was even expressed in verse in the *Evening World* article: "She loves home and family / She's everything the converse of the flighty flapper" (4). At the same time, her feminized image was designed to counter the prejudice against women and strenuous physical activity—the idea that even if such activity did not prove directly injurious to a woman's "weaker" constitution, it was likely to make a woman into a muscle-bound amazon unattractive to men. Even so, press accounts of Ederle tended to combine praise for her physical prowess with snide comments about her lack of feminine allure. A piece in *The Literary Digest*, for example, praised her "strapping, wholesome, fun-loving" nature but ended by suggesting that her "muscles of steel . . . would never lure a good sailor-man on the rocks" (quoted in Guttmann 1991, 147).

Savi's choice of swimming as her means to escape her life is affected by both personal and historical circumstances. The main personal reason for her choice is a simple one: she's good at it. Higgins, her crusty old coach, tells her that she has "physical intelligence"—and, Savi tells us, this "lit a fire in my rib cage" (Warwick 2008, 9). History, however, also plays a part. At the time of Savi's story, swimming was one of the few competitive activities open to women. It was also, importantly, an Olympic event. There were, in fact, only four events open to women at the 1924 Olympics—swimming, diving, tennis, and fencing (Guttmann 1991, 164); there were no track and field events, no gymnastics, and none of the "combat" sports for which resistance against women's participation was especially strong and long lasting (wrestling and boxing were only introduced in 2004 and 2012, respectively). At the Paris Olympics of 1924, of the 2,956 participants only 136 were women (Senn 1999, 41). What drives Savi early on is a desire for something like the fame and fortune traditionally available through Olympic success. To achieve that fame and fortune, she needs to find a way to be one of the few women allowed to compete at the Olympics—and swimming is her best option.

After Savi's Olympic hopes are dashed, she swims in the other events available to her—two Hudson River swims, the English Channel swim (aborted), and, finally, the Wrigley Ocean Marathon. Each event rekindles her competitive spirit. Of the river swims, for example, she says that she is "exhilarated by [...] the chase" (Warwick 2008, 43). The progression of events also takes her away from the artificial environment of the tank and into deeper and deeper water—both literally and metaphorically. The natural environment in the Hudson River exhilarates her in a way that takes on mythic qualities: "I felt wild in the river, as though I had regressed to a primal state of simplicity, where humans lived in the ocean, travelled by sea, and could breathe underwater" (43). When she begins training for the Wrigley Ocean Marathon, mythic associations become even more pronounced. In the ocean, she realizes, there are no "borders" or "concrete walls" (19).

Savi's journey from the tank to the borderless environment of the ocean has the characteristics of a traditional hero journey, in which a hero leaves the familiarity of home to face the challenges of an unknown place (e.g., the wilderness, the underworld) as part of a quest for glory and self-knowledge. Key to Savi's heroic journey is how the extreme environment of the Catalina Island swim allows her to shed her former self. As she puts it during the last stages of the swim, "I must exhaust my former self, exhaust her out, [...] the dread, the failures, the not-being-good-enough" (212). In *The*

Hero of a Thousand Faces, Joseph Campbell suggests that in hero myths, the annihilation of the old self is always necessary for rebirth and renewal, and crossing the threshold into the place where the hero's trials are to be found is "a form of self-annihilation" (1949, 77). *Sage Island* suggests that this is what happens to Savi during the Wrigley Ocean Marathon. Indeed, her moment of personal redemption is described in classically mythic terms:

> This monotonous repetition of stroking through wild, open water—a primal sense of peace, cleansing atonement, the peeling, stripping, moulting out of myself, out of my skin, an estrangement from all things human, social constraints, expectations, the disease of materialism, sex. The clearing out of everything, wipe the mind's slate clear—*tabula rasa*. (Warwick 2008, 212)

This description of Savi's epiphany—with its repetition of the phrase "*tabula rasa*"—directly echoes the opening of *Sage Island*. The climax, then, brings the novel full circle back to the mythic portrayal of swimming in the prologue.

Even with its mythic climax, however, the novel makes clear that history has an important role to play in Savi's heroic act. The obvious indicator of history has to do with the fact that Savi's swim takes place as part of the Wrigley Ocean Marathon, a historical competition organized by William Wrigley Jr. (of chewing gum fame) that took place in January 1927. The competition involved swimming the San Pedro Channel from Santa Catalina Island to the mainland of California just outside of Los Angeles, a distance of twenty-two miles—the same distance as the English Channel, but with especially treacherous currents and even colder water. Wrigley's idea was to hold the race to generate publicity for Catalina, which he owned and was trying to develop into a year-round tourist destination. To lure swimmers to the race, he offered a prize of $25,000 to the winner and $15,000 to the first woman to finish (Campbell 1977, 65–67). Money turns out not to be Savi's primary motivation; indeed, it is part of her overall journey that she becomes less concerned with traditional fame and fortune and more concerned with self-renewal. Her focus does not, however, alter the fact that material conditions profoundly shaped the Wrigley Ocean Marathon. The race itself would not have happened without Wrigley's promise of prize money, and, given Savi's life circumstances, she almost certainly would not have participated without the lure of a cash reward.

Wrigley's offer of prize money (today worth about $350,000 and $200,000, respectively, according to dollartimes.com) shapes the environment of the marathon in other ways as well. When Savi arrives at Catalina Island to train, she discovers a carnival-like atmosphere seemingly filled with hucksters and schemers. Like many heroes arriving in a wild place away from home, she finds it difficult to tell friend from foe. One of the first characters she meets is Loot, a shell-shocked veteran of World War I, whom she misunderstands as a threat (Warwick 2008, 5). Conversely, she is befriended by a journalist named Bea, who seems to have her best interests at heart but who, it turns out, is secretly working to undermine her on behalf of another competitor (149). The lure of prize money suggests a heightening of the competitive stakes. Savi recognizes that many of the competitors in the marathon are desperate, like herself, and wonders if "this whole event is fuelled by failures wanting to redeem themselves" (52). This contributes to an aura of ruthless competition. Finally, the disparity between prizes for men and women suggests a continuation of the sexism Savi has encountered before. That disparity and her experiences on Catalina Island give Savi the message that "women are not yet viewed in the same league as men" and that their presence in the race "is a bit of sideshow" (62).

The darker side of the commercial element in the Wrigley Ocean Marathon is perhaps most dramatically conveyed by the sub-plot involving the historical George Young, the seventeen-year-old Canadian who was the winner, and only finisher, of the Catalina Island swim. As the novel indicates, Young was exploited by a man who acted as his agent and who took 40 percent of his prize money and later earnings (Campbell 1977, 65; Warwick 2008, 65). Bea, despite her ulterior motives, accurately points out that Savi and George Young have backgrounds that are "remarkably similar." Both come from working-class families, both quit school at "about fourteen" to work, both started swimming out of "no-name tanks," and both—by implication—have tried to parlay their gift for swimming into better lives (Warwick 2009, 83–84). Without saying it directly, Bea suggests that Savi's background makes her vulnerable to exploitation in the same way as George. The obvious proof of this is in Savi's own past—how easily she was seduced into the world of the Laswells, including the bed of Tad Laswell, and how summarily she was dismissed again, as competitor and lover, when her project to swim the English Channel fell apart.

Wrigley's decision to hold a swimming event to promote his resort is itself shaped by history. According to Bruce Wigo, president of the International Swimming Hall of Fame, swimming was "the most popular recreational activity in America in the 1920s and 1930s" (quoted in Sherr 2012, 33). The popularity of swimming was related to the fact that major team sports had not yet become dominant in America (this would come with the help of radio, movies, and television); as a result, certain individual athletes, like marathon runners and swimmers, were accorded a status higher than they are given today (Campbell 1977, 10). Wrigley's idea was probably not only to generate publicity but also to create a new hero through his event, someone like Trudy Ederle after her English Channel swim, a new hero who would then be forever associated with Catalina Island. To some extent, this did happen: George Young, after his victory, was dubbed the Catalina Kid, and Wrigley made a considerable profit—in part, because of him (Campbell 1977, 68).

The extreme nature of the Catalina Island swim also reflects the transitional nature of sport in the Roaring Twenties. A key aspect of sport in this era was the celebration of extreme physical challenges, firsts of all kinds, and feats of daring do—activities that had their roots in earlier versions of sport but that would give way to more professionalized (and sanitized) competitions by the middle decades of the twentieth century. David Leach suggests that during the earlier years of the century, things like "placing the first mountaineer atop the world's highest peak" took on the character of "national urgency for glory-hungry governments in the United Kingdom and elsewhere" (2008, 116). It is worth noting that the Wrigley Ocean Marathon occurred within living memory of the first expeditions to the North and South Poles (Cook and Peary to the North in 1908 and 1909 and Amundsen to the South in 1911) and only a year before Amelia Earhart's pioneering flight across the Atlantic in 1928. This was also the heyday of Houdini, who died at the age of fifty-two in 1926. This transitional sporting culture also helps to account for the emergence of Johnny Weismuller as perhaps the first crossover athlete–Hollywood star. Weismuller won swimming medals in the 1924 and 1928 Olympics before going on to gain a different kind of fame with his portrayals of Tarzan, a historical background that is subtly hinted at by Weismuller's cameo appearances in *Sage Island*.

One way to read Savi's *tabula rasa* moment in *Sage Island* is that it represents a transcending of the material conditions that made her swim possible, a common experience of athletes in general. When an athlete steps onto the track or court, or into the water, anything outside the space of competition seems to disappear. The politics of the Olympics may be corrupt, but the track is still the track, the pool the pool, and so on. And doesn't a great athletic performance achieve a timelessness of its own? In *The Joy of Sports*, an early classic of sports criticism, Michael Novak supports this idea. Although "corruptions of various sorts" exist in sports, he argues, the lasting value of sporting activities has to do with something fundamentally religious: "The hunger for perfection in sports cleaves closely to the driving core of the human spirit" (1988, 27). Perhaps Savi's *tabula rasa* moment expresses her moment of contact with the "core of the human spirit."

According to Joseph Campbell (1949), the final phase of the hero's quest involves a rebirth of the self. This rebirth is accompanied by a series of boons. Something along these lines happens in *Sage Island*: after Savi is pulled from the water, she ends up in the hospital, where she receives a number of visitors. Her brother, Michael, arrives to effect a personal reconciliation, bringing with him a letter of best wishes from Maizee (Warwick 2008, 219). Sol also appears. The subplot involving Solomon—the doctor on Catalina Island who becomes Savi's navigator, protector, and potential love interest—intersects with Savi's hero journey in a complicated way. That Savi "wins" Sol as one of her boons might seem problematic at first: a strong woman on a hero-like quest fails to finish her swim (despite her *tabula rasa* moment) and is rescued from near death by a strong male. *Sage Island*, however, mitigates against a stereotypical reading of these elements. Sol is clearly a better choice of possible mate for Savi than Tad; in various ways, he represents the possibility of a relationship of equals. The novel remains silent on what the actual shape of their future relationship will be. The last words Savi and Sol exchange are, in fact, about Loot—who, as it turns out, is the brother of Sol—and the reason for his presence on Catalina Island (it seemed like a good place to care for him out of "the path of the authorities" [227]). The novel's last scene takes place on the beach after Savi has been released from hospital. After their exchange about Loot, Sol and Savi fall silent, lie back on the sand to watch the sky, and share a cigar—not a stereotypical "happily ever after" moment.

The mention of Loot at the end of *Sage Island* is a reminder that, far from being timelessly mythic, the boons Savi receives are shaped by history. A shell-shocked soldier in a novel of the Roaring Twenties is, of course, not surprising; it is a reflection of the historical environment of the time. (Savi remembers seeing comparable figures on the streets of New York.) Loot's character, however, takes on special significance in relation to Savi's quest. That Savi travels so far away for the Catalina Island swim only to immediately encounter a disabled veteran is a reminder that history cannot be escaped, even when one is on a mythic-like journey for self-renewal. The interactions between Loot and Savi also subtly point to different forms of heroism. To what extent is Savi's quest for personal redemption comparable to the experiences of a returned soldier like Loot? The novel does not force the comparison, nor does it use it to diminish what Savi ultimately achieves, but the presence of Loot is a reminder of the larger frame of history in which Savi's personal journey takes place.

The hand of history is more directly visible in the most tangible boon Savi receives. This comes from Rhea James. Rhea is a swimming coach who has been on the periphery during Savi's training period for the race. It turns out that she is affiliated with a girls' college on Santa Monica Bay. After watching Savi swim, Rhea invites Savi to join the college's swim team, to compete with the team in long-distance swimming competitions, and to attend the college on a scholarship (226–27). Rhea's offer addresses a number of issues for Savi at once, especially those related to the opportunities available for women (or not) in the 1920s. It is also a reminder that opportunities to compete do not appear in a historical vacuum: the development of competitive sports for women is related to improvements in opportunities for women more generally. Finally, Rhea councils Savi on the importance of women supporting one another. She asks her not to resent Trudy Ederle too much; after all, she reminds Savi, it was Ederle "who lit the fire under you that ultimately brought you here," and Savi might be "surprised how tight-knit the swimming fellowship is" (225–26). The implication is that a key to progress for women is for women to act in concert, even if part of that acting involves competition against one another in sporting events.

One thing that the novel is interestingly silent about at the end is prize money. Although Savi fails to finish her swim, the novel hints that she represents one of the two historical swimmers—both women—who came nearest to finishing after George Young. These two women, Margaret Hauser and Martha Sager, managed to swim for just over nineteen hours, the same length of time as Savi swims in the race (Campbell 1977, 67; Warwick 2008, 225). In recognition of their accomplishment, Wrigley awarded them each

$2,500. The lack of mention of such a prize for Savi serves a number of potential purposes. From a novelistic point of view, it makes the scholarship offer from Rhea more meaningful and avoids the anti-climax of Savi being offered financial support after she has just won a sizable sum of money. Thematically—and perhaps more significantly—it reinforces the novel's resistance to a triumphant ending of the kind found in most sports fiction. As Michard Oriard puts it in *Dreaming of Heroes*, sports novels tend to conclude "with a big game . . . in which the hero achieves his greatest triumph" (1982, 35). Savi does not win her big game; she does not even win a second-place-style consolation prize. She certainly does not get to be like the conventional hero-athlete who "simply glories in his new adulation with a sense of self-completeness from the task fulfilled" (38). Instead, Savi's meaningful failure shifts emphasis from the end of her journey to the journey itself. What turns out to be most important to her is not winning the Wrigley Ocean Marathon but what she learns—and who she meets—during the process of competing.

Savi's heroic failure, then, can be read as consistent with the classic hero model, which suggests that the middle of the mythic journey is where maturation—the making of a true hero—is found. Yet the mythic dimensions of Savi's swim are not the product of a timeless potential inherent in the water she swims in. That Savi chooses swimming for her self-journey is, in large measure, a result of historical circumstance, and the historical and material conditions of the Wrigley Ocean Marathon both make her swim possible and shape the rebirth that comes from it. If Savi takes to heart the lessons of losing, and works even harder, she may triumph at the next big event. Rhea James hints that a future victory for Savi might occur at a Lake Ontario swim the next August starting in Toronto. Even if this turns out to be the case, however, history will have its say. The sponsor of the event, according to Rhea, will be none other than William Wrigley Jr. (Warwick 2008, 227).

WORKS CITED

Atwood, Margaret. *Surfacing*. 2010. Toronto: McClelland and Stewart. First published 1972.

Barthes, Roland. *Mythologies*. 1972. Translated by Annette Lavers. New York: Hill and Wang.

Campbell, Gail. 1977. *Marathon: The World of the Long-Distance Athlete.* New York: Sterling.

Campbell, Joseph. 2008. *The Hero with a Thousand Faces.* Princeton, NJ: Princeton University Press. First published in 1949.

Dahlberg, Tim, Mary Ederle Ward, and Brenda Greene. 2009. *America's Girl: The Incredible Story of How Swimmer Gertrude Ederle Changed the Nation.* New York: St. Martin's.

Guttmann, Allen. 1991. *Women's Sports: A History.* New York: Columbia University Press.

Harris, Barbara J. 1978. *Beyond Her Sphere: Women and the Professions in American History.* Westport: Greenwood.

Klein, A. M. 1974. "Lone Bather." In *The Collected Poems of A. M. Klein.* Compiled and with an introduction by Miriam Waddington, 321. Toronto: McGraw-Hill Ryerson.

Leach, David. 2008. *Fatal Tide: When the Race of a Lifetime Goes Wrong.* Toronto: Viking.

Novak, Michael. 1988. *The Joy of Sports: End Zones, Bases, Baskets, Balls, and the Consecration of the American Spirit.* New York: Hamilton Press. First published 1967.

Oriard, Michael. 1982. *Dreaming of Heroes: American Sports Fiction, 1868–1980.* Chicago: Nelson-Hall.

Robinson, Eden. 2000. *Monkey Beach.* Toronto: Vintage.

Senn, Alfred E. 1999. *Power, Politics, and the Olympic Games.* Champaign, IL: Human Kinetics.

Sherr, Lynn. 2012. *Swim: Why We Love the Water.* New York: Public Affairs.

Warwick, Samantha. 2008. *Sage Island.* Victoria: Brindle and Glass.

Weissmuller, Johnny. 1930. *Swimming the American Crawl.* London: Putnam.

Wilson, Ethel. 1990. *Swamp Angel.* Toronto: McClelland and Stewart. First published 1954.

10   *Laura K. Davis*

Identity and the Athlete
Alexander MacLeod's "Miracle Mile"

Despite its title, Alexander MacLeod's "Miracle Mile" is not an inspirational tale that celebrates the great feats of sports heroes who, in apparent defiance of human limitations, are able to overcome all obstacles and win glory. A tightly woven short fictional story about two young elite runners, "Miracle Mile" culminates with the race toward which it builds, yet it is far from a narrative about victory. As the narrator and protagonist of the story, Mikey, puts it, "The most interesting stories [. . .] don't have anything to do with winning" (MacLeod 2010, 38).

The story is, in part, about how athletes might feel a sense of belonging in or exclusion from their own athletic communities. The protagonist, Mikey, like many athletes in competitive sports, feels a strange combination of rivalry and support for his fellow runner and friend, Burner. He is both a part of and apart from the running community he inhabits. Mikey's friendship with Burner and his own self-understanding are necessarily impacted in complicated ways when Burner emerges as the more dominant athlete of the two. "Miracle Mile" explores this fraught friendship in order to examine larger questions about the complexities of identity and the nature of relationships between individuals and their communities: How do we understand ourselves and our private experiences in relation to public events and discourses? How do we identify ourselves in relation to other people? What is our place in the world and what does it have to do with the past? For both the narrator and the reader, the answers to these questions emerge in fragments to reveal a dark and layered sport story.

With the first sentence of his story, MacLeod grounds it in an (in)famous moment in sport history: "This was the day after Mike Tyson bit off Evander Holyfield's ear" (9). Mikey and Burner are in a hotel room watching the Tyson moment on TV, while waiting to leave for their race, and, by blurring the boundaries between the boxer's act of violence and their wait in the hotel room, MacLeod deftly draws a connection between Tyson's story and the one that Mikey is about to tell. Indeed, Tyson's story is not separate from Mikey's own. "Mike kept coming at us through the screen," Mikey says, as if he himself were the object of Tyson's attack, and the effects linger: "I turned the TV off but the leftover buzz hanging in the air still hurt my eyes" (10). Just as Mikey is seemingly assaulted by Tyson and mesmerized by the TV coverage, so too is Burner, who sits "staring straight into the same dark place where the picture used to be," his eyes "kind of glossed over." Like the boxer's victim, or like Tyson himself, Burner has been "fading in and out," as if absent, in a different world (10).

Mikey experiences Tyson's violence as what Freud calls an "uncanny" moment—a moment in which one paradoxically experiences that which is both familiar and unfamiliar. In Freud's theory, the uncanny is associated with the self and the home, and it is infused with the horrific (Freud 1955). Mikey describes watching Tyson's act of violence on TV as repetitive and routine, yet he recognizes its horror: "If you look at the same pictures long enough even the worst things start to feel too familiar, even boring" (Macleod 2010, 10). Mikey's recognition of the Tyson moment as familiar implies that he sees something of himself in Tyson's act of violence. In the context of Freud's theory, Mikey intuits a hidden truth about himself when he experiences the uncanny—the familiar, his own self, made strange in Tyson's image. Later in the story, Mikey emphasizes the similarities between "freak show people" and competitive track athletes: "I used to think that's what we were like, the track people. Each of us had one of those strange bodies designed to do only one thing" (25). MacLeod reminds readers of Tyson's violence once again at the end of "Miracle Mile," when he implies that Burner might commit a similar act to Tyson's: "Burner had already closed the gap. [. . .] It all disintegrated after that" (44). Indeed, Tyson's presence, invoked at the beginning of the story, haunts it throughout. The story thus suggests that there is a fine line between the competitor and the "freak," the human and the monstrous.

Furthermore, MacLeod emphasizes Mikey's experience of Tyson's act of violence as mediated—as an image ("Cameras showed it from different angles and at different speeds" [10]) and as a story open to interpretation ("Commentators took turns explaining [. . .] what it all meant" [10]). On the one hand, MacLeod blurs the boundaries between Tyson and Mikey, each a part of the other, an interpretation that is supported by the similarity of their names. On the other hand, he highlights the mediation and constructedness of Tyson's story, and that too applies as much to Mikey as it does to Tyson. Just as Mikey views Tyson on TV, so we, the readers, read about Mikey in this story, a story in which Mikey is both character and narrator. MacLeod draws attention to Mikey's reading of Tyson's image on the screen; likewise, with his use of second-person narration, he draws attention to our reading of Mikey in the story: "*You* remember that" and "*You* know how it gets" (9, 10, emphasis mine). Therefore, the reader tends to feel a sense of discomfort similar to that which Mikey feels when he negotiates Tyson's image on the screen. We, like Mikey, might recognize deep within ourselves, within our own human nature, the dark animalistic violence that Tyson represents.

If Tyson's story is related to Mikey's, then so too is the story of Roger Bannister and John Landy, who ran the Miracle Mile at the Commonwealth Games in Vancouver in 1954, "the Tyson/Holyfield of its time" (37). Mikey narrates both races—Bannister and Landy's and his and Burner's—moving back and forth between the two stories. Just as Landy takes the lead early in the 1954 race, so too does the runner Eric Dawson in Mikey and Burner's race. And just as Bannister pulls ahead to beat Landy in 1954, so too does Burner pull ahead to beat Dawson in MacLeod's "Miracle Mile." Moreover, as mentioned above, Mikey and Mike Tyson share a name; in the same way, Bannister and Landy's race shares the same name—the Miracle Mile—as Mikey and Burner's. Thus, the legendary story of the Vancouver race and the story of Mikey's race conflate: one folds into and becomes the other.

By juxtaposing these two stories, MacLeod probes the issue of recognition and fame in competitive running. Elite runners like Mikey and Burner strive for recognition and fame by excelling in their sport, yet that achievement depends on various factors, including historical time. Mikey and Burner's story will never take on the significance of Bannister and Landy's because they will not be the first ones to run a mile in under four minutes. Similarly, Mikey falls into Burner's shadow in the race as Burner takes the lead. Burner is the one who experiences recognition and fame, even if momentarily, while Mikey does not: after the race, "[e]very eye was on Burner" (41). "Miracle Mile" demonstrates how athletes strive for recognition and public acknowledgement in sport, but it also shows how temporary and fleeting such fame is. After the story's penultimate race, Mikey and Burner run to cool down in a suburban neighbourhood, on "anonymous sidewalks" (43) where "nobody cared" (42). The story presents and ponders the significance of public recognition and fame in the lives of professional athletes, showing how prominent fame can be for elite athletes but also how temporary and tenuous it often is.

MacLeod parallels the Bannister-Landy and Mikey-Burner stories not only to contemplate recognition and fame but also to draw attention to them *as stories*. He highlights the stories' mediation. "That's the story they tell," Mikey says of Bannister and Landy, "but it's not true" (37). The Bannister-Landy story becomes consecrated in time with a "famous statue" (37); similarly, after his race, Mikey feels that his past is "crystallizing [...] and freezing into permanence" (41)—like the statue itself. Significantly, in Mikey's version of the Bannister-Landy race, there is an unnoticed presence, a "phantom" or "ghost" (37) that does not enter into the public domain, and yet the "phantom" is not who he appears to be. The official story maintains that Landy looked over the wrong shoulder and missed Bannister, "[a]s if Bannister was like some ghost, slipping past unseen" (37). But Mikey asserts that Landy knew Bannister was there and was looking for Richard Ferguson, the Canadian who came third, to see if he, Landy, could still make second place. "[T]he important missing character," Mikey says, was Ferguson, "the one who didn't make it into the statue" (38).

Thus, MacLeod, through Mikey's narration, challenges the "truth" of the historical narrative, the accepted public version of the race: he opens it up to a different possible interpretation. Referring to Herb Wylie's work, Andrea Cabajsky and Brett Josef Grubisic explain that Canadian historical novels have a "double-sidedness" (2010, xii), "a skepticism toward historical master narratives and simultaneous reluctance to dispose entirely of communally informed historical consciousness" (xiii–xiv). This is true of MacLeod's story as well, which challenges the publicly accepted version of the Bannister-Landy race and yet relies on it to create and propel the story of Mikey and Burner's race. As Georg Lukács argues, "what matters" in a historical narrative "is not the retelling of great historical events, but the poetic awakening of the people who figured in those events" (cited in Cabajsky and Grubisic 2010, vii). MacLeod's "Miracle Mile" is a "poetic awakening" for Bannister and Landy (since it offers an alternate interpretive possibility) and for Mikey and Burner (since it relies on the historical narrative to imagine the new one).

During the ultimate race in MacLeod's story, Mikey makes clear that he and Burner are acutely aware of each other. At the beginning of the race, he tells us, "I came up behind Burner and put my hand on his back, just kind of gently, so he'd know I was there" (MacLeod 2010, 34). And when, later in the race, Burner comes up behind him, Mikey feels "this hand reach out and touch the middle of my back [. . .] just a tap" (39). This mutual physical acknowledgement legitimizes and solidifies their presence for one another. However, Burner, as winner of the race, might be remembered, as Bannister is, whereas Mikey, like Ferguson in the Bannister-Landy narrative, is the "phantom" (37): he is out of the public picture. As Mikey anticipates earlier in the story, "I knew I wouldn't be close enough to be in the photograph when the first guy crossed the line" (15). Thus, MacLeod's story is self-reflexive, a metanarrative that examines the parts of stories that get told—"freezing into permanence" (41)—and those that do not. In such stories, writes Richard Lane, "the grand narratives of truth and reason are no longer believed in, or regarded, as universals, and are replaced by local expressions, little stories or narratives" (2011, 180). MacLeod juxtaposes those "little stories or narratives"—Ferguson in the Bannister-Landy race, Mikey in the Burner-Dawson one—in order to expose the mediation, chance, and constructedness of storytelling itself.

Yet the boundaries between the "grand narratives" and the "little stories" are not always easily defined. For example, on one interpretation, Burner, as the winner of the ultimate race in the story, enters into public discourse, whereas Mikey does not and falls into Burner's shadow, yet neither Burner nor Mikey really becomes legend, since, unlike Bannister and Landy, they are not the first runners to break the four-minute mile. On this interpretation, Mikey and Burner are the shadows of the former racers. The race that really matters—in terms of the public imagination—is the one at the Commonwealth Games in Vancouver in 1954. Therefore, what makes a sport story meaningful is not victory but the breaking of human barriers, in the time and at the place where those barriers matter.

In a 2013 interview, John Landy stated that at the time of the Vancouver race, "people really questioned whether a four-minute mile was humanly possible" (Commonwealth Games Federation 2013). While both Landy and Bannister had run a mile in under four minutes weeks before the Commonwealth Games, the Miracle Mile race in 1954 was significant, since it would be the first time after those runs that they would compete against each other. In MacLeod's "Miracle Mile," when Burner wins the race, Mikey says that "everyone [. . .] was trying to find a place for it in their own personal histories" (MacLeod 2010, 41). That statement is true not only for the Mikey-Burner race but also for the historical Bannister-Landy one. It signified breaking both the four-minute-mile barrier and, more generally, human boundaries of all kinds. In that way, the race came to signify nothing less than hope itself.

Mikey and Burner are the shadows of Landy and Bannister, and Mikey, as the narrator of "Miracle Mile," is Burner's "phantom" throughout the story. When the two of them are on the bus to the race, Mikey interprets Burner's erratic behaviour to one of the other athletes: "I said 'Nerves' as if that single word could explain everything about Burner" (24). Mikey is like the commentators broadcasting Tyson's violence, "explaining what was happening and what it all meant" (10). In both cases, MacLeod foregrounds the inability to narrate what cannot be completely understood—Tyson's violence and Burner's strange behaviour. Before they go to the race, Mikey names each racer, and after each one, Burner responds by describing "the guy's weaknesses"; with the speaking of each name, Burner defines himself as the winner against those who are not (15). Like Adam in the Garden of Eden, Mikey performs this ritual act of naming: "I just released the words into the air" (15). His "release" of words brings Burner and the other athletes into existence; similarly, for Mikey, Burner's "release" from the tunnel when they race the train brings Burner back to life. Likewise, Burner's "release" across the finish line at the final race of the story brings him into the public eye. Ultimately, Mikey is the narrator, Burner's "phantom," who creates and sustains Burner's character throughout the story. In this way, MacLeod conflates himself as author and Mikey as narrator of the text he writes.

The race itself is narrated by both Mikey and the sports announcer. While Mikey is the vehicle by which we come to know the story of the race, we hear the commentator's voice too, overriding the narrator's. In an uncanny moment, as Mikey listens to the commentator speak about him, he feels unfamiliar to himself: "Even as it was happening, the voice said, 'There goes Michael Campbell, moving into second place. [. . .]' It was like being inside and outside of yourself at the same time" (35). As he listens to the commentator speak about Burner, he again feels unfamiliar to himself—as if he and Burner are one and the same: "I heard the voice say something like 'Jamie Burns is safely tucked in at fifth or sixth place.' I remember this only because the announcer used Burner's real name and it sounded so strange to me" (35). In these instances, MacLeod suddenly foregrounds Mikey's role as character rather than narrator. One might say that Mikey has "lost control of the story" (40), since the "voice"—which parallels MacLeod himself— has taken control. Mikey's loss of control of the story finds its epitome at the end, when he has left both the sport of running and the ability or the willingness to continue to narrate Burner's fate. W. H. New explains that "postmodern techniques in the 1970s and 1980s emphasized the power of the storyteller to disrupt illusions of reality" and instead to "highlight the artifice of narrative" (2003, 347), a statement that easily applies to "Miracle Mile." In this instance, though, MacLeod highlights Mikey's receding voice. Mikey loses his narrative power to the commentator and author during the race, as the story moves into the public sphere and is no longer just his own. Indeed, in this scene, MacLeod foregrounds and undermines Mikey's role as narrator, simultaneously emphasizing both Mikey's authority to tell the story and the tenuousness of that authority.

Mikey does not seem to race *against* Burner but *for* him. When Mikey narrates Burner's win, he describes it as his own, as if he and Burner are one: "I knew I had never wanted anything more than this," Mikey tells us; "this little victory [. . .] mattered to me in some serious way" (40). Moreover, he describes his experience of watching Burner's win as a spiritual one: "I was caught up, caught up for the first and only time in my life, in one of those pure ecstatic surges that I believed only religious people ever experienced" (39–40). That experience, for Mikey, results in a kind of revelation, not about Burner but about himself. He states that his wish for Burner's win "told me something I had never known about myself before. We are what we want most and there are no miracles without desire" (40). The outcome of the race is a win for both Mikey and Burner, but in different ways. Burner wins by crossing the finish line first; in contrast, Mikey wins by experiencing an awakening to philosophical knowledge about possibilities. For the first time, he realizes that deep desire and caring can result in significant and unexpected outcomes, that "wishes" and "miracles" are connected, and that one can indeed lead to the other.

This moment situates "Miracle Mile" as metamodernist rather than postmodernist. Timotheus Vermeulen and Robin van den Akker define the metamodern as "constituted by the tension, no, the double-bind, of a modern desire for *sens* and a postmodern doubt about the sense of it all" (2010, 6), a tension that is manifest in the oscillation between "a modern enthusiasm and postmodern irony, between hope and melancholy, between naïveté and knowingness" (5–6). In MacLeod's story, Mikey's spiritual and intellectual experience is a turn toward the modernist desire for meaning and can be read as sincere. Nevertheless, his epiphany is tempered by the fact that his race does not hold meaning or have historical weight in the way that the Bannister-Landy race does—nor does it, to the same extent, enter into the realm of public or historical discourse. "Miracle Mile" thus vacillates between the achievement of meaning and purpose and the possibility that such meaning cannot be sustained: Mikey and Burner have missed the moment when the four-minute mile had meaning and purpose because they ran years too late.

Both Mikey's conflation with Burner and his spiritual experience at the moment of the race parallel his previous experience running with Burner in the train tunnel. Mikey runs the tunnel first, and when he finally sees Burner come through it, the train close behind him, he yells, "Come on, come on" and waves his "whole arm in a big circle, as if I could scoop out that space between us" (22). Mikey's attempt to reduce any space between him and Burner implies a oneness between them. The description of the tunnel as the underworld—a dark place in which there is "straight fear" and "rats" and from which one emerges "on the other side" (19)—also implies that Mikey and Burner could each be a part of the other. Within a Freudian framework, we might interpret Burner as Mikey's id, a part of Mikey himself, a "repressed impulse" that "can exert driving force without the ego noticing the compulsion" (Freud 1989, 634). Mikey is unaware of Burner until he emerges on the other side of the tunnel; in the same way, the ego, according to Freud, is unaware of the driving force of the id in one's own unconscious. The drive of the id is represented by the motivation and speed that is Burner as he runs through the tunnel. In addition, Freud's id is a base, animal-like instinct, and Burner himself is described as an animal: he "had this long line of spit hanging out of his mouth like a dog and the look on his face wasn't fear but something more like rage" (MacLeod 2010, 22). This description recalls Tyson's animal-like act of violence and anticipates the inconclusive end to the story, where the reader is invited to consider that Burner himself might commit such an act. Whereas Mikey is the shadow of Burner at the ultimate race, Burner is the shadow of Mikey—deep within the underworld or his unconscious—in the race against the train. Mikey and Burner vacillate, taking turns mirroring and upholding the identity of the other.

It is significant that Mikey has a spiritual experience in both of these moments—the final race of the story and the race against the train. He explains the dangers of racing the train: "The other thing they always talked about was the light. They said that if the light ever touched you, if that big glare of the freighter ever landed on you, then that would be the end" (20). Here, Mikey's explanation is literal—to view the train's headlight is to be crushed by the train—but it is also metaphorical: it suggests the witnessing of God or the spiritual at the moment of death while also signifying a moment of enlightenment or knowledge. Already waiting outside the tunnel, Mikey sees the light of the train as Burner emerges from it: "I saw the big round light and it touched me and filled up the whole space, illuminating everything" (21). At the race, Mikey comes to understand that a wish or deep desire can produce results; at the tunnel, he sees the light, an image of that understanding or illumination. In both cases, MacLeod describes the moment of epiphany as both intellectual and spiritual, a "miraculous desperation" (40).

MacLeod puns on the words "training" and "train" when he indicates that Mikey and Burner are "training" together when they begin to race the "train" (17). Likewise, he hints at the expression "light at the end of the tunnel" when Mikey narrates his witnessing of the "light." Indeed, that "light" refers both to Mikey's new intellectual or spiritual awakening and to Burner's "release" into first place at the final race. That MacLeod draws attention to the meanings of words and phrases here suggests that the "light" could also signal the spark of the imagination, the creation of meaning by the storyteller. This reading is supported by the ways in which the author foregrounds Mikey as the narrator of the story and posits "Miracle Mile" as a metanarrative. It also marks the story not only as metamodern, as discussed above, but also as historiographic metafiction—fiction that, according to Linda Hutcheon, brings together the historical and the literary and foregrounds both as "linguistic constructs, highly conventionalized in their narrative forms" (1988, 105). MacLeod's story addresses the historical through extensive references—to Mike Tyson, Bannister and Landy, the 9/11 attack, and the Canadian runner Ben Johnson (MacLeod 2010, 9). "Miracle Mile" also emphasizes the telling and retelling of those histories, and the "light" that is the act of creation itself.

Not only does the author draw attention to and blur the boundaries between meanings of words and phrases; he also blurs the boundaries between worlds or modes of being in the story. The boundary of the finish line is perhaps the most important example, and this boundary gains special significance for the person who crosses over it first, as Burner does in the final race of the story. As noted above, Burner's win at the race results in his entrance into the public realm. As Mikey puts it after Burner wins, "Other people, strangers I had never seen before, were coming around slapping him on the back and giving their congratulations" (41). Interestingly, though, Mikey and Burner's last run through the train tunnel has just the opposite result—a deliberate avoidance of the public eye, of what could be the so-called official story. "We knew they'd be making their calls and trying to track us down," Mikey tells us, referring to the train driver and engineers who had witnessed their race against the train, "so we spent the next half an hour running and hiding behind a few dumpsters and trying to make our way back to my car" (22). In contrast to Burner's public win in the ultimate race, Mikey and Burner's race through the train tunnel is to be hidden, kept unseen and unknown. It is the journey into the underworld, the id or the unconscious, and the coming through "on the other side" (19).

In addition to blurring the boundaries between Mikey and Burner, the public and the private, the ego and the id, MacLeod blurs the lines between the human and the so-called superhuman, the "regular guy" and the hero or villain. For instance, he uses hyperbole to describe the elite athletes on the bus: "The long jumpers could leap over a mid-sized station wagon and the shot putters could bench press it" (26). Alongside such descriptions, however, Mikey notes the athletes' vulnerable, human-like qualities, pointing out that "some of those hundred metre guys are built up like superheroes [. . .], but when the race gets close, every one of them is scared" (23). Similarly, he discusses the athletes who "cross over" (29) such boundaries, using drugs to test the extent to which they can push the limits of what is humanly possible. Mikey and Burner get "giant horse pills" (29) from a vet who works on race horses, and Mikey gets six cortisone injections in five months, despite knowing that "you're only supposed to take three of those in your whole life" (30). The reference to Mike Tyson, as discussed earlier, epitomizes this notion: he has "crossed over" into an act—the biting off of an opponent's ear—that evokes the villainous, the inhuman, the incomprehensible. In a particularly gothic image, Mikey describes what athletes call "'rigging,' short for rigor mortis," the process at the point of exhaustion by which the muscles in the body constrict one by one, "dying right underneath you" (37). MacLeod explores the idea that humans can break barriers and overcome setbacks of any kind, inspiring hope, yet he simultaneously emphasizes the dark side of that equation. To "cross over" might be to become not human but animal, not hero but villain. Hope and inspiration, the author suggests, can be overridden by the ugly and the horrific.

Although Mikey strives to be superhuman, he is also consistently reminded that he is not, since he suffers from a recurring injury to his Achilles tendon. Like Achilles himself, a warrior in Homer's *Iliad*, he is courageous and loyal, yet he suffers from one weakness, his Achilles heel, which makes him human and separates him from the gods. The attributes that make the characters human in both *The Iliad* and "Miracle Mile" invoke the reader's understanding and sympathy. MacLeod thus questions the extent to which it is desirable to exceed human boundaries. Should we attempt to be god-like by pushing the boundaries of what is humanly impossible? Or does the breaking of such boundaries, the desire to be "flawless," hover dangerously near the inhuman, oppressive, and violent? "Miracle Mile" seems to offer both possibilities. In addition, MacLeod situates his own character within literary history by aligning him with Homer's. Thus, through his narrator, the author enables a "poetic awakening" (Lukács again) of history in the realms of both sport and literature: in sport, Mikey's race is the shadow of the Bannister-Landy race, and in literature, Mikey is the shadow of Homer's Achilles. Once again, Mac-Leod intertwines history and fiction and emphasizes Mikey and his story as literary artifice.

MacLeod also extends the blurring of boundaries to include space and time. The tunnel through which Mikey and Burner run, for instance, spans the distance from Detroit, Michigan, to Windsor, Ontario, and therefore crosses the border between the United States and Canada. Similarly, after Mikey and Burner finish their race, they run to cool down in a suburban neighbourhood, crossing the boundary from one kind of geographical space (the public race) to another (the private, domestic space)—"past all those houses where nobody cared" (42).

Just as national and geographical boundaries are crossed in the story, so too are boundaries of time. The story and its references, for instance, cover a wide span of time, from Homer's *Iliad*, probably composed during the eighth century BC, to the Bannister-Landy race at the Commonwealth Games in 1954, to June 1997, when Tyson bit Holyfield's ear and the fictional characters of Mikey and Burner ran their race on 28 June 1997. Mikey and Burner simultaneously wait, filling in a seemingly endless amount of time, and speed, racing against their own times and the times of others. Mikey notes that his and Burner's lives "kept rolling along, filling in all this extra time" (22), yet when they are racing, there is real significance in just a few seconds, "the difference between 3:36 and 3:39" (16). Furthermore, the narrator not only oscillates between waiting and speeding, slow time and fast, but also captures the past and the future in a single image. Mikey imagines a future in which he has a kid who enters school track meets, painting a rosy and nostalgic picture of the scene that seems to be both a remembrance of his own past and a projection into the future (27–28). Finally, he conflates not only the past and the future but also, with his use of second-person narration in this scene, himself and his readers. "*You*," as a school-aged child, are "holding all your first-place ribbons in the middle of a weedy field" (28, emphasis mine). The narrator juxtaposes the "ribbons," a symbol of hope and happiness, with the "weeds," a representation of the ugliness of life. In "Miracle Mile," then, MacLeod brilliantly collapses space and time in images that obscure the distinction between the past and the future, the moment the story is written and the moment it is read, the good times and the bad, hope and despair, happiness and ruin.

MacLeod's story thus suggests that private experiences relate in significant ways to public events and histories, that individuals in the present gesture back to those in the past. In order to make meaning, the story implies, we continually forge such connections, assessing and evaluating how moments in our lives relate to those that have already entered the public realm, "freezing into permanence" (41). Athletes consistently attempt to measure up against the last race or the top record holder, yet "Miracle Mile" suggests that this act is not limited to the athlete but is common to all who engage in acts of creation. Therefore, Mikey celebrates Burner's "release" (15) into first place because he is not only his competitor but also his creator, "illuminating" (21) his character as he pushes Burner into public discourse, which is the story itself. In this way, "Miracle Mile" is aligned with and draws upon other stories, both literary and historical: from Homer's *Iliad*, to the story of Mike Tyson, to Landy and Bannister's Miracle Mile. MacLeod's story tests its literary identity in the same way that Mikey and Burner test their identities against one another and, relatedly, against their own fragmented, inner selves.

"Miracle Mile" adheres to the tendency in Canadian literature to contemplate the present in relation to the past. In *Canadian Literature and Cultural Memory*, Cynthia Sugars and Eleanor Ty argue that memory is the impetus of contemporary Canadian literature: "Articulations of a retrievable or 'forgotten' authentic memory, often linked to ideas of national commemoration, have in more recent years been supplemented by critical attention to instances of counter-memory or 'memory from below,' which considers communities that have been omitted from official discourses of historical commemoration" (Sugars and Ty 2014, 4). Certainly, MacLeod's story presents "memory from below," at once tying the present to a known and unknown past: the author interrogates the validity of athletic heroism (with reference to Ben Johnson and others), and he questions the intertwining of violence and sport (with reference to Tyson's act of violence during a boxing match). Moreover, he presents an alternate interpretation of the Landy-Bannister story by introducing a "phantom" (MacLeod 2010, 37)—that "counter-memory" or version that lurks in the shadows, just about to take form and substance. The way in which "Miracle Mile" intertwines the present with the past implies that memory is the substance of identity. While the story momentarily engages in nostalgia, it ultimately posits athletic identities as "imbued with simultaneous resonance and ambivalence" (Sugars and Ty 2014, 9). The telling of sport histories are nonetheless reiterations of stories. And perhaps they end, as Mikey's and Burner's identities do and "Miracle Mile" itself does, with a closing of "the gap" and a disintegration (MacLeod 2010, 44). Ultimately, then, MacLeod's "Miracle Mile" upsets and complicates our common and easy perceptions and understandings of sports, memories, stories, and identities.

Cabajsky, Andrea, and Brett Josef Grubisic. 2010. "Introduction." In *National Plots: Historical Fiction and Changing Ideas of Canada*, edited by Andrea Cabajsky and Brett Josef Grubisic, vii–xxiv. Waterloo, ON: Wilfrid Laurier University Press.

Commonwealth Games Federation. 2013. *Ten Commonwealth Games Moments: The Miracle Mile*. YouTube video. https://www.youtube.com/watch?v=P7dROEOn_20.

Freud, Sigmund. 1955. "The Uncanny." In *The Standard Edition of the Complete Psychological Works of Sigmund Freud, Volume XVII (1917–1919): An Infantile Neurosis and Other Works*, edited and translated by James Strachey and Anna Freud, 217–56. London: Hogarth Press and the Institute of Psycho-analysis. First published 1919.

———. 1989. "The Ego and the Id." In *The Freud Reader*, edited by Peter Gay, 626–58. New York: W. W. Norton.

Homer. 2007. *The Iliad*. Translated by W. H. D. Rouse. With an introduction by Seth L. Schein. New York: Signet Classics.

Hutcheon, Linda. 1988. *A Poetics of Postmodernism: History, Theory, Fiction*. London and New York: Routledge.

Lane, Richard. 2011. *The Routledge Concise History of Canadian Literature*. London and New York: Routledge.

MacLeod, Alexander. 2010. *Light Lifting*. Windsor, ON: Biblioasis.

New, W. H. 2003. *A History of Canadian Literature*. 2nd ed. Montréal and Kingston: McGill-Queen's University Press.

Sugars, Cynthia, and Eleanor Ty. 2014. "Introduction." In *Canadian Literature and Cultural Memory*, edited by Cynthia Sugars and Eleanor Ty, 1–19. Oxford: Oxford University Press.

Vermeulen, Timotheus, and Robin van den Akker. 2010. "Notes on Metamodernism." *Journal of Aesthetics and Culture* 2. doi: 10.3402/jac.v2i0.5677.

11

Sam McKegney and Trevor J. Phillips

Decolonizing the Hockey Novel
Ambivalence and Apotheosis in Richard Wagamese's *Indian Horse*

"White ice, white players," I said. "You gonna tell me that isn't the case everywhere? That they don't think it's their game wherever a guy goes?"

He took his time answering. "It's not a perfect country," he said. "But it is a perfect game."

Richard Wagamese, *Indian Horse* (149–50)

Through the story of Saul Indian Horse, an Ojibway hockey prodigy who learns the game in residential school and whose potential rise to hockey stardom is hindered by traumatic legacies of personal abuse and the entrenched racism of Canadian hockey culture, Ojibway novelist Richard Wagamese lays bare, in his 2012 novel *Indian Horse*, heinous transgressions conducted in the name of Canadian nationhood. Yet part of what has made the novel such a commercial success in Canada is its fluency with and seamless incorporation of popular cultural tropes about the game—tropes that tend to glorify white settler citizenship, thereby normalizing senses of territorial belonging for white players, fans, and coaches while clouding the history of dispossession of Indigenous lands and the dehumanization of Indigenous peoples through which the Canadian nation state has been forged.

In this essay, we seek to understand and unpack the ambivalence of Wagamese's portrayal of hockey as both confining and liberating, as both a tool of Canadian nationalism and a means of Indigenous self-expression and resilience. Despite awareness expressed in the novel that hockey has functioned as a tool of settler colonialism in Canada and that it continues to be implicated in nationalist mythologies that normalize white privilege while effacing colonial transgressions, *Indian Horse* conveys such an abiding affection for hockey's beauty, grace, and artistry that it seems open to the claim articulated in the epigraph above: "But it is a perfect game." Ultimately, we argue that *Indian Horse* does not tear down popular conceptions of hockey in Canada and offer some radically decolonial alternative in its stead; rather, in order to depict the healing journey at the novel's core, it tears those representations open in order to expose the traumatic colonial foundations upon which hockey narratives are frequently built and which they often work to conceal.

And herein lies the novel's decolonial potential: written during the Truth and Reconciliation Commission's exploration into the legacy of Indian residential schools, *Indian Horse* adopts the form of both a retrospective retirement narrative, so common to sport literature, and a residential school survivor's testimony. In the retirement narrative form, much of the story's overarching pathos emerges from the reader's recognition that, although he is still a relatively young person at age thirty-three, Saul, the narrator, considers his best self forever confined to the past; the narrative arc conscripts remembrance of past glory and past failure in a struggle to grieve the loss of the elite athletic self and to reconcile with an altered life stage in search of a renewed sense of purpose. In the testimony form, residential school survivors share personal truths about their experiences in order to embolden the public record and disseminate greater knowledge that might form a foundation of understanding upon which various forms of reconciliation—with oneself, one's family, one's community, perhaps even one's oppressors—might become possible. Wagamese weaves these narrative postures together meticulously to speak in a semiotic register that resonates with urgent Indigenous concerns and that is simultaneously capable of leveraging hockey's popular cultural caché to illuminate ongoing colonial oppression in Canada. In this way, Wagamese's novel targets both Indigenous and settler audiences, opening up sovereign spaces for Indigenous reflection while struggling to change the nation by changing how Canadians understand "their" game. Thus, although *Indian Horse* is defiantly not a decolonial novel, we argue in what follows that it performs significant decolonial work by imagining an indigenized apotheosis of hockey that might foster individual healing by elaborating an ethic of community; rather than locating the wounded Indigenous player as the primary site for pursuing positive change, *Indian Horse* concludes with an awareness of the vitality of Indigenous communities as the foundation upon which such individual healing is contingent. The game that readers experience at the novel's conclusion is thus an indigenized form of hockey that reaffirms the game's collaborative energies in the cause of Indigenous communal empowerment.[1]

INDIGENOUS AMBIVALENCE AND SETTLER BELONGING THROUGH HOCKEY

As the Calgary poet Richard Harrison has argued, hockey is a vehicle through which Canadians "make meaning out of winter" and thereby establish a sense of belonging in the northern landscape (personal communication). Popular discourse celebrating hockey as "Canada's game" naturalizes the Canadian nation state while valorizing those who participate in it (players, coaches, and spectators) as authentic inhabitants of the "True North" from which the game has supposedly sprung. According to Michael Buma, the central pillars of what he calls "the Canadian hockey myth" are the resilient beliefs (1) that hockey arises naturally from the Canadian landscape, (2) that the game fosters social cohesion and civic virtue, and (3) that the game ultimately offers a synecdoche for Canadian culture (2012, 37). In this way, hockey has functioned as a vehicle for what

---

1 As settler scholar Patrick Wolfe argues, "invasion is a structure not an event" (2006, 388) because in settler colonial contexts, the colonizers have not left, they often outnumber the Indigenous inhabitants they have displaced, and they continually work to naturalize and re-entrench logics and institutions that reify the legitimacy of their sense of belonging. We consider "decolonization" an expansive collection of activist practices and ideas that works to destabilize the authority of that structure, mute the expressions of its power, and open up possibilities for alternative ways of being in the world that emerge from Indigenous world views. Because hockey literature tends to obfuscate the horrific realities of settler colonial history and to reify the Canadian nation state, we write from the position that hockey literature is most often a colonial genre.

literary critic Terry Goldie terms "indigenization," a process through which settlers confront "the impossible necessity of becoming indigenous" (1989, 13): responding to the psychological compulsion to legitimize entitlement *to* the land, settlers seek to manufacture senses of belonging *in* the land. As hockey becomes reified as a natural by-product of the Canadian landscape, purveyors of the game promote senses of "Native Canadian" identity among those who play it, in the process erasing—or denying—differential senses of belonging among First Nations, Inuit, and Métis people who may or may not self-identify as "Canadian." Saul's narrative in *Indian Horse* exposes the incongruously exclusionary nature of this process of claiming territory through sport: "The white people thought it was their game. They thought it was their world" (Wagamese 2012, 136).

Ironically, the semiotic capital of indigeneity is often retained in this process of national legitimation via the circulation of language and images that conjure a stereotyped Indigenous-warrior past in team logos, mascots, and names—Warriors, Blackhawks, Braves, Redmen—while ignoring the political persistence of Indigenous nations. It is unsurprising that the first non-Indigenous team against which Saul's Manitouwadge Moose play is the "Chiefs." Goldie frames this form of semiotic accumulation as "indigenization by inclusion for the white who, one might say, 'acquires Indian.' Note that my word is 'acquires,' not 'becomes.' . . . The indigene is acquired, the white is not abandoned" (215). In this way, the characteristics associated with (imagined) Indigenous hypermasculinity are absorbed within an almost exclusively white settler arena, thereby advancing the colonial imperative that the future belongs to white settler Canadians and living Indigenous people remain anachronistic. Thus, the imagined relationship between hockey and landscape in Canada has tended to foster a sense of "authentic" belonging for settler and other non-Indigenous Canadians while obfuscating the relationships to land that continue to obtain for Indigenous individuals, communities, and nations. It is hardly surprising, then, that *Hockey Night in Canada* was a cornerstone of nationalist programming on radio and then television for the Canadian Broadcasting Corporation for more than eighty years: the program, now under licence by other networks, continues to enable settler populations—including those who have never set a booted blade upon a frozen pond or lake anywhere in lands claimed by Canada—to collectively envision and indeed participate in the "imagined community" of the Canadian nation.[2]

Complicating matters further, hockey was mobilized historically in residential schools as a tool of colonial social engineering designed to encourage Indigenous youth to shed connections with Indigenous cultural values and self-identify as Canadian citizens. Several historical studies have documented (generally male) students playing hockey at residential schools (Milloy 1999, Miller 1996, Johnston 1988, etc.), activities permitted according to the belief that sport fosters civic virtue. As such, the sport is also laden with the historical weight of its use within systemic structures designed to "kill the Indian, and save the man." In *Indian Horse*, upon arrival at the residential school, Saul is told, "At St. Jerome's we work to remove the Indian from our children so that the blessings of the Lord may be evidenced upon them." Father Quinney continues: "Industry, boys. [. . .] Good, honest work and earnest study. That's what you'll do here. That's what will prepare you for the world" (Wagamese 2012, 47). Hockey and other recreational activities become what Michael Robidoux calls "disciplining device[s]" (2012, 13) within the residential school's pedagogical arsenal designed to inculcate Eurocentric notions of "industry" among the students.

However, despite the game's deployment to enforce prescriptive identity formations in young players like Saul, the experiences of Indigenous residential school students playing the game did not always—nor perhaps even regularly—align with the motivations of institutional overseers. At the celebrations for the delivery of the Truth and Reconciliation Commission's *Final Report*, chairperson Chief Wilton Littlechild, of the Maskwacîs Cree Nation, explained how playing hockey was imperative to his ability to endure the trauma of his residential school years, an experience corroborated by scores of survivors throughout the TRC's statement gathering process. The summary of the TRC's final report states that sport "helped them [students] make it through residential school" (TRCC 2015b, 112), and the final report itself says that "the opportunity to play sports at residential schools made their lives more bearable and gave them a sense of identity, accomplishment, and pride" (TRCC 2015a, 199). Evan Habkirk

---

2 Tellingly, Saul describes *Hockey Night in Canada* as "the personification of magic" (Wagamese 2012, 59) when he encounters it in Father Leboutilier's quarters at the residential school. Here, we rely on Benedict Anderson's theorization of imagined communities (2006).

and Janice Forsyth (2016) write that although these statements are "certainly true," they worry that this

> glosses over the distinct and diverse ways to understand the role and significance of physical activities in these schools. We wonder, for instance, to what extent did school officials, including instructors, missionaries, and government agents, use physical activities to exploit the students for social, political, and economic gain? And how did the students transform the meanings that were attached to these activities to "make it through" these highly oppressive environments, especially since many of the activities were intended to eradicate and replace traditional Aboriginal values and practices?

THE FALSE PROMISE OF INCLUSION

Wagamese's novel takes as its thematic core the tensions between hockey as a means of achieving momentary emancipation from the carceral space of the residential school and hockey as an activity laden with racist, sexist, and anthropocentric ideological baggage that has served to mask and make possible the abuse of Indigenous youth. Wagamese thus lays bare two significant contradictions that conspire to marginalize Indigenous peoples in Canada: the first pertains to the insidious false promise of assimilation through residential school social engineering, and the second involves the pervasive lie (so often treated as truth within Canadian hockey literature) that hockey is inevitably a vehicle for intercultural inclusion and social harmony. We explore each of these contradictions below.

In 1887, Prime Minister John A. Macdonald explained the motivations behind the Indian Act: "The great aim of our legislation has been to do away with the tribal system and assimilate the Indian people in all respects with the inhabitants of the Dominion as speedily as they are fit for the change" (quoted in Ennamorato 1998, 72). Minister of Indian Affairs Duncan Campbell Scott famously related this assimilative objective to residential school policy, arguing, "I want to get rid of the Indian problem. . . . Our objective is to continue until there is not a single Indian in Canada that has not been absorbed into the body politic, and there is no Indian question, and no Indian Department" (quoted in Milloy 1999, 46). Beyond signalling the culturally genocidal motivations behind both the Indian Act and residential schooling, these quotations express strategic goals of absorption and inclusion that residential schools were fundamentally incapable of facilitating because of structural limitations and widespread racism within the broader cultural milieu.

While official rhetoric suggested that residential schooling would place Indigenous students on par with their mainstream Canadian counterparts in order to foster equality, the education they received was so far below that received by mainstream Canadian students as to engender profound disadvantages (even apart from the debilitating traumatic cultural loss, separation from loved ones, and rampant abuse). Most residential school students received formal education for only a fraction of their school day, with the rest taken up by prayer and the manual labour upon which the institutions relied, and the instruction they did receive was commonly delivered by religious staff with no formal pedagogical training. Furthermore, Indigenous students tended to be taught outmoded skills related to domestic work, manual trades, and farming, while most other students across the country experienced a breadth of instruction designed to prepare them for entry into an industrialized Canadian economy (see Milloy 1999, 157-80). When they finally emerged from residential school, Indigenous students needed to compete for jobs within a labour market characterized by racist hiring practices of employers whose views about Indigenous people were influenced by the very cultural biases that undergirded residential school policies in the first place. Thus, the supposed goal of integration and assimilation through social engineering was disingenuous from the very beginning.

In fact, at the same time that the residential school system was expanding to its peak in the 1940s and 50s, Indian Affairs was embarking on a policy of "centralization" on the East Coast designed to relocate Mi'kmaq people from sundry communities and small reserves to two large reserves at Eskasoni and Shubenacadie as a means of ensuring the *absence* of Indigenous peoples within or around white communities in Nova Scotia. Clearly the goals of assimilation and absorption articulated by Macdonald and Scott ran counter to the segregationist thrust of centralization. Such are the contradictions within the federal government's treatment of Indigenous peoples over time. As one of us has written elsewhere,

> Residential school policy has always been . . . perplexed with its 'cultural progressivist' agenda dogged by endemic racism; never

has the political goal of assimilating the Native population, and thereby abolishing their distinct rights, truly contained the social corollary of ignoring ethnic difference and abandoning white perceptions regarding the inferiority of Native blood, nor has it striven to ease the divide between white economic superiority and Indigenous poverty. (McKegney 2017, 115)

This is why policies and practices purportedly designed to engender equality have consistently entrenched difference and exacerbated marginalization.

Indian Horse demonstrates how the contradictions embedded within public discourse on residential schooling are mirrored by those relating to the social function of hockey in Canadian culture. As mentioned above, hockey is often conceived as a vehicle for manufacturing settler belonging, and Indigenous iconography is often marshalled as inclusive of "indigenization" (Goldie 1989, 13).[3] While Indigenous-inspired images may adorn the fronts of jerseys and teams may adopt Indigenous-themed names, the game's "proper" player in the popular imaginary remains fundamentally a white settler Canadian. Indigenous iconography in hockey culture therefore constitutes what Anishinaabe writer Gerald Vizenor calls an "inscribed absence" (2009, 3) that stands in for and serves to replace the lived realities of Indigenous peoples; Indigenous emblems are desired, while Indigenous people are not. This is why the landscape of frozen lakes and rivers that is conceptualized as the "True North" and replicated in NHL advertising and beer commercials is one that tends to be portrayed as devoid of Indigenous presence. The irony here, of course, is that while hockey is imagined as a force of social cohesion that works to "indigenize" the nation, Indigenous peoples are either ignored or actively excluded from full participation in the game.

Wagamese's novel depicts just how anxiously the limits on Indigenous inclusion in Canadian hockey culture have historically been policed. Despite the fact that Saul is repeatedly shown to be the best player in each level at which he plays, he is actively—and often violently—discouraged from feeling as though he fully belongs by white coaches, players, fans, and the media. In one notable example, Saul arrives at the rink to play with the non-Indigenous competitive midget team for which he has scored

3 Note, however, that in Goldie's use of "indigenization," indigeneity is trapped within the semiotic, as images of indigeneity are mobilized by settlers in the absence of Indigenous people.

a scorching fourteen points in ten games as a thirteen-year-old underager. There, he finds he has been cut from the team because "[t]he parents of other players want their own kids to play." Seeking clarification, Saul asks, "It's because I'm Indian, isn't it?" which Father Leboutilier confirms, before adding, "They think it's their game" (Wagamese 2012, 91–92). Although Saul had been brought onto the roster to help the team win, such inclusion is tenuous and proves contingent on his not disturbing the game's—not to mention the team's—naturalized culture of white entitlement. Even though Saul proves an asset on the scoresheet, his presence troubles the untouchable "rights" of his white teammates to the ice, and he is cut unceremoniously.

White entitlement is enforced even more vehemently when the all-Indigenous Manitouwadge Moose squad enters the non-Indigenous hockey circuit and begins defeating white teams. Unable to simply eliminate the team (as the midget squad had axed Saul), fans engage in acts of performative disavowal designed to mark the bodies of the Indigenous players as other, as out of place, as ultimately disposable: they pelt the Moose players with garbage, slash the tires of their van, and urinate and defecate in their dressing room. When the Moose win an otherwise all-white tournament, anxieties about white ownership of the game are heightened and such performative disavowal takes a violent turn. Stopping at a small-town café en route home from the tournament, the Moose team is confronted by a mob of "working men, big and strong-looking with stern faces," one of whom declares: "You boys got kinda big for the britches. [. . .] [Y]ou win a little hockey tournament and then you think you got the right to come in here and eat like white people" (133). Framing the conversation in a juridical vernacular of "rights" that delineates insider and outsider status, the man elaborates racialized distinctions between those who belong—"white people"—and those whose access to the space is provisional and contingent. Because the men's belief in white superiority has been challenged by the Moose team's tournament victory, the men prove sadistically eager to reinscribe a colonial hierarchy of white entitlement and Indigenous inferiority onto the bodies of the Moose players, taking each member of the team, with the exception of Saul, out back of the café, where they beat them mercilessly before showering them with spit and urine. The beatings mark the men with signifiers of supposed racialized inferiority, with spit and urine signalling their dehumanization. The use of bodily excretions to shame the players seems tactically concocted to register their disposability in the service of colonial erasure. Whereas the white men present themselves as entitled to eat at the restaurant, and thereby to be nourished and endure as a community, the Indigenous players are performatively associated with detritus to signal their symbolic elimination in the service of white progress. The Indigenous players become associated with the casualties of modernity as the white future is heralded and the Indians vanish.

Like residential school technologies of discipline, the violence here constitutes a form of social engineering designed to remind the Indigenous men of their "place." And the brutality of the lesson proves chillingly effective. On the long van ride back to Manitouwadge, one of the victims explains the incident to Saul, stating, "We crossed a line. Their line. They figure they got the right to make us pay for that." When Saul inquires, "Do they?" his teammate responds: "Sometimes I think so" (136). The effects of this incident and ones like it cast a protracted shadow over the novel. Saul notes that, although they never speak about it, "there were moments when you'd catch another boy's eye and know that you were both thinking about it. Everything was contained in that glance. All the hurt. All the shame. All the rage. The white people thought it was their game. They thought it was their world" (136).

Returning to a cadence found throughout the novel—that white Canadians think it is "their game"—Wagamese again demonstrates how the belief that hockey is a space of white authority, power, and privilege comes to be leveraged in the often violent naturalization of white entitlement in Canada and thereby in the reification of settler colonialism as an unquestioned norm. Wagamese's novel thus forces both Indigenous and settler readers to ask certain questions: Is it indeed "their/our game"? Does hockey belong only to white Canadians? And if not, how might exposure of these claims' falsity be mobilized to trouble the colonial corollary that it is "their world"?[4] In the final section of this essay, we interrogate the

---

4 To reiterate, the ideological collapse between the game itself and the northern territory from which it is imagined "naturally" to have sprung enables white settler participants to marshal hockey in the (re)production of beliefs that *they belong* in the land they and their ancestors have colonized and that both the land and the game, in turn, *belong to them*—a self-perpetuating dynamic that undergirds Saul's repeated lament that white players "think it's their game" (31). *Indian Horse* is actively engaged with the destabilization of these persistent beliefs while making use of the very representational inheritance through which they have historically been reified.

resilient affection for the game that is evident in *Indian Horse* and Wagamese's use of apotheosis to examine hockey's capacity to participate in the individual and collective transformations necessary to pursue a more just and balanced world.

FROM AMBIVALENCE TO APOTHEOSIS: INDIVIDUAL ACHIEVEMENT AND COMMUNAL RESURGENCE

By the end of the novel, it seems as though Saul's unshakable faith in hockey as something sacred and incorruptible is criminally naïve. For many readers, the novel's eventual disclosure that Father Leboutilier had used his power as a coach—along with the secret practices, the private hockey-viewing sessions in the priest's quarters, and Saul's vulnerability as an orphaned residential school student desperate for affection—to exploit and sexually abuse the young protagonist would inspire rejection of any romantic vestiges the game might retain. Curiously though, it does not. Rather than turning away from hockey completely while facing the return of his repressed past in the contemporary time frame of the novel's final section, Saul concedes that hockey was and perhaps still is his salvation: "As long as I could escape into it, I could fly away. Fly away and never have to land on the scorched earth of my boyhood" (199). The declaration sounds remarkably similar to those quoted by Halkirk and Forsyth from the TRC's *Final Report* (2015). Hockey, in Saul's opinion, in spite of itself, retains its ability to lift a man up, an apotheosis rather than a metamorphosis. Whether or not hockey has "an alchemy that transforms ordinary men into great ones" (57), as Saul gushes earlier in the novel, the game continues to present definitive opportunities for individual acts of athletic brilliance that are transformative—even at this late point in the novel; the novel expresses skepticism, however, about whether such individual transformations work in the service of decolonization. Saul had come the closest to his own apotheosis earlier in the novel during his otherworldly performance at the Espanola tournament, during which he seemed to rise above both his teammates and opponents, yet even this transformation had proven incapable of fostering the genuine healing towards which the novel is directed and which ultimately led Saul to the New Dawn Centre, where he began to craft his life narrative.

If hockey is a symbolic playing out of white Canadianness, then the Espanola tournament acts as a collision point between white entitlement and Indigenous embodied sovereignty. The Moose is the first Indigenous team to participate in the tournament, where all the teams have "a pedigree" and "only the best teams got invited" (137). White teams from cities like North Bay and Owen Sound attempt to subdue Saul's dazzling skill and speed with physicality, racist verbal assaults, and irritating stick infractions designed to goad him into fighting or taking retaliatory penalties. This style of play bends the rules of gentlemanly decorum and white civility that pervade white Canada's self-perception as performed through the national winter sport. Saul sits neatly astride both the white teams' hostility and his teammates' insistence that he retaliate. Instead of taking the bait and throwing punches, he "stepped out onto the ice and reclaimed the game" (144) with speed, skill, and imagination.

The connection to the game that Saul displays in Espanola transcends time and space, representing the consummation of the clairvoyance he experienced upon being introduced to the game as a young child—an innate sense of the pace and rhythm of hockey that was passed on to him from his ancestors. Saul tells the story of his family:

> There are teachers among our people who could determine where a particular moose was, a bear, the exact time the fish would make their spawning runs. My great-grandfather Shabogeesick, the original Indian Horse, had that gift. The world spoke to him. It told him where to look. Shabogeesick's gift had been passed on to me. There's no other explanation for how I was able to see this foreign game so completely right away. (58)

Saul's invocation of the term "foreign" here is telling, since it registers both a rejection of residential schooling's assimilative objective of domesticating Indigenous youth within the Canadian nation state *and* an autonomous intervention in Canadian hockey literature by an Anishinaabe world view in which intergenerational knowledge-sharing and land-based foresight regarding the world's rhythms are not only possible but necessary to survival.

For Saul, hockey is a sensory experience—one involving foresight and anticipation in a predatory way, like hunting, but also one attuned harmoniously to the natural spiritual energies of the earth and nature. In this way, Saul seems to be divining his mythical and spiritual aptitude for the game from his heritage, which is antithetical to the typical codifications of the game as inherently settler Canadian. Yet, in doing so, Saul relies upon one of the dominant representations of the Canadian hockey novel: that the game arises naturally from the Canadian landscape and is therefore attuned to the Canadian environment (only in this case, the landscape need not be coded "Canadian" but could as readily be framed "Anishinaabe" or, more generally, "Indigenous"). Nonetheless, the tournament in Espanola becomes a turning point in the novel, as Saul's initial experience of love for the game, a love that facilitated transcendence, is attacked relentlessly by settler opponents and fans. Their affronts to Saul's spiritual connection, their repeated assaults to his body, and their dehumanizing racist chants are epistemological strikes to Saul's spirit and style. In literary terms, hockey played Saul's way is an act of what Anishinaabe intellectual Gerald Vizenor calls "survivance" or the expression of ongoing, creative, evolutionary/revolutionary Indigenous culture through imagination in prose, plays, and poetry: "Natives, by communal stories, memory, and potentiality create a sense of presence not an inscribed absence" (2009, 3). Saul reaches to the spiritual and practical modes of being of his forbears, but rather than ossifying that knowledge as a fixed, romanticized set of stereotypes—like the "inscribed absence" implied by settler imaginings of an Indigenous hypermasculine past on team logos and in team names—he expresses it anew through what 'Ōiwi scholar Ty Tengan might call "embodied discursive action" within the "foreign" arena of elite hockey (2008, 17).[5]

The irony of Saul's success in Espanola is that he earns an invitation to try out with a major junior team out of Toronto, for which he eventually plays. Wagamese's novel exposes ambivalences within the Canadian culture of the game in which, despite the continual reification and policing of settler entitlement, admiration for exceptional skill occasionally intervenes in the game's general exclusivity. For example, after receiving first star in the Espanola tournament's final game, Saul expected "boos to rain down" during his "turn around centre ice," but instead he was surrounded by "applause and stamping feet [. . .] like thunder rolling around the arena" (Wagamese 2012, 128); in addition, as noted above, Saul was the only

---

5 In *Native Men Remade*, Tengan describes the "embodied discursive practice," in which Indigenous "men come to perform and know themselves and their bodies in a new way" (2008, 151). Referring to rituals enacted at an event in Pu'ukoholā, Hawai'i, in 1991, Tengan explains that "bodily experience, action, and movement played a fundamental role in the creation of new subjectivities of culture and gender" (87).

player not to be assaulted in the diner after the Espanola victory. Nonetheless, upon his arrival in Toronto, now alone and in the big city, Saul feels the resistance to his presence manifest ever more vociferously. Facing the reality of ongoing Indigenous persistence, white media and audiences prove fanatically invested in returning the living body of Saul Indian Horse to the falsified myths of a colonial past: "The press would not let me be. [. . .] When I made a dash down the ice and brought the crowd to their feet, I was on a raid. If I inadvertently high-sticked someone during a tussle in the corner, I was taking scalps. When I did not react to getting a penalty, I was the stoic Indian" (163). The reinscription of Saul's hockey actions with stereotypically "Indian" representations is a dual act of erasure—first of Saul's skills, which are above and beyond those of the average player, and then again of Indigenous presence in the Canadian game. What's more, Saul is demoralized by the representations, conceding, "I wanted to rise to new heights, be one of the glittering few. But they wouldn't let me be just a hockey player. I always had to be the Indian" (164).

The individualist myth of apotheosis through hockey, which Saul had learned about "from those books" back at residential school (56), is proven time and again to be inadequate or incomplete for an Indigenous player like Saul. Although he does receive accolades for his transcendent performances on the ice, the dominant, nationalistic culture in which those performances occur actively prevents Saul's internalization of a sense of belonging, of purpose, and of valued personhood. In other words, while Saul's hockey skill allows him to be elevated beyond the quotidian crowd of the average player, the persistent racism of the game's dominant culture ensures that such elevation for the individual Indigenous player does not translate into a resilient apotheosis characterized by healing. Early in the novel, Wagamese prepares readers expertly for this Catch-22 by following Saul's discovery that hockey had "an alchemy that could transform ordinary men into great ones" with the resonant sentence fragment, "The white glory of the rink" (57). So long as the hockey rink's "glory" remains forcibly bound to a culture of "white" entitlement steeped in individualism and hypermasculinity—as the "ordinary men" and "great ones" would suggest—the potential for the game to participate in genuine decolonial change remains hampered. Under such circumstances, Saul's defection from the Toronto Marlboros and his subsequent spiral into alcoholism constitutes a rational response to the corrosive effects of Canadian hockey culture. Saul's singularity as a player emerges from the visionary skill set inherited from his Anishinaabe ancestors, enlivened and enacted in the contemporary moment. Yet Saul's living and evolving cultural knowledge is continually denied and overwritten by settler stereotypes of bygone and backward indigeneity; his unique gifts are obscured within a racialized, nationalistic discourse that works not only to disempower Saul but to further dispossess the Anishinaabe nation and Indigenous peoples more generally. To confront such unjust conditions, Saul cannot reach simply to his own "greatness" but must in fact envisage more community-based solutions.

In rehab for alcoholism at the New Dawn Centre, Saul has a spiritual transformation in the form of a vision of communal regeneration. While out in the bush, he watches the beavers work on their home in unison and is distracted from getting back to the centre before dark; he is forced to camp among "the cedars" on "a flat table of rock" (191). In an interstitial space between "awake or dreaming" (192), Saul is visited by his great-grandfather Shabogeesick, the person from whom he inherited his special hockey skills, and his grandmother, whom he loved more than anyone. The effect of the vision is immediate: Saul needs to return to Manitouwadge and hand his skills down to the next generation. Ultimately, the novel's depictions of the residential school survivor's healing journey and the nostalgic elite athlete past his prime fuse together in a triumphant gesture of Anishinaabe survivance expressed through communal agency and solidarity. Returning to skate with his old teammates on the Manitouwadge rink, Saul finds that behind a full line of the "original Moose [. . .] were some kids of assorted ages and sizes and behind them were young girls and older women. Everyone had a hockey stick." With at least eighteen skaters on the ice—at different life stages, levels of ability, and genders—Saul asks Virgil, his former teammate, confidante, and surrogate brother, "How are we gonna do this? [. . .] I mean with all these people. How are we gonna play the game?" Virgil responds, "Together. . . . Like we shoulda all along" (221).

CONCLUSION: TO TRANSFORM A GAME, NOT AN INDIVIDUAL

Saul Indian Horse was first introduced to the game of hockey through literature within the racist, nationalistic, and assimilative space of the residential school. "From those books," he declares, "I got the idea that hockey had an alchemy that could transform ordinary men into great ones" (57).

Saul's journey throughout the novel is structured as a (perhaps doomed) search for such greatness. The novel tracks its protagonist's development as a seer and a gifted athlete, but the apotheosis that Saul imagines as a child proves consistently unachievable in the context of ongoing colonial power relations configured to ensure his second-class status. The healing arc of the novel as a residential school survival narrative offers other transformative possibilities; however, it too cannot point in the direction of the narrator's personal well-being until he has broadened the individualist focus on "ordinary men" and "great ones" to encompass the realities of living Indigenous communities.

This is why the novel concludes with Indigenous players of various ages and genders playing "together." Rather than seeking after his own singular transformation to hockey superstar (or even to healthy and sober individual), Saul needs to recognize that his capacity to become the fullest expression of himself is deeply interdependent with his community's capacity to transform the game—to disentangle it from the threads of individualism, racism, sexism, and capitalism that together form the web of ideological inheritance from colonial heteropatriachy.

In this way, Wagamese's novel has richly decolonizing properties. These properties, however, persist through a deep and abiding love for the game of hockey rather than in opposition to it. But in order for that love to begin to engender positive social change, the racism of hockey culture must be exposed; its implicatedness in violent colonial history must be laid bare; and the ongoing capacity of Indigenous players, fans, coaches, and communities to reimagine the game within the frameworks of their own world views must be recognized and affirmed. These are the lessons gifted to both settler and Indigenous audiences within Wagamese's forcefully noncolonial—as opposed to *decolonial*—hockey novel.

WORKS CITED

Anderson, Benedict. 2006. *Imagined Communities: Reflections on the Origin and Spread of Nationalism*. London: Verso.

Blake, Jason. 2010. *Canadian Hockey Literature: A Thematic Study*. Toronto: University of Toronto Press.

Buma, Michael. 2012. *Refereeing Identity: The Cultural Work of Canadian Hockey Novels*. Montréal and Kingston: McGill-Queen's University Press.

Dopp, Jamie, and Richard Harrison. 2009. *Now Is the Winter: Thinking About Hockey*. Hamilton, ON: Wolsak and Wynn.

Dowbiggin, Bruce. 2011. *The Meaning of Puck: How Hockey Explains Modern Canada*. Red Deer, AB: Red Deer Press.

Dryden, Ken, and Roy MacGregor. 1989. *Home Game: Hockey and Life in Canada*. Toronto: McClelland and Stewart.

Ennamorato, Judith. 1998. *Sing the Brave Song*. Schomberg, ON: Raven Press.

Goldie, Terry. 1989. *Fear and Temptation: The Image of the Indigene in Canadian, Australian, and New Zealand Literatures*. Montréal and Kingston: McGill-Queen's University Press.

Gruneau, Richard, and David Whitson. 1993. *Hockey Night in Canada: Sport, Identities and Cultural Politics*. Toronto: Garamond Press.

Habkirk, Evan J., and Janice Forsyth. 2016. "Truth, Reconciliation, and the Politics of the Body in Indian Residential School History." *ActiveHistory. ca*, 27 January. http://activehistory.ca/papers/truth-reconciliation-and-the-politics-of-the-body-in-indian-residential-school-history/.

Howell, Colin D. 2001. *Blood, Sweat, and Cheers: Sport and the Making of Modern Canada*. Toronto: University of Toronto Press.

Hughes-Fuller, Patricia. 2002. "The Good Old Game: Hockey, Nostalgia, Identity." PhD diss., University of Alberta.

Johnston, Basil H. 1988. *Indian School Days*. Norman, OK: University of Oklahama Press.

McKegney, Sam. 2017. *Magic Weapons: Aboriginal Writers Remaking Community After Residential School*. Winnipeg: University of Manitoba Press.

McKinley, Michael. 2001. *Putting a Roof on Winter: Hockey's Rise from Sport to Spectacle*. Vancouver: GreyStone Books.

Miller, J. R. 1996. *Shingwauk's Vision: A History of Native Residential Schools*. Toronto: University of Toronto Press.

Milloy, John S. 1999. *"A National Crime": The Canadian Government and the Residential School System, 1879 to 1986*. Winnipeg: University of Manitoba Press.

Robidoux, Michael A. 2012. *Stickhandling through the Margins: First Nations Hockey in Canada*. Toronto: University of Toronto Press.

Tengan, Ty P. Kāwika. 2008. *Native Men Remade: Gender and Nation in Contemporary Hawai'i*. Durham, NC: Duke University Press.

TRCC (Truth and Reconciliation Commission of Canada). 2015a. *Canada's Residential Schools: Reconciliation*. Vol. 6 of *The Final Report of the*

Truth and Reconciliation Commission of Canada. Montréal and Kingston: McGill-Queen's University Press.

————. 2015b. *Honouring the Truth, Reconciling for the Future: Summary of the Final Report of the Truth and Reconciliation Commission of Canada.* Winnipeg: Truth and Reconciliation Commission of Canada. http://www.trc.ca/websites/trcinstitution/File/2015/Findings/Exec_Summary_2015_05_31_web_o.pdf.

Vizenor, Gerald. 2009. *Native Liberty: Natural Reason and Cultural Survivance.* Lincoln: University of Nebraska Press.

Wagamese, Richard. 2012. *Indian Horse.* Vancouver: Douglas and McIntyre.

Wolfe, Patrick. 2006. "Settler Colonialism and the Elimination of the Native." *Journal of Genocide Research* 8, no. 4: 387–409.

Contributors

Angie Abdou is an associate professor of creative writing at Athabasca University and a regular book reviewer for *Quill and Quire*. She has published one short story collection and four novels. Her first novel, *The Bone Cage*, was a CBC Canada Reads finalist in 2011, defended by NHL star Georges Laraque. *The Bone Cage* was also chosen for the inaugural One Book One Kootenay in 2009 and as MacEwan University's 2011/12 Book of the Year. The novel was included on *Canadian Literature* magazine's "All-Time Top Ten List of Best Canadian Sport Literature" and was number one on the CBC Book Club's "Top 10 Sport Books."

Jason Blake teaches in the English Department at the University of Ljubljana. He is the author of *Canadian Hockey Literature* and the coeditor of *The Same but Different: Hockey in Quebec* (2017). His nonhockey books include *Culture Smart! Slovenia* (2011).

Laura K. Davis teaches English at Red Deer College and holds a PhD from the University of Alberta. Her books include *Margaret Laurence Writes Africa and Canada* (2017); *Margaret Laurence and Jack McClelland, Letters*, coedited with Linda M. Morra (2018), and *Essay Writing for Canadian Students*, coauthored with Roger Davis (2016).

Jamie Dopp is an associate professor of Canadian literature at the University of Victoria, where he has taught a course in hockey and literature for a number of years. His poetry, fiction, reviews, and scholarly articles have appeared in many journals. He has also published two collections of poetry and a novel. In 2009, he coedited a collection of essays with Richard Harrison titled *Now Is the Winter: Thinking About Hockey*.

Cara Hedley is the author of *Twenty Miles*, the first Canadian hockey novel about women players. *Twenty Miles* was nominated for the Margaret Laurence Award for Fiction and included on the CBC Books "list of Canada's greatest hockey books." With a PhD in English literature from the University of Calgary, Hedley is an editor and writing instructor in the University of Calgary's Faculty of Continuing Education.

Paul Martin splits his time between teaching and writing about the literatures of Canada and serving as MacEwan University's faculty development coordinator. His book *Sanctioned Ignorance: The Politics of Knowledge Production and the Teaching of the Literatures of Canada* (2013) won the Gabrielle Roy Prize for Canadian literary criticism (English).

Fred Mason teaches sport history and sociology in the Faculty of Kinesiology at the University of New Brunswick. His work ranges across both areas, including the history of parasports and sociological perspectives on ultrarunning. He has research interests in sport in fiction and film, especially science fiction versions of sport.

Sam McKegney is a settler scholar of Indigenous literatures. He has published a collection of interviews titled *Masculindians: Conversations About Indigenous Manhood*; a monograph titled *Magic Weapons: Aboriginal Writers Remaking Community After Residential School*; and articles on such topics as environmental kinship, masculinity theory, prison writing, Indigenous governance, and Canadian hockey mythologies.

Gyllian Phillips is an associate professor in the English Studies Department at Nipissing University in North Bay, Ontario. She teaches a first-year course called "Sport in Literature and Film." Her chapter in this volume is her first foray into sport literature scholarship. Other publications include articles on 1930s British film and on women writers of the 1920s and 1930s, as well as, with Allan Pero, a coedited volume, *The Many Facades of Edith Sitwell* (2017).

Trevor J. Phillips is a Métis PhD candidate in English literature at Queen's University. He is the Indigenous graduate student success coordinator at the University of Manitoba, where he hosts the podcast *At the Edge of Canada: On Indigenous Research*, teaches courses on Indigenous masculinities and literatures, and is the radio voice of Bison's Hockey.

Cory Willard is working on his PhD in English literary and cultural studies at the University of Nebraska–Lincoln, where he focuses on ecocriticism, environmental literature, and place studies. His primary interest is fly fishing and fly-fishing literature. When he is not trapped at a desk reading or writing, you can find him streamside.